15 —
New Guinea

Don't Go Up
 KETTLE CREEK

Don't

Go Up

KETTLE CREEK

Verbal Legacy

of the Upper Cumberland

by William Lynwood Montell

THE UNIVERSITY OF TENNESSEE PRESS / *Knoxville*

Library of Congress Cataloging in Publication Data
Montell, William Lynwood, 1931–
  Don't go up Kettle Creek.
  Bibliography: p.
  Includes indexes.
  1. Cumberland River Valley (Ky. and Tenn.)—Social
life and customs.   2. Cumberland River Valley (Ky. and
Tenn.)—History.   3. Cumberland River Valley (Ky. and
Tenn.)—Biography.   4. Folklore—Cumberland River
Valley (Ky. and Tenn.)   5. Oral history.   I. Title.
F442.2.M66   1983   976.8'5   82-8566
ISBN 0-87049-365-5   AACR2

Dedicated to my parents
HAZEL CHAPMAN MONTELL
WILLIE G. MONTELL, 1908–1979

Preface

Although much of my academic career has been spent studying various aspects of the Upper Cumberland region of Kentucky and Tennessee, I began library and archival research for this particular book in August 1975. By December I was ready to go into the field to tape record information from narrators and to seek out any local history manuscripts and books available in the area from Carthage to Burnside. The success I had in taping oral interviews and gathering supporting materials to do an oral history for a region this size was due to the generous help and willing cooperation which I received from people everywhere I went. Their excitement and enthusiasm drove me at a constant pace, and I never grew tired of meeting new persons and recording their priceless and time-honored oral traditions.

The interviews were finished in December 1980. I wish to acknowledge my debt to these people first of all. They are recognized by name in the Biographies of Narrators, but I want to add this special word of thanks; without them there would be no book.

In addition, some of the narrators volunteered to act as guides, to contact other persons and act as go-betweens in the community, to help as researchers, and to serve as subject-matter consultants. Worthy of mention in this regard are Landon Anderson, Ona Barton, Iva Butler, Katherine Cassetty, E. Ray Gaskin, and Curtis and Edwina Upton, all Tennesseans; and Keith Byrd, Benjamin Coffey, Bernice Mitchell, Hiram Parrish, and Garnet Walker, all of Kentucky. Miss Mitchell read and criticized the manuscript in its final stages of completion.

I wish to thank the archivists and librarians in the Folklore, Folklife, and Oral History Archives at Western Kentucky University, Bowling Green; those in the Kentucky Library at that same institution; and the personnel in the Tennessee State Library and Archives, Nashville. Thanks also go to the local librarians in virtually every county of the Upper Cumberland. They spent hours on my behalf locating obscure documents and providing me with copies. Mrs. Jewell Thomas, deputy regional librarian, of Burkesville, Kentucky, deserves a special note of recognition for the splendid work she is doing in gathering and making available oral history interviews through the office of the Lake Cumberland Library District. All the taped interviews and available transcriptions done by her staff have been deposited with the Kentucky State Library, Frankfort. Finally, I wish to acknowledge the research help and the privilege of copying documents accorded me at the Nashville Office, Army Corps of Engineers.

My debt is heavy to the undergraduate and graduate students in Folk Studies at Western Kentucky University who assisted in this project in many ways, such as transcribing tapes, typing transcriptions, and running down elusive library titles. Space limitations preclude listing all of their names, but I do feel compelled to single out four persons for special recognition. Carolyn Day Best, a graduate student, interviewed several Metcalfe County, Kentucky, residents; transcribed the tapes; and made several follow-up telephone calls. Tom Ayres and Kate Parker, graduate students, assisted me with interviewing in 1975–76; and Becky Morse, graduate student, began work on the project as editorial assistant in June 1976. She read the initial drafts, offered criticisms, and coordinated much of the clerical work done by other students.

Valerie Kinder and Joan Oldham, executive secretaries in the Department of Folk and Intercultural Studies at Western deserve my thanks, not only for typing the manuscript in its various stages but also for patiently assisting everyone else who was clamoring for their professional expertise and services at the same time. Thanks also to Linda Gensler, student assistant and later departmental secretary.

Western Kentucky University provided me with a sabbatical leave for the spring semester 1977 to work on the manuscript, and my folklore faculty colleagues graciously consented to assume my departmental duties during my absence.

Dr. Barbara Allen—my wife, research companion, staunch supporter, and helpful critic—deserves the biggest thank you of all. Her careful and painstaking reading helped me reshape the manuscript into its final form.

William Lynwood Montell
Bowling Green, Kentucky
February 1982

Contents

Illustrations

"Don't Go Up Kettle Creek"

As big a thing as a steamboat, you wouldn't think it would save time but they's a lot of difference in plying right at the middle of the river or catching these eddies and dragging the brush.... And the [Cumberland] river was up.... When it was up ... all you needed to see was that water. And keep it in there close. ...

And I had them lights cut around short, you know, and was dragging them willows and bushes along there. Well, I passed Celina! I seen that! But right above Celina, I touched the far side and I jerked that headlight over there. It was narrow, and there was a log raft tied up and a gasoline boat over here. Big sycamores hanging out, and I couldn't figure it, for I knowed I had just passed Celina. ...

Directly Joe [the captain] raised up, "Where are you at!"

I said, "Right above Celina."

He said, "Stop!"

I rung the bell. He commenced laughing, "Kinda backwards, ain't you, old boy! ..."

And I was going up Obey's River [a tributary]. I'd failed to see it! Well, we backed it out in the river. Joe said, "Now don't go up Kettle Creek!"

    —John Stone

Introduction

In the past decade and a half, the fields of oral history and folklore studies have come together to shed light on the historical experiences of heretofore unknown or unrecognized persons and on racial and ethnic communities in both rural and urban areas. The merger has already yielded a dozen or more significant works,[1] but numerous additional case studies are needed to give substance to the general suggestions made and issues raised by theorists in oral history studies. This book proposes to help fill this void and to illustrate that folklorists, because of their sensitivity to the oral tradition process, are especially well equipped to deal with oral history.

Specifically, this book attempts to reconstruct the history of a river region as it is perceived from the vernacular point of view, relying on personal reminiscences, oral traditions, balladry and song, and printed materials (which were themselves derived from oral history data) as primary sources of information.[2] The river is the Cumberland—more specifically, the navigable waters of its upper reaches—from Carthage, Tennessee, to Burnside, Kentucky. The region is the Upper Cumberland, virtually unknown to the world at large, yet a distinct cultural-geographic entity to the people who have lived and worked within its boundaries through the years.

The Cumberland River, which dominates the region's

physical character, heads in the mountains of eastern Kentucky near Whitesburg. On its long westward journey, it flows through Harlan, Pineville, and Williamsburg before dropping over a high ledge to form Cumberland Falls, sixty-eight nautical miles above Burnside. At Burnside the Cumberland becomes a major river, for it is there that it converges with the Big South Fork River, which flows northward from New River, Tennessee, picking up the waters of the Little South Fork en route to Burnside.

From Burnside the Cumberland flows in great loops in a generally southwesterly direction across south central Kentucky before it enters Tennessee a few miles north of Celina. It continues to meander in a sinuous channel while forming a great southward arc, via Nashville, before heading northward to join the Ohio River at Kuttawa, Kentucky.

The Obey River, a tributary, drains much of the rugged portions of Clay, Overton, Fentress, and Pickett counties, Tennessee. En route to Celina, where it empties into the Cumberland, the Obey converges at Lillydale with the Wolf River, a flashy mountain stream that rises in the Valley of the Three Forks of the Wolf near Jamestown, Tennessee, and drains the area on both sides of the state line. (Both the Obey and the Wolf were bottled up in the early 1940s to form the Dale Hollow Reservoir.) The Roaring River, another swift-flowing stream, with tributaries reaching almost to Livingston, Tennessee, joins the Cumberland at Gainesboro, Tennessee; and the Caney Fork River, which drains the Cookeville-Smithville-Sparta hinterland, flows into the Cumberland one mile above Carthage.

For the purposes of this study, we may outline the boundaries of the Upper Cumberland region as follows: begin at Carthage, then draw a line northward through Red Boiling Springs, Tennessee, to Edmonton, Kentucky. Extend the line eastward through Russell Springs to Somerset, then southward to Whitley City. From there, continue to Crossville, Tennessee, then via Sparta to the starting point at Carthage. Kentucky and Tennessee make up equal parts of the region, but its history transcends state boundaries. The state line was not fixed at its present location, in fact, until 1804—more than twenty years after the first white settlers arrived.

It cannot be established when or by whom this area astraddle the

2

midpoint of the Kentucky-Tennessee state line was first called the Upper Cumberland. It likely came about in the early 1830s with the arrival of the steamboat on the river above Carthage. Many of the riverboat captains of the day worked the Cumberland both above and below Carthage; along with the warehousemen and lumbermen in Nashville, they made a rather clear distinction between the upper river and the lower river, for the upper waters were more treacherous and the cargoes were different.[3] Nashville newspapers made frequent reference to the Upper Cumberland in the 1860s, as news about upper river boats was commonly carried on their pages. The term was employed by the Upper Cumberland Medical Society beginning in 1894;[4] in advertisements by the Hawk's and Company general store in Celina prior to the turn of the century;[5] and by the Hotel Celina, which was heralded as "one of the best hotels on the Upper Cumberland" in 1906.[6]

Across the years thousands of native sons and daughters have left the area for northern industrial cities with fond expectations of returning home someday. But since the 1940s, the Dale Hollow, Wolf Creek, Center Hill, and Cordell Hull reservoirs have inundated many of the older settlements and burial grounds of the pioneers in this low mountain fastness. As a result, the term *Upper Cumberland* is laden with nostalgia for present and past residents of the area; signage in Tennessee's hill country and the adjacent Cumberland Plateau makes clear the inhabitants' preference that their territory be referred to by this name. The Upper Cumberland Tourist Association in Cookeville has issued a directory of *The Upper Cumberlands: Tennessee's Family Funland*. Included is a map of Middle Tennessee with bold demarcation around the counties which comprise the "Fabulous Upper Cumberlands." Electric and telephone cooperatives, lumber companies, federal planning and social work agencies, bookstores, banks, and other institutions from Carthage to Celina to Crossville prominently display the words *Upper Cumberland* as part of their official names.

The topography of the Upper Cumberland generally ranges from fairly well-developed flood plains located along the Cumberland River and its tributaries to rugged hills, low mountains, and deep, narrow, U-shaped valleys resulting from the erosional action of wild

3

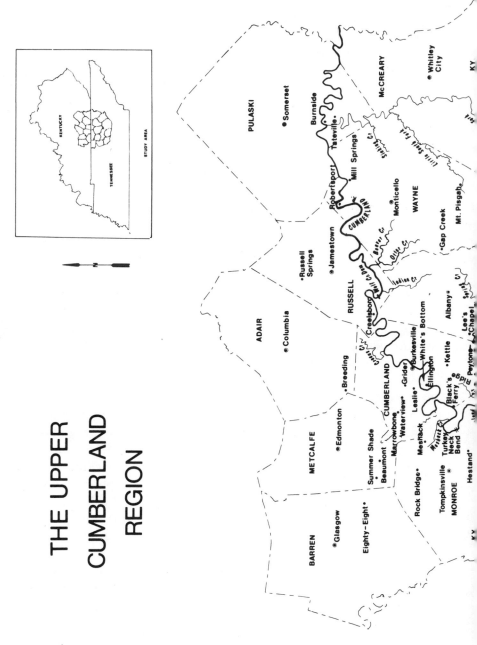

THE UPPER CUMBERLAND REGION

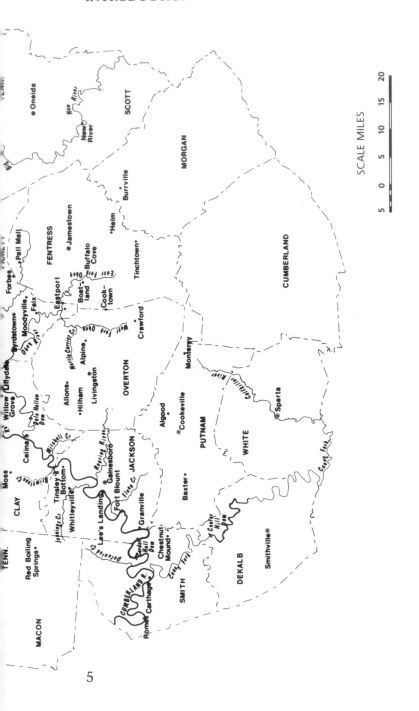

SCALE MILES

5   0   5   10   15   20

streams on the susceptible geological strata of the Cumberland Plateau. These physical features dictated the emergence of small farms in the upland areas and larger ones along the rivers. The timber that flourished on the hilly slopes and the presence of the rivers combined to provide lucrative logging, rafting, and sawmilling activities between 1870 and 1930. The rugged terrain of the region precluded extensive development of roads and railroads, so the river served as the major means of transporting farm products and timber to market for more than a century. The river not only dominated the region physically but also controlled it economically; thus, the lives of the people were intimately bound up with the river, as is reflected in the oral traditions and personal experiences recounted in this book.

The people of the Upper Cumberland are by no means homogeneous. There are hill farmers and river farmers, loggers and coal miners, steamboatmen and merchants, Republicans and Democrats, Baptists and Methodists, whites and blacks, the employed and the unemployed. Yet they have lived together long enough to develop a sense of economic interdependence and to share certain historical experiences. A common core of spoken and sung traditions attests to these experiences and to a strong sense of identification with the region. An elderly resident of Double Top Mountain, located along the Fentress-Pickett county border, refuses to visit members of his family in Indiana; he is afraid that he might die there and not be returned home for burial. Dave Wright, the former patriarch of Wright Mountain in western Fentress County, stated in the winter of 1973 that if he lived until that summer he was going home again. "When I get up there [on the mountain], I'm going to kiss every tree there and say, 'Hello, old tree, I'm home.'" And persons who migrated from the region forty to sixty years ago, and who have seldom visited the Upper Cumberland since, often request to be taken "home" at death for burial alongside parents and grandparents.

Virtually all forms of folklore are found in every community across the Upper Cumberland, although some types are more plentiful than others. Traditional ballads from the British Isles are vanishing, but local ballads and lyric songs are abundant; fairy tales are nonexistent, but migratory legends flourish; fables are scarce, but ghost tales are

6

told by blacks and whites alike. We may define *local ballads* as songs that recount an event in a community's past. "The Battle of Mill Springs" and "Beanie Short," both described in Chapter 2, are illustrative of local ballads. *Lyric songs* express mood or emotion without providing the narrative details often found in ballads. "Away Up On Fishing Creek," also to be found in Chapter 2, is representative of the lyric genre. *Migratory legends* are traditional narratives which move from one geographical area to another, incorporating the names of local persons and places in the process of relocation. While it is usually impossible to prove or disprove the veracity of these stories, they are likely not true, as they could not have occurred under essentially identical circumstances in the various areas where they are told. Yet they sound logical and are thus told to be true. Numerous migratory legends are included herein, including the account in Chapter 1 of how a frontier heroine eluded a pursuing panther by tossing items of her clothing behind her into the road, piece by piece, until she reached home safely. Synopses of the migratory legends contained in this book are presented in Appendix A along with references to known published parallels of the legends. Appendix A also contains recognizable *motifs* (free-floating narrative elements) and *traditional beliefs* (those mental constructs upon which individual and group action often is based).

The one genre that is present above all others in the region is the *oral historical narrative,* in the form of both traditional stories and accounts of personal experiences. There is every indication that this form of expression was characteristic of the Upper Cumberland from the earliest times to the present. The people there like a good story, and conditions and events within the region provided grist for narrators. People especially enjoy talking about the exploits of local folk heroes. Narrators in Clay County know about the Confederate renegade Champ Ferguson of Clinton County, Kentucky, for example, but they prefer to recount the escapades of their own Confederate Colonel Oliver Hamilton. Similarly, the folk in Burnside have heard of legendary steamboat captain Tim Armstrong of Celina, but they have their own steamboat family to talk about in Dave Heath and his sons.

Most of all, people like to relate *personal experience narratives* about people and events within their own lifetimes. John I. Cummings of Clinton County, for example, admitted having knowledge of guerrillas such as Champ Ferguson and Dave Beaty and of divided loyalties during the Civil War, but he brushed aside questions about them in order to talk about his personal logging and rafting experiences on the Wolf River.

It might be helpful at this point to draw a distinction between personal experience narratives and oral traditional narratives, both of which appear in this book. The personal experience narrative is an *eyewitness* or *firsthand* account; the narrator says, in essence, "I was there, I saw the action, and this is the way it happened." Accounts of the same event by two or more narrators may vary in structure and content, depending on the individuals' perceptions and recollections, but these accounts generally can be relied upon for their historical content, and the scholar can obtain from them a relatively full and meaningful description of the event in question.

Oral traditional narratives, on the other hand, are *secondhand* ("I wasn't there, but my grandmother was, and she described it like this") or *thirdhand* reminiscences. Secondhand accounts, which make up the bulk of oral traditional stories, are not as historically reliable as eyewitness accounts but logically are more so than thirdhand stories, the category under which migratory legends fall. This last category is more revealing of attitudes and aspirations of narrators than of facts to be used in reconstructing the past.

Since the material for this book came primarily from the words of the people who lived the history, the narratives not only describe historical events and conditions, but also reflect narrators' paramount concerns, attitudes, and feelings. Scholars interested in oral recollections, especially oral traditional reminiscences, recognize that people talk about the past in terms meaningful to them in the present. Personal prejudices serve as filters through which local history is passed on orally from one generation to the next. From stories about characters such as the rebel raider Champ Ferguson, for example, we may learn as much about the attitudes of the narrators as about Ferguson himself. He is remembered in oral tradition on the one hand as a thief, counterfeiter, robber, murderer, and bloodthirsty guerrilla, and on the other hand as a respected family man and law-abiding citizen who was compelled by circumstances to kill in defense of his family and the Confederate cause.

A study of all the oral historical traditions of the people of the Upper Cumberland affords a strikingly clear picture of the history of the region from the earliest days of settlement to the present, although the standard historical topics (politics, religion, education, and the like) largely are ignored in these pages. Residents of the area unquestionably are interested in and knowledgeable about these subjects, and I had initially intended to include them in this work. In the final analysis, however, I dropped them in favor of those topics which had the most impact on the daily lives of the people, topics they still discuss among themselves with fervor. The subjects that dominate the conversations of both past and present generations must be seen as the most significant facets of the region's heritage. Thus, I made the final selection of the topics to be included here, but only after I had interviewed enough residents to have a clear perception of what they consider to be the cords that bind together the fabric of their historical experience.

The people interviewed for this study viewed their region's history not along a chronological continuum interspersed with dates but rather in terms of events and conditions that most vitally affected their own lives and the lives of their ancestors. The divisions of the book retain this topical orientation while organizing the material within a broad chronological frame. Chapter 1 presents the oral traditions surrounding the progression from frontier times to the farming era—a period fraught with dangers and marked by cooperation among families and friends in their quest for self-sufficiency. Just when economic independence was within the grasp of the people of the Upper Cumberland, their dreams were shattered and their loyalties divided over the question of national unity. Chapter 2 describes the effects of the Civil War, indelibly stamped on the region's psyche by the criss-crossing of the area by opposing armies and cutthroat guerrilla bands. Logging, rafting, and sawmilling provided major sources of income for area residents during three quarters of a century after the Civil War; Chapter 3 describes these important economic activities. Chapter 4 contains both oral traditions and personal testimonies about the importance of steamboats in the Upper Cumberland as a mode of transportation and as the region's only viable link with mainstream America between 1830 and 1930. The final chapter looks at the Upper Cumberland in modern times, focusing on the changes in lifestyles brought about mainly by improved road construction, modern technology, and the ready availability of mass-produced wares.

All of the information in *Don't Go Up Kettle Creek*, unless otherwise stipulated, is based on oral traditions and personal reminiscences drawn from three sources: accounts in locally printed histories and newspapers, those written by area residents and available only in unpublished manuscript form, and those tape recorded from narrators between December 1975 and December 1980. Almost without exception, information contained in the written documents is derived from the personal experiences or word-of-mouth testimonies and traditions of older people. These printed or unpublished items demonstrate the ease with which certain oral traditions in the Upper Cumberland have entered local print. The notes for each chapter and comments within the chapters cite specific sources of information and indicate whether they are in print, manuscript, or tape-recorded form. In many cases, information provided orally was the only information available, particularly for the occupations associated with the timber industry. In other instances, oral information could be corroborated by printed sources; thus, notes may include references to published materials along with data about the interview.

My own interviews with narrators provided the bulk of the oral material for the book. (Other sources of oral information are identified in the notes and in the bibliography.) In conducting interviews, I went to narrators' homes and offices, and I often accompanied them in an automobile or on foot to local cemeteries, riverboat landings, and other points of historic interest and significance. When tape recording was not feasible, I jotted down items on a notepad. Within the book, I present these oral materials in two ways. First, whenever possible I have included entire oral texts. When an oral item is used in

10

its entirety, I have introduced the narrator and the text with a lead-in sentence that attempts to convey the spirit in which the oral account was uttered. Second, I have extracted and summarized information from various oral sources and then cited each narrator in a note.

Because it is generally necessary to edit oral historical narratives to make them adaptable to the printed page, a word about my own editing practices is in order. In transcribing the tapes, no attempt was made to reproduce regional accents. Spelling and word forms have been standardized: *talking*, not *talkin'*; *heard*, not *heerd*; *get*, not *git*. My feeling is that since the oral speech patterns are recorded on tape and the tapes will be preserved as a permanent record, attempts to reproduce dialect in print are unnecessary. Furthermore, such attempts are distracting to the reader and often are offensive to the original speakers.

Terms used in the narratives that denote special meanings, however, have been retained. These words are marked by an asterisk upon their first appearance in this book and are defined in Appendix B.

In addition to standardizing speech in the oral texts, I have deleted all false starts, stutterings, and crutch words and phrases if their presence adds nothing to the content of the text and their absence in no way changes the spirit or intent of the narrator. Brackets indicate my additions for clarity. Other than applying these editorial practices, I have in no way altered the transcripts. In no instance have I collated two or more texts into an "acceptable" one, nor have I tampered with word order or the internal structure of these oral documents. When oral texts were too unwieldy to present intact, I have summarized the words of the narrators, while retaining direct quotes so as to impart the spirit and flavor of the spoken word. The account of Coonrod Pyle in Chapter 1 illustrates this practice.

All of the oral accounts I recorded were told to me as factual history by people who have a great respect for the past and a passionate desire to see that it is not lost to the ravages of time. The names of people and places identified in the book are real, and the events or conditions described are very real in the minds of the narrators. This, then, is their history, put together in such a way as to reflect an esoteric point of view.[7] As I am personally committed to the premise that works based on oral history should reflect the insider's point of view, I prefer to let the people tell their own story without undue interference from me. In the body of the present work, I have made no attempt to editorialize or to correct. Any editorial comments I have regarding these materials are made in the notes to each chapter.

CHAPTER 1

From Frontier to Farm

etween the years 1761 and 1774, explorers from Virginia and North Carolina came to the Upper Cumberland area to explore and to hunt. These "Long Hunters," so named because of their lengthy stays in the wilderness, combed the Upper Cumberland, charting and naming the creeks, rivers, knobs, and other landmarks, usually after themselves. For example, Obediah Terrill, who is still remembered as "a chunky, small man with a club foot," spent a few years farming and hunting the area around Celina—the point where the Obey River converges with the Cumberland. Named by and for himself, the Obey was first called Obed, later Obeds, and now Obey.[1] Some of the Long Hunters laid claims to parcels of land, then went back east to get their families. Just how many did this is not known. We do know, however, that every county in the Upper Cumberland still has families that bear the same surnames as the Long Hunters, and numerous oral family legends trace kinship to these men.

Some of the Long Hunters are recalled in oral tradition better than others. Conrad Pyle, remembered today as Coonrod in the Fentress-Pickett County area, "stopped off on Wolf River and built himself a little log cabin" by splitting out a big tree. Coonrod liked his new home but longed for a woman companion. He returned to Virginia and "stole him a redheaded woman." Her people tracked them down, kidnapped the woman, and headed back to Virginia with her. Upon his return from a hunting trip, Coonrod found her gone. He overtook her and her friendly captors and "fetched her back with him." This frontier couple raised a large family and had numerous descendants, including great-great-grandson Sergeant Alvin C. York of World War I fame.[2]

Gladys Williams of Fentress County, a descendant of Coonrod Pyle, had never heard of the "stolen woman" episode. She did, however, share other insights into his life and times by reading from an unpublished manuscript that she had written on the basis of oral testimonies told by her grandmother, who had known Coonrod personally:

> On one of these [hunting and exploring] expeditions was a long, tall, red-headed boy named Conrad Pyle. To his friends he was nicknamed "Coonrod." He had left a girl back in Virginia and he couldn't get her out of his thoughts. After the hunt was over, Coonrod set out a few days ahead of his companions to rejoin this girl whom he referred to as Pretty Mary. And while traveling across what is now called Middle Eastern Tennessee he came upon a little valley in the heart of the mountains. And this valley was well watered with springs and streams and surrounded by high mountains. On the banks of the river which ran through this little valley, Conrad Pyle shot a wolf. And he named the stream Wolf River. [She added extemporaneously: "That's the river right down here; that's how it happened to be Wolf River. He shot a wolf."] Because Wolf River split into three forks at the entrance to the valley, he named it the Valley of the Three Forks of the Wolf.
>
> The Long Hunter remained in this valley for several days, sleeping at night in a cave on the mountainside. Then he returned to Virginia, married Pretty Mary and brought her back to his valley. They were one of the first white families to settle in the Valley of the Three Forks of the Wolf River. Conrad built a log cabin near the site where he made his first camp and where he killed his first deer. It was in this log cabin he and Mary reared their family of eight children. . . .

14

In 1829 Conrad Pyle, along with a group of interested citizens, petitioned the general assembly of the State of Tennessee for a road to the north of the Cumberland Mountains. The petition was granted and Old Coonrod engineered the building of the pike, Pyle's Turnpike. . . . The Pyle's Turnpike was a state road coming by way of Tinchtown, through Jamestown, down the Pyle's Mountain, and into Clinton County, Kentucky.

When Coonrod built his home, he built one room without windows, with only one door. He used this room as a bank or safe to keep his valuables in. He kept his rifle by the door and a pitchfork with the prongs straightened and sharpened as his burglary insurance. In this room he always kept a keg covered with animal skins. And when he sold a slave or made a trade in which he received a gold coin, he always tossed it in this keg—covered it with the hides. There is a legend in the valley that this keg was full of gold pieces, but after his death no trace of the gold was ever found.

The story is that he tried to give his son Elijah a message on his death bed but could never finish it. It is thought that he wanted to tell where the keg was hidden. Some of his neighbors didn't believe he had a keg of gold, but others did. [They] hunted in vain for it. In 1933, one dark night where there was no moon shining, ghouls came to the Wolf River Cemetery searching for this legendary keg of gold. Coonrod had fashioned huge stone covers shaped like the lid of a coffin for his wife's and daughter's graves. These stones were removed by the ghouls and it is believed by the Wolf River folk that the keg of gold was found in his daughter's grave.

Jasper Pyle and A.W. Pyle, both residents of the valley, were among the first people to discover the work of the ghouls. And they both stated that an impression was left in the soil from which it appeared an object had been removed. Coonrod's keg of gold still remains an unsolved mystery.[3]

The Upper Cumberland generally was not populated by settlers until about 1780. Hugh Roberts, a Pennsylvania Quaker who migrated to what is now Clay County to avoid military service, was among the first.[4] Tradition has it that William Dale settled on the Obey River just above the Roberts place in 1782.[5] In 1786, a few families whose names are unknown bought some land on the Wolf River, a tributary of the Obey, from Judge Richard Henderson of North Carolina and settled near Lillydale, also in Clay County.[6] Later that same year, the Franklin, Robbins and Huddleston families settled farther up the Wolf in Pickett and Fentress counties.[7] Local historians presume these families to be the first permanent white settlers on the Upper Cumberland in what is now Tennessee.

Probably the first settlement in the entire Upper Cumberland occurred in Kentucky at Parmleysville in 1780.[8] It was Cherokee country then; today it is in Wayne County. Legend holds that these first settlers were little less than thieves and indeed may have hidden stolen horses in what is now called the Horse Hollow.[9] Just prior to 1790, Monroe, Metcalfe, and Cumberland counties, Kentucky, witnessed the arrival of a handful of families at or near present-day Tompkinsville, Edmonton, and Burkesville. (If oral tradition is correct, around Meshack in Monroe County, in 1776 the Kirkpatrick family built the first brick house south of Green River, a structure which still stands.)

In 1791, a district was set apart for the Cherokees, who still laid claim to much of the region, the western boundary of which extended in a southwesterly direction from the Big South Fork River in Kentucky near Burnside to a dividing ridge separating the Cumberland and Duck rivers forty-five miles above Nashville. This line (running just east of present-day Livingston) divided Tennessee's Upper Cumberland into two equal parts. The west was open to settlement, but the mountainous area to the east was reserved for the Cherokees,[10] except that the whites were granted permission to "have a free and unmolested use of a road" from east Tennessee to the Cumberland settlements.[11] The Treaty of Tellico in 1805 extinguished all Indian hopes of remaining in the area. After that time, the whole of the eastern Upper Cumberland in both Tennessee and Kentucky was open to white settlement.[12]

One small band of Indians, however, lived on undetected near Alpine in Overton County in the shadow of the Cumberland Mountains. They were an offshoot from the Cherokee nation and went by the name of Nettle Carrier Indians; they lived in Nettle Carrier Village on Nettle Carrier Creek, and they answered to the leadership of Chief Nettle Carrier at the death of Chief Obeds. The tribe's members were lovers of peace and home, it is said, and never roamed more than a few miles from their dwellings for meat and skins. Like their North Carolina counterparts, the Nettle Carrier Indians were farmers, potters, and basket makers.[13]

An explanation for the name Nettle Carrier was passed through oral tradition. In the Alpine village lived two young braves who were in love with the same Indian girl. They sought the advice of the chief as to which one would marry her. The old chief told each brave to throw a sprig into the water of the nearby creek; the one whose object was carried farther by the water would marry the girl. One threw a thorn, the other a nettle. The nettle floated farther. Its owner claimed his bride, and from that day he was called Nettle Carrier. He was the last Indian chief to reside in this part of the Upper Cumberland. Tradition has it that he lived there until 1799 and then departed for East Tennessee.[14] The remaining members of the tribe were eventually absorbed into the nearby white race at the Alpine community (still locally referred to by some as Nettle Carrier) and at Oak Grove.

The Nettle Carrier tribe is likely the one referred to in the following oral tradition perpetuated within the family of narrator Sarah Jane Koger of Jamestown, Tennessee:

> Grandmother told things, you know, that had happened back then and she also talked about her—her parents was a-living back when the Indians was in the Obey River country.
>
> She said her father was a awful good friend to one Indian chief, but I forget his name. So he invited her father to go home with him one night for supper. Of course, said her dad said he hated to go, but said he knowed not to would make him mad. So he went home with him and they went in the Indian village and said they started down through the village. Said they was a-cooking—squaws a-cooking. Said they went by one. Said she's a-churning a dog hide—they'd killed a dog,

17

skinned it and had it hung, and she was churning that dog hide. Says my great-grandfather said he didn't think he could eat a bite of anything. But he went on home with this chief and said his wife had a pretty decent supper. She baked her bread on a board, you know, in front of the fire, what they called johnny-cakes. And said she had venison cooked and said she had a pretty good supper. Said he eat a right smart [of] supper.[15]

There were virtually no Indian attacks on white families in the Upper Cumberland. Only an occasional conflict between the races took place, and most of these have been neglected by oral tradition. One such oral legend recounts that Meshack Kirkpatrick was scalped by Indians and hanged from a tree over the stream in Monroe County that now bears the name Meshack Creek.[16] Another story, perhaps a migratory legend, concerns Jim Crockett (likely related to Davy Crockett) of Fentress County, who was deaf and dumb. He was captured by a band of Indians and held a prisoner for several years. While a captive, he was taken blindfolded to a lead mine on the East Fork of Obey, where the Indians got a load of lead for him and themselves to carry.[17]

Sarah Jane Koger claimed traditional knowledge of a renegade Indian attack on members of her family:

> And she [Mrs. Koger's grandmother] had a cousin; she also had a cousin that the Indians captured. They was a-taking her off and she said her people, the Choates, was all big, big people, big men. They called them the Big Choates. And they was four or five of them up so close on them that they scalped this girl and left her for dead, the Indians did, and got away. But Grandmother said she lived. But said she never did have any hair up there where they took the scalp off. And her name was Omie, Omie Choate.[18]

All that is currently known of the Indians of the Upper Cumberland is that a few were there when the whites penetrated this rugged hinterland. Some of the initial contacts between the two races resulted in bloodshed while others resulted in the convergence of the two cultures, lasting friendships, and intermarriage and assimilation. The admixture of races resulted in the almost total disappearance of Indian traits and characteristics. Today, many white and black people of the region proudly boast of an ancestor—three, four, or five times removed—who was "full-blooded Cherokee." This is likely a valid assertion.

Following favorable land legislation in the late 1790s, coupled with the 1805 treaty calling for removal of the Cherokees from the Upper Cumberland, the region received hundreds of land-hungry farming families and artisans lured ever westward by tales of lush lands beyond the mountains. They were mainly from Virginia, the Carolinas, East Tennessee, and Pennsylvania, possessing English, Scottish, German, Swiss, and French ancestry.

In order to understand these people of the Upper Cumberland who moved into the region nearly 200 years ago and who worked to build a future for themselves and their posterity, it is necessary to understand their concepts of fear, security, cooperation, self-sufficiency, family, community, and personal conflict. Oral narratives, traditional beliefs, and folksongs still current in the region revolve around these concepts.

Fear and anxiety lay heavily on the minds of the people of the Upper Cumberland during the initial years of frontier settlement. These feelings were not manifested overtly; on the surface, settlers feared neither the known enemies—such as Indians, wild animals, floods, droughts, or blizzards—nor the unknown enemies, epitomized by death and supernatural creatures. Beliefs and feelings subtly couched in oral traditions, however, reveal that fear was indeed a compelling force, and the lifestyle which the pioneers developed also attests to this.

The frontier era was characterized by efforts directed toward survival. The need for shelter was a paramount consideration, to be addressed before anything else. Whether the new home in the wilderness was a cave, an overhanging rock ledge, or a single-room cabin crudely fashioned from native logs, rocks, and clay, it shielded the frontier family against such natural forces as rain and cold. The home also offered protection from attacks by the Indians and forest animals,

19

which constantly jeopardized the lives of the settlers. Traditional stories from that period reflect the survival instinct of the first generation.

Verda Cook Wright has written that as a child in Pickett County she sat spellbound listening to pioneer tales told by her grandmother, Mrs. Margaret Barton, who had learned them from her mother. These accounts describe the wild mountain country during the first years of settlement and tell of a life full of hardships and anxiety as the family cut the trees for their first cabin in the shadow of Huddleston Knob. One story the grandmother related concerned an attack on two men of the family by a howling pack of wolves. The wolves killed two dogs and would have mutilated the men also had not two other hunters arrived on the scene to fight off the hungry wild animals.

Mrs. Wright also recalled that the pioneers placed bells on grazing horses and cattle so they could be found if they strayed too far from home. When children were sent to bring the cattle home for milking, their feet were first rubbed with gunpowder, for it was believed that wolves feared the smell.

Bears also were a source of danger for the early settlers. Mrs. Wright recounted a traditional story of a bear's attack on the pig pen: "One morning they heard a brood of pigs squealing in the pen, and when they looked out they saw a big bear trying to get out of the pen with a pig held tight in his great paws. My great-grandfather shot the bear and made a lovely rug from the skin."

Panthers have been gone from the area for years, but the first settlers suffered depredations because of their presence. Panther legends are still common throughout the region, indicating that the panther was the favored animal for placing human beings in jeopardy in real and imagined situations. Mrs. Wright remembered the time her great-grandmother was at the spring washing clothes and saw a large panther staring at her from a nearby tree. The woman ran to the house in time to elude the pursuing beast. Her husband later shot and killed the creature.[19]

Two migratory legends, commonly known elsewhere but also told in the Upper Cumberland, concern a panther on the roof of a cabin making strenuous efforts to get inside, and a panther in pursuit of a woman who escapes the animal by ripping off pieces of her clothing

20

and tossing them in the road for the panther to smell. A brief, local-ized version of this latter story was told by a woman from Forbus, Tennessee:

> One time, Great-grandmother—everyone called her Aunt Betty—she had been out in the vicinity where Aunt Betsy Ann Moody lived down there somewhere. And somebody give her a mess of meat. And as she was on her way back, this panther was following her and she first throwed down her bonnet, I think and it tore it up. And I think finally she had to give her meat up.[20]

Another Tennessee encounter with a panther, this one just after the Civil War, was recounted from family tradition by the same elderly woman in Jamestown who told two of the foregoing stories about encounters with Indians:

> I have an uncle that killed a panther one time. He lived way back out on the mountain and it was all wilderness, you know. And they [panthers] was plentiful out there, I reckon, at that time. He had went to mill and he walked and carried his turn* across his shoulders. He went down here on Wolf [River]; somebody was running a mill down here on Wolf. Now I don't know who. As he was going back, he was going around the path—I know where the place is—he went down around and around, turned up like that. They was a stopping tree that come over that path there and there was a spring there. He said he got up pretty close to that tree and said he heard a noise and he looked up and one was patting on that tree; it was fixing to jump on him. Of course, he had his gun, so he killed it. And they always called him Panther Bill after that.
>
> And he was my uncle. He was brother to my daddy.[21]

Snakes share equal billing with panthers in regional legendry. Albert Bilbrey of Whitleyville, Tennessee, identified some snakes native to the area as the "rattlesnake, copperhead, viper, chicken snake, black snake, water moccasin, garter snake, and blue racer." Unlike the first two named, the viper, or spreading viper, is harmless

21

except that in folk belief it will suck cattle.[22] Chicken snakes, black snakes, and racers are the farmer's friends, since they will rid barns and cribs of mice and other rodents. "Most of the old-timers used to keep a black snake in the barn to catch rats," according to Landon Anderson of Celina, and apparently the farmers were not surprised to find a reptile hiding in the corn shucks.[23] Numerous family legends tell of a farmer or child bitten by a poisonous snake mistaken for one of the harmless black species. Lives were saved by a quick-thinking father or older brother who whipped out a pocket knife, lanced the bitten area, and sucked out the lethal poison by mouth. "They'd split the bite with a knife," according to Anderson, "and if they had no hollow teeth or anything, they'd suck that poison out. And if they had a breast pump, they'd use that. And lots of them used coal oil and turpentine."[24] Bilbrey chimed in, "Well, back in olden times they had whiskey. When you got bit, you drank enough whiskey to kill that poison. . . . And a lot of them would kill a live chicken and split it open and slop it on there."[25]

Virtually any snake was believed to be able to charm a person. Widespread across the region is the migratory legend of a child charmed into helpless submission by a snake.[26] The most common snake tale of all, however, relates how two snakes, generally poisonous ones, engage in a death struggle. One keeps breaking away and going to a certain type of weed or bush for life-giving sustenance. Elsworth Carter of northern Monroe County described a fight-to-the-death struggle he heard about as a boy:

> I've heard Lanny Miller tell about the snake tale. He said that a black snake could whip a copperhead. He said they was setting out one Sunday evening, a big bunch of boys and girls. They heard this racket down at the corner of the house, old house. And they went down there and they seen this black snake and copperhead a-fighting. And this black snake, he had him a weed that he'd fight this copperhead awhile, then he'd run out there and suck that weed and he'd come back and fight this copperhead. And said they kept a-watching him and followed him to where he was a-going to this weed. Just had a certain kind of weed. He didn't say what kind it was. But they

22

cut this weed down and these snakes, this black snake whipped the copperhead and killed him. But this here one, he'd suck this weed to get that stuff out of it to kill the poison of that copperhead. And he said that they cut this weed down and took it away where this black snake couldn't find it, and that black snake soon died. He didn't live long. But they claimed he would have lived. He got that stuff that killed this copperhead's poison.

And Lanny knowed that weed. He said he knowed the weed it took, but he never did say what kind of weed it was.[27]

In addition to these natural annoyances and hazards, the early settlers constantly faced the problems associated with providing adequate food, clothing, and shelter for themselves and their families. Typical frontier homes generally were unpretentious. Most furnishings—tables, beds, chairs, benches, buckets, churns, and trays—were handcrafted on the spot, since the settlers had carried along a minimum of baggage when they headed for the western frontier. Early houses and furnishings were not built to last forever; they were designed to meet the needs of survival at a specific time and place.

Cooperation among most persons and a willingness to help one's neighbors grew out of the pioneer sense of survival. When a new family moved into the Upper Cumberland area, people already there supported the newcomers until they could raise and harvest their first crop. When anyone sustained a loss by fire or other means, neighbors customarily donated time, labor, money, or other valuables to help rebuild or replace what had been destroyed. Often the entire loss was covered in this manner. Thus, the settlement of the region was not an act of rugged individualism, as typically depicted in most history books, but was a result of cooperation and joint assistance.

Mutual assistance in order to survive the rigors and hardships of frontier life was probably most important in clearing new ground, planting seeds, and harvesting crops. The men and boys cleared land for "new grounds"* at every opportunity. They cut away the small bushes and saplings and girdled the large trees to kill them. The brush was piled up and burned on the spot. Some preferred to cut the trees so that they could be removed completely from the land. Log rollings

23

An Upper Cumberland couple photographed in Russell County, Kentucky. Print from a glass negative, ca. 1890.

Two young women in Russell County, Kentucky, pose with their favorite horse and dog. Print from a glass negative, ca. 1890.

were held in the spring and were attended by other members of the community. Since there was no heavy equipment, all the rolling and lifting was done by hand with sharpened poles and crude hooks. After the logs were rolled into position, they were burned. The men would set fire to the log heap at several spots, then rake back the ground leaves to keep the adjoining timber land from catching on fire. Clearing land provided ample justification for a neighborhood gathering; not to receive an invitation to a log rolling or other communal function, in fact, was considered an insult. Women wore their Sunday aprons and bonnets and brought along large baskets of food.[28]

After the land was cleared, it was broken with a bull tongue plow* (named for its shape and large wooden beam) pulled by oxen. This also was a cooperative venture between husband and wife or father and son. One drove the work animals while the other steered the plow and held it in the ground. In those times, the land received little or no preparation beyond plowing.

Next came planting the seed, all by hand. This was the job of women and children. The men walked behind them, covering the seed with a broad-bitted, hand-forged hoe, often referred to as a chopping-out hoe* since it was used to hand-groom the rows (that is, "chop out" the weeds) when the plants were young and tender. Things were not vastly different a century later. Virgil Beaty of Byrdstown, Tennessee, recalls plowing the land and planting seeds during his childhood:

> Well, back when I was a little boy, that's the way they put out all the crops. We didn't have no machines to put out. Take an old mule or a horse and a bull tongue plow and marked their rows off. Well, there'd be one go along, they dropped this corn and they followed it with a hoe and cover it.[29]

Albert Bilbrey remembers dropping seed peas by hand and the licking he got from his father for sowing them too thickly:

> I'll tell you about a joke on myself. My daddy put me to dropping peas. Back yonder in olden times that's the way we got our winter clothes is picking peas. And he give me a two-gallon bucket over half full of peas to take up on a hillside. Said, "I want two dropped in a hill."

26

> Well, I took them old peas and in about six, seven rows up
> through there, I run out. And he come out there, and he said,
> "What are you a-doing?"
>
> I said, "I ain't got no more peas."
>
> He said, "You don't mean you've dropped all them peas!"
>
> I said, "Yeah."
>
> He just stopped that mule and my mother was with him.
> He said, "Kate, you watch that mule." He went out over the
> end of that row and cut him an elm, and I want you to know,
> you talk about dropping peas!" [Laughter]
>
> He said, "I'm going to tell you something, young man;
> when them comes up, you've got to thin every one of them
> out of there but two in a hill."
>
> And I had that to do! And, boys, it took me a right smart bit
> to get them [thinned].[30]

In addition to preparing the land for the field crops, the men broke
soil for the family's vegetable garden and laid off the rows for planting. From that point on, gardening was delegated to women and
children. In their gardens, frontier families grew regular cabbage, a
variety of blue cabbage, English peas, six weeks' beans, cucumbers,
black crease-back beans, early October beans, shelly beans, turnips,
and other staple vegetables. In at least one Kentucky community, the
tradition still persists of naming bean varieties after the person from
whom the seeds were obtained. Thus, for example, Ollie beans were
named for Ollie Birch, "Old Man Millard Birch's mother"; Pearl
beans were brought into the community by Pearl Johns from East
Tennessee during pioneer days; Granny Rasner beans are the name-
sake of Eliza Witty Rasner, who was born a few years prior to the Civil
War; Mammy beans are named for Martha Strode Chapman; and
Grandma Strode beans are called after Martha's mother.[31]

Preserving food for out-of-season consumption afforded frontier
families a great degree of security and self-reliance. Family members
killed and cured their own meat; they dried beans (hung up on a
string, the beans were called shucky beans*), pumpkins, apples,
peaches, and pears; they buried potatoes and turnips in conical
mounds; and they kept apples and sweet potatoes in cellars, if available, or in caves, along with turnips and potatoes.

Frontier women worked in the fields with their men. Albert Bilbrey recalled that "women back then went to the field just the same as men went, with a hoe, to get them weeds out of that corn!"[32] The women also cared for the garden, milked the cows, and tended to other livestock, in addition to washing clothes, keeping house, cooking, and bearing children. They also found time to learn and practice various domestic craft forms necessary to keep a household running: carding wool and cotton, spinning and weaving cloth and coverlets, making dresses and coats for the female members of the family and overalls and other work garments for the males, piecing and quilting covers for bedding, and making lye soap. For frontier women, men, and children alike, cooperation was a prerequisite for survival. But cooperative work sharing also afforded occasions for socializing among friends. People looked forward to candy breakings, quilting bees, house raisings, pea shellings, corn huskings, grain harvests, and hunting, fishing, and nut and herb gathering expeditions.

After a few years on the remote Upper Cumberland frontier, the occupants no longer were faced with the immediate problems of survival. They expanded their self-reliance and self-sufficiency, as reflected in larger homes, larger farms, and more acreage cleared for agriculture. The quest for economic security went on continually—a goal that characterized the farming era, which lasted from 1830 to 1930.

With survival no longer a constant challenge, the people of the Upper Cumberland were free to concentrate on developing their communities. More counties were created, more representative officials were elected, and courthouse societies developed. Society in general became stabilized, and people identified strongly with individual counties. Pride and provincialism ensued. The sense of community was heightened with the establishment of a church, public one-room school, general store, and post office within reach of all.

Artisan industries, introduced during the frontier period, spanned the entire farming era and continued in some instances through the Depression years. There were great numbers of blacksmiths, millers, tanners, shoemakers, saddle makers, harness makers, brick makers, cabinet makers, tinkers, and other craftspersons who supported themselves by their labors. Census schedules indicate that by the

28

1830s there was an abundance of these artisans in each county. The figures do not include craftspersons who could fashion commodities such as oak split baskets, groundhog-hide shoe strings, and groundhog-hide banjo heads[33] from elements of the natural environment.

The blacksmith was extremely important to an agricultural economy. He manufactured wagons, plows, cutting knives with double blades, axes, hoes, plow points, and harrow teeth; he fabricated singletrees,* doubletrees,* and clevises*; he made and adjusted steel wagon rims and shod horses.[34] Many large farms had their own blacksmith shops for minor jobs and repairs. Richard Blair of Russell County, Kentucky, superbly documented the home blacksmith industry in the following recollection of his grandfather's blacksmith shop:

> Another thing I like to remember about my Grandfather Wilson was the old blacksmith shop. He and Uncle Bryant lived on the same tract of land, but each one of them had his own personal, private blacksmith shop. A lot of people nowadays seem to hate cold, rainy days in winter time, but I don't. Those were the days that Granddad would go to the shop and I would go with him as a little boy. He would let me pull the bellows to keep the fire going.
>
> During the winter months when no work could be done on the farm, Granddad would take each piece of farm machinery; if there was a piece that was broken, he would mend or replace it with a new one. He would see that all the bearings, all the wheels, and all the moving parts of that particular piece of farm machinery was in good order. He would take all the hoes, the grubbing hoes, and axes that we used for general farming purposes or to make a crop with, and see that every one was sharpened that wasn't sharp. Then he would take shoes—horse shoes and mule shoes—that he would buy as blanks in the store up on Gosser Ridge and he would make and fit two pair of shoes for each work animal on the farm. As those shoes the following season would wear thin, then Granddad would take those shoes off and replace them with new shoes. But you never saw him throw those old shoes out in the weeds, over in the creek, or in a junk heap. He piled

29

This Cumberland County, Kentucky, farmer still splits his own fence rails, using the froe and mallet. Photograph 1972 by David Sutherland.

30

Split oak baskets made in the Upper Cumberland were functional adjuncts to domestic and agrarian activities. Photograph 1972 by David Sutherland.

31

them up in a pile over in the corner of the blacksmith shop. Then the following winter, he would take those shoes and take the nails out, if there was some left hanging with them, and put them in the fire and heat them red hot and then he would make those horse shoes and mule shoes into hinges. They already had the holes in them for driving nails and he would use them on farm gates and on the barn doors and other places where we needed hinges.

Now there is one thing about those hinges of Granddad's: they not only lasted a long time, these hinges that he would make from horse shoes and use on the farm would squeak to high heaven. You could hear those things squeak for a mile up the creek or down the creek.[35]

Water-powered mills supported a variety of industries in the Upper Cumberland region. Grist,* roller,* paper, textile, and saw mills were operated by huge water wheels of both the undershot* and overshot* varieties, and later by turbines. Some of the old mills were made entirely of wood, with the exception of the tin water buckets on the wheel and the buhrstones.* The cogs of the wheels were made of seasoned hickory.[36] Some communities had water-powered mills as early as 1800 for grinding grains into meal and flour, but it was not until between 1830 and 1840 that virtually every community boasted of its own mill.[37] Most of the water-powered mills were gone by World War I, but the old grist mill at Mill Springs in Wayne County—reputedly the tallest metal wheel in the world—was in commercial operation until 1948.

E.R. Gaskin, formerly of Russell County, recalled that an "average family would use a bushel of corn meal each week. Some of the larger families would need two bushels. It was a familiar sight to see one riding his horse along the narrow sandy roads, with long white bags filled with corn, headed for one of the grist mills located on some small stream."[38] The miller was paid for his grinding services when he extracted a toll,* generally one-eighth, from the "turn" or sack of corn brought in by the farmer. Will H. Jones of Cumberland County remembered that the miller used a *toll dish:*

I reckon it held one-eighth of a bushel. He would fill that

toll dish with corn before they got a bushel in the hopper.* If they had two bushel, he would take it out twice. . . . I heard it said that Mr.——— lost his half bushel [container] and he looked everywhere for it and when he picked up his toll dish, he found his half bushel. His toll dish was supposed to be only one-eighth, but when he found his half bushel, he found his toll dish to be bigger than his half bushel.[39]

While millers' reputations were not always untarnished, neither were those of customers. And customers were sometimes hard to please, at least the ones described by Charlie Burtram of southern Wayne County:

> Uncle Reuben [Dishman] ground corn at the water mill. Old Uncle Dad Denny, he was queer. He had to have his meal just exactly the way he wanted it. Not too fine, not too coarse. Uncle Reuben had a little thing to step on, and reach up there and turn the buhrs, you know, with a string. And he'd turn the buhrs, fine or coarse, whatever you wanted.
>
> And Old Uncle Dad, he'd come and he'd tell Uncle Reuben, "I want this meal just so and so."
>
> "Now you get right here and whenever I turn it to where it suits you, why, you tell me."
>
> "That's it."
>
> He said, "I never did move that peg up!" He said, "If I had, I would have ruined it."
>
> I know that from experience. Dad used to grind right out there where them roads fork. And I've ground bushels and bushels, and there's lots of people come back and grumble about the meal not being fine enough. And you can put them down there to feel of the meal, and never turn them buhrs a bit, and finally they'd say it was all right.[40]

Many people have clear memories of milling activities and of the mill and mill dam as places for socializing and courting. Picnics and community outings frequently were held there, boys swam in the pond, and lovers gazed into the waters or strolled in the shaded areas along the bank.

33

Tanbark milling merits mention here because it was of importance to those narrators who like to talk about the tanyards, the process of tanning, and the colorful tanners themselves. Cumberland County, in fact, has a community named Tanbark.

Frontier families used the skins of both domestic and wild animals in various ways, and so tanning was one of the first industries in the area. The tanner was an appreciated person in the community fortunate enough to have one, the odorific smell which he produced notwithstanding. Deerskins from which the hair had been removed were used for men's trousers, hunting shirts, and underclothing. Hides tanned with the fur on them produced rugs, robes, and upholstery. Buffalo and bear hides were used to make robes and coverlets,[41] while cattle and horse hides provided rawhide leather for shoes, saddles, and bridles.[42] The tanner was equipped with lime vats, a tanner's beam* (a split log bench with two legs in one end), a curved knife for scraping, hoppers to place the tanbark in, and steers to power the hoppers.[43]

Bark was taken in strips from the appropriate kinds of trees and was dried before being ground up in the hoppers. White oak bark was used very infrequently. Chestnut oak, a species between red oak and white oak, was a good producer of tannic acid. Red oak, which produced a reddish-brown hue, also was used in normal tanning processes. Maple was used to produce gray, and walnut yielded a rich brown color.[44] Some farmers cut and hauled tanbark during late spring and early summer, while the sap was up and running freely. Extracted at any other time, the bark could not be peeled from the tree trunk in sizeable pieces.[45]

Tanning was a slow and expensive process. It took a cord of wood to tan ten hides, and the process of removing the hair, dyeing the hides, and repeatedly rubbing in oil and tallow to make the skins soft took almost a year to complete.[46] The hides and leather not used to manufacture items for domestic consumption were shipped by flatboats and steamboats to New Orleans; later they were sent to Nashville when that market opened up. Leather goods constituted a significant proportion of local exports for many years after the Civil War. The general stores of the area had little use for them except as items received as barter to be exported by steamboat.

34

This Kentucky trapper from Cumberland County prefers to earn a living at hunting-fishing-gathering activities rather than farming. Photograph 1972 by David Sutherland.

35

Two sisters in eastern Wayne County, Kentucky, live much like their fore-bears a century ago. Photograph 1976 by the author.

Prior to 1800, before the coming of steamboats, even before the establishment of general stores throughout the area, Yankee peddlers penetrated the Upper Cumberland with pack horses laden with dress and coat materials, hats and coats, and a vast array of small items such as needles, hat pins, and miscellaneous trinkets. Individual peddlers made up a part of the local scene for more than a century, and descriptions of them are still available from older people. A Wayne County resident offered this memory of one of them:

> We loved to see them come. They would come and leave little trinkets. They would come and show their products. If they stayed all night, they would leave a little trinket. But I will tell you of one time a man came to our home. It was around midnight; he came naked. He hollered. Mama heard him. She told Papa, and he asked him what he wanted. He said he was about to freeze to death. Papa picked up a quilt and told him to put it around him and come in. Papa gave him some quinine to help him from getting a cold and Mama fixed him some supper. She came upstairs; she was scared. She didn't know what he was or who he was: "He is down there and getting some quinine to keep him from getting a cold."
>
> She had fixed his supper. Papa had never turned anyone away. So he stayed all night. . . .[47]

The presence of a general store was one means by which a community established an identity. Throughout the nineteenth century, the general store was unsurpassed as a gathering place. Its influence extended well into the twentieth century and is still prominent in many rural communities throughout the Upper Cumberland. The store attracted those who wanted to hear the neighborhood news as well as news from other places carried in by travelers and salesmen. If a farmer killed an especially large snake or grew a whopper watermelon, he displayed it at the store. His wife did the same for products from the garden. Here also family members bartered such items as beeswax, furs, chestnuts, peas, feathers, eggs, and poultry for plow points, flax wheels, coffee, salt, pepper, a piece of pretty calico, or any of a host of other items brought in by steamboat or freight wagon* from outside the region.[48] Lists of these and similar bartering items are common in many local history books. Rarely, however, do they reveal the human element that lies behind such lists in the way that personal narratives do, such as that recounted by Clyde White:

> Well, back when us young ones was raised up, our mother raised a bunch of hens every year. Along in the spring, she'd sell those hens and get us all a pair of shoes and some clothes to do that summer, you know, and some food to eat out of those hens.
>
> We'd go of a night and climb up in the trees and catch those hens and hand them down out of the trees. We'd have a coop to put them in. The next day we'd take them to the store and sell them in a wagon, a road wagon.
>
> Mother always thought if they brought a dollar or a dollar and a quarter apiece, that was the most money ever was.[49]

The mercantile business flourished in the river communities throughout the steamboat century. Some general stores in county seat towns acquired inventories larger than modern-day department stores. An example is the J.D. Irvin store in Creelsboro in Russell County, which around 1900 reputedly sold more goods than all the stores in Russell Springs and Jamestown, Kentucky, combined. People came from forty miles away to buy groceries there and to "outfit their families with shoes. Maybe there'd be eight or ten kids. A fellow told me that one time he counted thirty-eight wagons lined up down the road, all loaded with families waiting their turn to come in."[50] William Smith & Son of the Leslie community in Cumberland County also had a large clientele. The Smiths sent huckster wagons* drawn by pairs of mules out into the surrounding communities to sell and barter merchandise with people who never went to the county seat more than once each year.[51]

Huckster wagons, direct descendants of the Yankee peddlers, evolved into rolling stores* about 1930, with the advent of rubber-tired vehicles and improved roads. The rolling store, like the huckster wagon, traveled along established routes on a regular schedule. Schoolchildren and housewives looked forward with eagerness to these scheduled visits. The children had a penny or two set aside to spend on pencils, paper, and candy. Their mothers stuck with the barter economy, exchanging chickens, eggs, and feathers for sugar, spices, and coffee.[52] The people had little money, but they owned or tended farms which gave them the means of acquiring what they needed. After all, "at ten cents a pound, coffee was not hard to come by."[53]

Farming gave sustenance to the people of the Upper Cumberland and became the way of life for most residents, despite the fact that many of the hills and low mountains were not suited to intensive cultivation. Families were large, and because there was the need for family self-sufficiency, everyone was taught to work in the house or in the fields at an early age. In the early days the population was small; consequently, there was an abundance of fertile new land. When a field wore out, more land was cleared to make a new one. A farm of 150 acres would last for a long time in this manner, for only a few acres were under cultivation at a given time. Conservation and reclamation came later, mainly since the 1940s.

Hill country farmers and bottomland farmers alike spent the first years of the farming era producing foodstuffs and other agricultural products that would make them economically self-sufficient: corn, oats, rye, wheat, and tobacco, and sometimes hemp, cotton, and flax. Along with agricultural crops, they raised horses, cattle, hogs, sheep, and turkeys, and they made maple sugar, molasses, pine tar, and other items for sale on local and regional markets.

Some farmers maintained livestock pastures and grew fields of hay, but open-range grazing was instituted at an early date and continued until World War I in most areas and through the 1930s on the Cumberland Plateau, near Byrdstown, Jamestown, and Livingston, Tennessee, and Monticello, Kentucky. It was common for poor mountain people, who did not have farms of their own, to turn their livestock into the woods to forage. Richard Blair, resident of Russell County, recalled that hogs and cattle foraged in the woods:

> When our folks first came here and settled, they began to clear out the timber and plant corn, beans, and other things they could use for food on the table, to feed their livestock, and generally make a living. They weren't worried about grass. Anytime they had extra cattle, they would turn them

39

loose out in the woods and then they would find fire-blackened spots where lightning had started fires; burned the timber off and the first thing came back was grass and weeds. Later the same territory would reforest itself and get back into forest like it was originally. Their hogs were turned loose in the woods to get fat on beech mast, chestnuts, and acorns.[54]

Hogs roamed the countryside foraging at will, sleeping under schoolhouses and in the woods and carrying fleas wherever they went.[55] Arlo Barnett of McCreary County, Kentucky, explained how he kept the hogs gentle: "Before they put stock laws in this end of the county, I had a lot of hogs. They didn't even know where home was. There was always a lot of mast. I'd go to them when it would come snows. I'd ride a horse and go and feed them. This would keep them gentle enough so I could get them up when I wanted to."[56]

Henry Powell of Wayne County, Kentucky, discussed the farm families' reliance on livestock for a little extra cash: "The people who lived [back on South Fork] raised lots of hogs. They followed the hogs on mast. That's what the farmers back in there depended on mostly. When they got away from these valleys, you know, they depended on their hogs altogether, and milch cows. Just raised their own living, you might say—lumber wasn't no good. They couldn't sell no lumber for anything."[57]

Daily Crouch of Fentress County remembered the free range era and the attendant branding of cattle and annual roundups: "We used to run cattle on Cumberland Mountain. My granddaddy lived out there and we'd put our cattle out there in the spring of the year. We'd ride horses out there on Cumberland Mountain and round up them cattle. They were branded. It was free range. Camp out of a night and look for cattle."[58]

Ira Bell of Wayne County talked about the manner in which animals were branded and the importance of the procedure:

> Well, one mark they had for cattle was a kind of instrument that made a circle or a hole in their ear. One hole in the right and one in the left. Now my father lived at Parmleysville; his mark, he cropped the ear and split each one, a crop and a split.

40

And then they had another called a swallow fork; I don't
know just what kind of a big mark that was. We never used
that. Sometimes in a part of the ear, they'd make a right angle
and take a little section of a square, just cut a little piece out
and make it not go back too far. In the neighborhood, why,
each had their own mark and if some new one come in, he'd
devise something else a little different.[59]

The following anecdote, related by Ira Bell, illustrates how deeply
open-range grazing was entrenched in the region:

During the Depression, some unemployed men from
southern Wayne County were sent to Indiana to work on
farms. One of these mountaineers was sent to the dairy barn
to clean the milking parlor. Pondering the situation, he said,
"I can't understand that. We don't scoop up fresh cow manure
where I'm from." Says, "We turn the cows out in the woods
and we dog them up when it's time to milk them, and their
bowels act while the dogs are running them. So we don't have
this stuff to clean out!"[60]

Upper Cumberland farmers across the years mostly were small-
time livestock raisers who kept only a few animals. Surpluses were
sold in local markets on "Court Day,"* a practice that was well
established by the 1830s. Breeders and trainers periodically visited
areas where they had previously contacted farmers about buying
sheep, hogs, and cattle to drive to nearby markets in central Kentucky, Nashville, or Knoxville, as well as distant markets in Baltimore, Philadelphia, and the Deep South.[61] A resident of Fentress
County provided a fairly detailed oral traditional account of early
animal drives from the Upper Cumberland to Baltimore—one of the
longest drives in the country during pre-Civil War times:

Pleasant Gatewood had a store down here in the Forbus-
Pall Mall area, and he would buy cattle and mules and other
things through the summer—take them in trade on his goods.
Then he would go through to Baltimore with them—sell the
livestock, buy wagons and goods, haul the goods back in the
wagons; sell the wagons and the goods for more stock to go
back again.

41

The route probably went through here by Burrville and Kingston and into the Knoxville area, and then up that valley to Baltimore.

This was before the Civil War, probably the 1840s, so the wagons he bought were probably the Tarskein Wagons. What they were, on their axles in place of having the metal part go on there like they used in later times for your metal hub to fit up on, they had a wooden axle then and used tar made out of pine. I've never seen one, but I've heard the old-timers say you could hear them coming for a mile or more with that thing squeaking when the tar began to dry up on it.[62]

The production of hogs and cattle developed rapidly across the Upper Cumberland. Following the Civil War, when drives could be made without fear of attack by scavenging bands of soldiers, "professional" livestock drovers* began operations under standardized practices. Drovers generally drove stock cattle, not fat ones. Hogs, however, were "top hogs" or of "finished" quality. A wagonload of corn was sometimes brought along to feed the hogs; since they were well cared for on the way, they lost very little weight. The first day on the road took the greatest toll.[63] Longer drives usually consisted of about 120 head of livestock, with a head drover on horseback and two men on foot, accompanied by a couple of dogs. There were farms en route where weary drovers found rest and food, and farmers sold them feed or rented grass lots for their livestock.

An old black drover from Cumberland County knew the secret for controlling hogs on the road: "Never let a hog know he's being driven. Just let him take his way, and keep him going in the right direction."[64]

Eugene Wilhelm noted that cattle, hog, and poultry drives served several social and cultural functions in the Blue Ridge country. His observations also hold true for livestock drives in the Upper Cumberland. They were a form of cooperative labor between local farm families and drovers, or between the families themselves in community drives. Driving provided contact with people outside one's own culture and surroundings. These annual events were a way of journeying into cities where goods were purchased and taken home, clothing styles and the making of clothes were discussed, new games were learned, newspapers were read, oral recollections and political stories were told, and local news items were exchanged.[65]

Very large herds of sheep, cattle, and hogs annually made their way along the Kentucky Stock Road which ran from northern Alabama through Sparta, Livingston, and Byrdstown. The road crossed the Wolf River at Dug Ford about three miles below the present bridge, recrossed the river into Clinton County at the mouth of Spring Creek in the vicinity of Lee's Chapel, and made its way through Albany, Kentucky, and Monticello to the Bluegrass region. Elvin Byrd, who viewed the passage of these herds on many occasions, recounted stories of the drovers, their dogs, and their horses. He remembered especially the lead cow with the bell that the other cattle followed in almost hypnotic rhythm.[66] Henry Rogers of Jamestown, Ed Harris of Byrdstown,[68] and Fred Littrell of Albany[69] were well-known stock buyers and drovers in that area. Al Cross of Albany was another.

> My dad, Al Cross, was a great cattle trader and mule trader. He'd go out and buy up seventy-five to a hundred head of cattle at a time from down on Obey River and Wolf River and Lillydale down in Tennessee. And he'd get those cattle together in maybe two or three weeks' time, and we'd take out to the market to what's called the Bluegrass. It's at the edge of the Bluegrass; up about Stanford is as far as we ever went. Sometimes they went to Richmond, but I never did go to Richmond. We'd have about a hundred cattle on Monday morning. We'd line them up and get them ready to start; go up through Duvall Valley and across Poplar Mountain; have one leader—an old cow who usually went in front. And it'd take four or five people to get them across the mountain and get them broke to the road. And we'd take horses and buggies and so on, and we'd take those cattle and get them broke. And then when we got them over about Gap Creek, about three people could handle them then. And we'd go on up, right this side of Monticello along there at Elmer Dunnington's and Tom Dick Denney's and Tom King's, which was about twenty-something miles and we'd stay all night.

43

They had a place to keep the cattle and feed them. Didn't feed them much and they's thin anyway. Next day, we'd get our cattle on up the road, on up through Monticello, on up about five miles this side of Burnside, which was about another twenty miles—made about twenty miles a day. And we'd stay with Old Man Wesley Cowan, wife named Nannie Mae. They's quite characters. And we'd stay at their house, but we'd keep our cattle over at a fellow's named Sam Weaver. He had a big farm and a good feedlot and so on.

The third night we'd go on across Waitsboro [Ferry] and ferry our cattle across and river on the ferry boat. We didn't go through Burnside. There was a cut-off into Somerset called Waitsboro. So we'd go up to about five or six miles the other side of Somerset, what they called Old Man Hurt's there; I forget his first name now. And that is the third night.

Fourth night we'd go on up right beyond King's Mountain, right this side of Hall's Gap. And they's a fellow name of Privette, John Privette; they'd take care of the cattle and the men too.

The fifth day, along about one or two o'clock, you'd get into Stanford. And that's Friday and the market was on Monday. All the farmers come in on Monday to buy these cattle; wasn't an auction—you'd just have these big yards there and you'd rent pens and put your cattle in them and sort your cattle according to grade and size and so on.

And you'd start selling these cattle on Saturday; some people would come in on Saturday and maybe Sunday they'd come in. And then they'd pick out their cattle and buy a few. You'd like to get them sold before the big day. And lots of times you'd trade them for mules and horses and bring them back down, and trade them to farmers here in the county. But some of them, during that time, took them to Richmond, went as far as Richmond and that took seven days.[70]

The importance of the dog in animal drives cannot be overstressed. Mary Littrell of Monticello claimed that she, her husband Fred, and one dog "drove one hundred sheep through this town to the valley."[71]

44

Henry H. Rogers of Jamestown, Tennessee, related the following
story of a drover and his dog:

> No trouble after you got started. They had dogs that was
> worth all the men in the world. Just one dog was all you
> needed for a hundred head of cattle.
>
> Everybody rode horses. When we got to Danville and sold
> the cattle, this man put that dog up in the saddle and brought
> him back.
>
> I remember selling one bunch of cattle to Herb Guinn of
> Danville and he stayed out three or four days there picking up
> cattle and delivering to our place till he got seventy-five head.
> When he turned them out, why, in just a few steps the road
> forked. He was going to turn left. He called his dog and said,
> "Go up yonder to that house and stay in the road and turn
> them cattle left." And he just shot over the fence and went up
> through the field. When we got up there with the cattle, he
> was standing in the road. And he done that all the way
> through, too.[72]

Turkeys and geese were driven in flocks of several hundred and
were not at all difficult to handle, at least not during the day. Sun-
down changed all of this, however; at that moment the fowl raised
their giant wings in flight and roosted on the nearest available perch.
One narrator described the dilemma this way: "My husband used to
buy and drive turkeys from near Jamestown [Tennessee] to Monticello. He said whenever night come, them turkeys went to roost; it
didn't matter where they was at. Nothing you could do about it
except let them go."[73] Often the excess weight on tree limbs caused
them to break. It then became necessary to guard the turkeys from
angry citizens whose shade trees had been damaged. Drovers sometimes were obliged to pay for damages done.[74] It is said that turkeys
were sometimes traded for whiskey along the road.

John Black Tooley of Meshack drove about 1,500 turkeys from the
Cumberland River to the railhead at Glasgow three or four times each
year. Assisted by four or five men on each trip, he took along a wagon
for cooking, sleeping, and hauling exhausted turkeys.[75]

Sam Watson, a drover from Metcalfe County, saw beauty in a flock of geese being driven down the road to market: "That was the prettiest drive of everything they drove. Every goose's head was the same height. . . . They'd just paddle along with them webbed feet."[76]

Will Peavyhouse of Buffalo Cove, Tennessee—a spot where Davy Crockett spent a few months—recalled his childhood memories of two stock buyers, Lewis Wright and Denton Buck. He observed that cattle and hogs were driven to Danville, while turkeys and geese were driven to nearby poultry markets in Jamestown or Livingston—all this in the days when a road was generally either a river of mud or a dust-choked artery which coated the lungs and nostrils and made breathing very difficult.[77] With the construction of better roads, it became easier to transport livestock by vehicles; by 1940, stock driving had diminished to the point where it was almost nonexistent.

Today, some area residents, both young and old, earn comfortable livings farming part-time and "pen-hooking"* the rest of the time. They roam from farm to farm and from community to community, hoping to buy one or more head of livestock in order to turn a quick dollar. They may haul the stock to market and take their chances of prices there, or they may sell to another jobber without ever loading up the animals in their own trucks. In classic form, the pen-hooker hangs around the regional livestock markets in places such as Gamaliel, Edmonton, and Monticello, Kentucky, and Livingston; he jumps onto trucks loaded with hogs or cattle and offers the owner "top dollar" for his cargo before he has the chance to yard the animals. Although today's transportation differs from that of the drover era, the actors and the roles are essentially the same in both time periods.

Just as new and improved roads heralded the end of animal drives in the Upper Cumberland, improvements in farm machinery ushered in a new era in agricultural practices. Most farm families aspired to being progressive and to introducing as much new agricultural technology (in the form of equipment and methods) as possible. Although new tools and ideas occasionally were introduced, the conservative, independent character of the economy largely was retained. For example, each family strove to provide for all of its sugar needs at home. As late as the early twentieth century, it was not at all uncommon for a single family to have thirty-five bee gums* situated on large, flat rocks at the side or to the rear of the vegetable garden. The gums were usually cut from hollow sections of the lin tree, a member of the gum family. Rodents disliked its taste, it is said, and thus would not chew an entry hole into the gum and take the honey. Later, hand-made beehives were fashioned from lumber to replace the gums.

More advanced agricultural practices did not come to the region until the 1880s. Prior to that time, progress meant giving up one type of horse-drawn plow for a new type of horse-drawn plow. The traditional bull tongue plow, with a jumping or cutting coulter,* broke up the land and made it loose so that planting could be accomplished more readily by hand. The new moldboard plow* pulverized the soil and led to the introduction of small plows for row cultivation, such as the A-harrow* and the double shovel.*[78] The hillside turning plow* was introduced around the turn of the century. This unique plow had a moldboard and landside that could be flipped onto the opposite side of the plow at the end of each row, and so it enabled hill country farmers to plow a little higher up the sides of the hills and practice soil conservation at the same time. The farmer could continue to throw the soil along parallel lines instead of making erosion-inducing furrows up and down the hill.[79]

The job-planters* preceded by many years the mechanized one-row planters such as those made by Oliver and John Deere. Operated by hand, the job-planter was jabbed into the soil and then triggered so that one or two grains were released. This new device was not much faster than dropping seed by hand, but it was a back-saver and therefore highly prized. It was later used during replanting sessions, following the introduction of one-row planters.[80]

Women helped their husbands during the hand-planting and job-planting years. They took their babies to the field and put them on straw or quilt pallets in a shady location so that the infants could be observed at all times. Family dogs were stationed nearby to watch for snakes and other threats to the babies.[81]

The introduction of fertilizer was another mark of progressive farming, but this did not occur in the main until the early years of the present century. When fertilizer came into use, it was considered a luxury to be enjoyed and profited from only by well-to-do farm families. Some farmers delicately dispensed the fertilizer into the soil with a teaspoon, each hill of corn receiving one measure.[82] If a bountiful corn havest did not result, people felt that "something was wrong with the seed."[83] Most would not buy high-test fertilizer when it was first introduced; dubious about the nutrient content in the product, they were afraid of being cheated by the manufacturer or the merchant.[84]

As a result of the skepticism with which people regarded commercial fertilizer, shippers and merchants were not without their financial problems during the first years of the fertilizer era. A 1921 issue of *The Burkesville News* carried the following letter from a small proprietor to a fertilizer dealer:

> Dear Sir, I received your letter about which I owe you. Now, be pachent, I ain't forget you yet. As soon as folks pay me I will pay you. If this was judgement day and you were no more prepared to meet your God than I am to meet your account, you are sure going to hell.[85]

With the advent of improved implements for cultivation and harvesting, farm families made a concerted effort to grow bigger and better crops to provide for a greater degree of self-sufficiency and to earn money to spend on improvements and bigger and better homes. The era of log cabin and log house construction was over by the late nineteenth century; most families built frame houses and covered them with yellow poplar weatherboards. Joshua Baxter, age ninety-eight, of Monroe County observed: "You can't imagine how things have improved since my early days. Every house and building in this country was put up out of hewed logs. I was born in that kind of house."[86]

Poor whites and blacks of the area contracted their services on a daily or weekly basis for labor on the farm and in the log woods. This was their major means of earning money for their families' needs. They worked twelve to fourteen hours a day during growing and harvesting periods—as they expressed it, "from sun to sun." For these long hours they were paid fifty to sixty cents a day and were fed dinner (lunch).[87] All too often the workers did not receive this much pay (one man claimed that he worked for fifteen cents a day), and many of them took their wages in food products. For a day's work, they might receive five pounds of pork side, jowl, or shoulder,[88] or a bushel of shelled corn which could be converted into meal at the local grist mill.[89] It should be noted, in defense of the farmer-employers, that they were often short of cash; some had none at all.[90]

Since the barter economy did not permit farmers to expand the base of agricultural practices, the need for money came into prominence. The crops farmers raised to create a cash economy were corn, wheat, potatoes, melons, hay, and tobacco.[91] Virtually all farmers cleared large fields for corn, for it was the major cash crop from 1830 to the present, as well as the prime source of food for humans and feed for animals. Charles S. Guthrie described corn as "The Mainstay of the Cumberland Valley" in an article which considers the vocabulary of corn production.[92] Yellow grain and white grain varieties were produced cross the years, both of which takes three to four weeks longer to mature than hybrid varieties. It was commonly thought that white corn meal tasted better than yellow.[93] Some farmers grew traditional strains of blue speckled corn, carried from Virginia; pokeberry corn, which grew especially large in the river bottoms; and blood and butcher corn, named for the red kernels ("blood") among the white ("butcher") on the ear.[94]

The open-range pastures were inadequate to support cattle through the winter months, so farmers often were compelled to cut the corn before it matured fully or to strip the brownish-green blades off the stalk as roughage for cattle and horses. This process, called foddering,* caused a low grain yield. By World War II, good quality hay made from crimson clover, red clover, lespedeza, red top, timothy, alfalfa, and soybeans had replaced the need for fodder.

Wheat, like corn, was a source of bread. It was sown in early fall, harvested the following July with a scythe, and tied into bundles with some of its own straw. One man could cut about one acre per day. After the wheat cradle was introduced, three to four acres per day could be harvested. In early times, the grain was trampled out with horses or oxen or flailed out with a flailing stick. It is still common to hear someone threatened with the admonition, "I'll flail the living daylight out of you!"

In the early 1870s, the groundhog thresher* was brought into the region. Powered by four teams pulling a sweep in a circle, it delivered straw, grain, and chaff onto a large sheet spread on the ground. Hay forks removed the straw, leaving the wheat and chaff to be scooped up and run through a separating machine called a wheat fan.* Modern separating machines (called threshing machines) made their appearance in the 1920s and 1930s. [95]

Threshing day was a significant event, with all the neighbors cooperating to do the work. This was one form of "swapping labor*; people donated their work to neighbors, who would in turn help them out when their crop was ready to be harvested. The women traveled with their husbands to cook for the threshing crew at each farm.[96]

Soon after threshing was completed each year, wheat was taken to the roller mill and ground into flour. Farmers and tenants (those who worked "on shares") alike shared the flour. All of them filled their bed ticks* with new straw,[97] and ample straw was stored to be fed to livestock during winter months and to provide stall bedding for animals.

Tobacco cultivation provided its own set of folk practices, customs, and unique vocabulary in the same fashion as corn and wheat. The first kind of tobacco grown in the Upper Cumberland was the "dark" variety. This was a coarser and hardier tobacco than burley, the type grown in the area since the 1920s. Dark tobacco was grown without fertilizer and was stripped from the stalk in grades, pressed into homemade wooden hogsheads,* rolled or hauled by ox-cart to the river, and shipped on steamboats to market.[98] This variety was important as a cash crop during the first decade following the Civil War, but prices dropped so low by 1874 that farmers were forced to quit raising the crop.[99] Generally, it brought no more than five cents per pound for several years before and after 1900 and could not be depended on even to pay the floor charges at the market center. Much of the tobacco grown then was used at home for chewing and smoking.[100]

When burley tobacco was introduced, it was necessary to cover the plant bed with a cloth mesh or canvas, which was expensive at that time. Consequently, the plant beds were covered only with two or three layers of cedar brush. The added revenue derived from burley allowed farmers to assume the added costs of producing the new variety, and by 1935 burley was established as the chief cash crop in the Upper Cumberland.[101]

50

The old ways of farming generally had disappeared by World War II. People today talk about earlier times with emotion and readily recount personal experience and oral traditional narratives to anyone who will listen to the tales of long ago. No one really wants to go back in time, however; people are painfully aware that during the agricultural era, hill slopes too often were destroyed by erosion, soils were sapped of their nutrients by a one-crop system, and roving livestock grazed the lands of others all too freely. A Pickett Countian summed it up very clearly:

> People back when I was growing up didn't know how to take care of the land. They just corned it to death. They didn't have no hay; sowed nothing. They just made enough to keep a pair of mules and a cow or two and a few hogs. Well, the hogs run out. . . . People didn't know how to take care of their land. There wasn't nobody, to tell you the truth, that farmed much. There didn't nobody try to get ahead. It's no trouble if you just want to do enough to live and get by. If you try to get ahead, it takes a little more effort.
>
> They didn't fertilize much then. People, when they cleaned up a field, first few years you got the best off of it. Then they'd kind of let it grow up and clean up more. It would wash in gullies. There was thousands of acres that ought to never have been cleaned up. It ought to have been left as a forest. There is a lot of land yet in this country that ought to be reforested.[102]

Farm families had a good living during the latter years of the agricultural era, for they measured progress against frontier times and conditions. The area's families achieved a significant degree of economic self-sufficiency, but they never discarded the practice of mutual cooperation when seasonal jobs had to be done. More than any other word, *cooperation* is the key to understanding the lifestyle of the agricultural era. Every thought and every act was bound up in the concept of helping one another. Oral traditions testify that in a time when all things had to be done with sheer human and animal strength, the farm families of the Upper Cumberland perfected the art of cooperation and community living.

CHAPTER 2

A Region Divided

The years between 1830 and 1860 were good ones in the Upper Cumberland. County governments were strengthened, churches were firmly rooted and wielded considerable influence on the lives of the people, general stores were within easy reach of everyone, and schools and post offices gave healthy boosts to community pride and development. Farming was important and was the major determinant of regional character, but trades and professions were especially important in the growth of such emerging towns as Carthage, Sparta, Cookeville, Livingston, Gainesboro, Tompkinsville, Burkesville, Monticello, and Somerset. Stores handling specialty goods were founded during that period, hotels were built to accommodate drummers* and travelers, banks were opened, and weekly newspapers began publication. People of the Upper Cumberland demonstrated a spirit of cooperation and their future looked bright.

In the spring and summer of 1861, the Civil War came upon the Upper Cumberland. For four years, the region was in turmoil. Civil courts were suspended; anarchy prevailed everywhere. Post offices and post roads were abandoned. Stores, with all their calicoes, shoes, hats, and fancy foodstuffs, were closed. Pastors abandoned their churches, and many homes were deserted by those who took sides at the onset of the war and moved to friendlier surroundings. Many

Unionists moved across the line into Kentucky to avoid the Tennessee militia, and those who favored the Confederacy moved farther south.[1] Slaveholding was not a major issue. Many Union sympathizers on both sides of the state line owned slaves. Across the Upper Cumberland, the war was a question of union or disunion; most people, especially in the mountainous areas, were Unionists.

When the Civil War broke out, the people of the Upper Cumberland were not ready psychologically for the crisis which was to lay heavy upon them. They had just come through a period of growth designed to achieve cultural and financial stability. Now they were being called upon to choose sides—a decision which was at times extremely hard to make and one which relatives, neighbors, and friends often considered to be the wrong one.

The people of this border country were touched during the war years as no other people in the nation. Their homes were not burned like those in the Valley of Virginia, but families were torn apart by divided allegiances, and guerrilla bands raided the region, taking what items they could carry away on horseback and killing or torturing those persons who resisted them. All too numerous are oral stories which tell of fathers and small sons brutally murdered and of traumatized wives and daughters raped and left behind to bury the mutilated bodies of their men. Cordell Hull, secretary of state under Franklin D. Roosevelt, described his Pickett County homeland during the Civil War as "a perfect hell."[2]

Immediately after the vote for secession was taken in June 1861, both Union and Confederate camps were established within the Upper Cumberland region to hold the line in behalf of their respective causes, and by late summer numerous deaths by ambush had occurred on both sides. By late summer, too, both sides of the state line witnessed the arrival of Yankee and Rebel soldiers who chased each other and occasionally drew blood as they vied for position in this low mountain terrain.

By winter of 1861, the rebels occupied the southern part of Kentucky as their strong line of defense. They had a line stretching from Forts Henry and Donelson on the Lower Cumberland in northwest Tennessee eastward through Tompkinsville, Burkesville, Monticello, and Somerset to Cumberland Gap. The key Confederate post

53

of the Upper Cumberland was in Wayne County near Mill Springs. This was also the first link to be broken in the long, loose Southern chain. The break came January 19, 1862, in the following manner.

In October 1861, General Felix Zollicoffer, C.S.A., was garrisoned at Cumberland Gap. He feared that Union forces would try to invade east Tennessee from Kentucky, possibly by crossing over between Albany, Kentucky, and Jamestown, Tennessee, and then traversing the rugged Cumberland Plateau. Zollicoffer moved westward during November in the direction of Jamestown with intentions of bolstering the Monticello-Somerset defense line. From Jamestown he moved into Kentucky, passing through Albany and Monticello, and took position at Mill Springs. This was, to his thinking, a strategic and easily defensible location, for it commanded the river, the ferry, and the approaches to Cumberland Gap and the Jacksboro Road into Tennessee.

General George H. Thomas moved into the area with a large Union force. Zollicoffer, uncertain as to what action to take, crossed the Cumberland during a heavy rain despite danger of flooding, which would cut off his retreat. With reinforcements present, General Thomas attacked early on the morning of January 19, 1862. After a bloody battle, General Zollicoffer was killed and his entire army routed.

The Confederates retreated through Monticello and passed through Fentress and Overton counties on their way to Gainesboro. Thomas moved into Smith County, Tennessee, two weeks later and established himself at Camp Fogg, between Chestnut Mound and Carthage.[3]

Zollicoffer's defeat at the Battle of Mill Springs is celebrated orally in both legend and song. Few events, in fact, are more talked about in the Upper Cumberland than this one, and at least three songs (two of which are included here) were written to commemorate that fateful day in 1862. Four testimonies are presented here to illustrate the richness of the oral traditions surrounding the Battle of Mill Springs. The first, told by Jean Dicken of Albany, illustrates the fear of and perhaps contempt for the rebels felt by many residents of the area:

> The first I remember hearing about the Civil War was from
> my Grandmother Dyer, who was a great storyteller. I can

54

remember sitting by her chair and watching her smoke her corncob pipe and listening to these stories. She was sort of like a queen on a throne. The whole family would come in and listen to her tell her stories.

Whenever she mentioned a rebel, it was just like saying a dirty word. I can remember that a rebel to me was the most terrible thing I ever heard of when I was a little bitty girl. The first I ever heard about the Confederate Army I heard through her. And I remember her telling me that when she was just very small, she sat in the window and watched the Confederate Army go by their house.

The way I remember her telling, the Confederate Army traveled all day and they were dressed in their finery and had the polished buttons on their pretty suits and plumes in their hats and all kinds of fancy weapons. Some were walking and some were riding, and they looked very gallant.

She was afraid. She said her mother was never afraid of anything. So she always got next to her mother's rocking chair, and her mother would knit. They watched them all day as they went by, and they knew that there was a big battle that was going to be held somewhere, but they had no idea where the battle would be. As it turned out, it was the battle of Mill Springs.

Whenever the battle was over, she said here they came back and the soldiers were all tattered and torn. They were a defeated group, and some of them were just almost dead. The way she told it, you could just imagine the suffering they had had.

One group come to their house. They camped down by the creek below their house, and they wanted to have the wounded to sleep in their house. So they slept in all the rooms of the house except one bedroom, and all the family stayed there—eight or nine children and mother and father.

And the wounded were all laying in all the beds and on the floor. She said that her sister wanted a drink of water and she woke her up in the middle of the night and she said, "Alice, Alice, I'm thirsty." Said, "Go with me to get a drink of water." The water was in the kitchen. Had to go through the room where all the rebels were. She said, "No, I'm not going, Sister. I'm not going to get a drink of water."

She said she laid back down, and said her sister came over and said, "Alice, Alice, I'm thirsty. Go with me to get a drink of water."

Said, she said, "No, Sis. I'm not going in there where all those rebels are."

She said she woke her up the third time, and Grandmother said, "I'd die of thirst before I'd go in there where those rebels are!"[4]

Jenny Hail of Wayne County recounted her grandmother's first-person account of hearing the shots during the battle:

My grandmother was living in this house during the Civil War, and she told us many, many Civil War stories. She stood out here in her back yard and listened to the battle when Zollicoffer was killed. And she said that she got on her horse, and rode over there about three days after that battle, and that the mound there had 150 men under it. And she said that when they went, somebody had thrown a few shovels of dirt on these men, but they were still piled up there. And one man had a sun bonnet on."[5]

Quinn Davidson of Pickett County told an oral traditional account of his own family's involvement in the conflict:

My great-grandfather Copeland on Mother's side fought in the regular army. He was a captain in the artillery. See, you had them both sides that way—he was a captain of the artillery. He and his two boys—Horace Copeland was one and Benton was the other one—was in the Battle of Mill Springs. I've heard my mother talk about it. Said she'd hear him talk about it.

They had to retreat there. And they had to cross the river. And he said a-getting them on the boat—he was a great big man, he weighed 250 pounds—he couldn't get them on fast and a lot of his boys was killed. He said he like to have fell and

56

somebody just grabbed him by the shoulders and shoved him on the boat and he looked around and it was one of his boys. He knowed that one was saved.

But they all come through and they was mustered out as regular soldiers—they didn't go in for none of this [guerrilla] killing."[6]

Cordell Dishman of Wayne County recalled talking with a woman who witnessed the passage of the rebel army to and from the Mill Springs encounter, and recounted her description this way:

Now this road over here, General Zollicoffer, you know, fortified Mill Springs up here. The soldiers went this road.

It went through Tennessee, you know, into Kentucky. And they passed that road a-going to Mill Springs and they retraced back through it. Same road.

Well, as they went on, they had plenty. They'd go to their camps, pick up all kinds of meat and stuff to eat where they camped along the road. But as they come back they was just a-living off of the country. And the old Hurt Place right down here (you can see it if you was on the outside, where Paul Burnett lives). They lived there then. And these soldiers, when they was retreating back south, they'd come there, you know, and they'd have to cook for the officers.

Debbie Hurt said she saw that whole hill over there of soldiers a-laying all over that hill. Just, you know, waiting for the officers to eat. And she told a little story. They come there, and I believe it was the captain come and told her father, you know, to go and put his horse up and feed him. Well, he went and put him up and fed him. When he got ready to leave, told him to go get him. (He [the officer] had placed his son there on guard of that horse, unbeknownst to Old Man Hurt.) Well, he went to get the horse and he went up and opened the door, and he said the next thing he knowed, there was a bayonet directly in front of him. He [the officer's son] marched him over to the house. Said it tickled that officer to death. Said he was just trying his son out.[7]

This family plows the tobacco patch in southern Wayne County, Kentucky.
Photograph 1976 by the author.

Some traditional farmers in the Upper Cumberland often prefer not to hire helpers. Photograph 1972 by David Sutherland.

"Away up on Fishing Creek," a disconnected lyric song composed after the Battle of Mill Springs, provides a sketchy scenario of the encounter:[8]

Away up on Fishing Creek

Old Crittenden called the Union boys Devils,
We marched out one night;
Zollicoffer to fight,
To clean up a few of his Rebels.

Refrain:
Cheer you up my Union boys,
And skip the windy weather;
Cheer you up my Union boys,
We'll all march out together.

Oh there is Thomas Brown,
Some call him a clever fellow;
We shot a cannon ball through his house,
And ran him into the cellar.

Refrain:
Old Colonel Fry, he did very well,
For the very first round;
Old Zollicoffer fell,
Get away home, get away home, for Dixie's land is gone.

A second song about this fateful battle, entitled "The Battle of Mill Springs" and identified in an index of native American ballads, actually has no more story content than the first title. The ballad lyrics are focused on a dying soldier and his final words to his comrades:

I am a dying soldier lying near the battle field,
My comrades gather around me, down by my side they kneel;
To gaze upon young Edward who rose his dropping head,
Saying who will care for mother when her soldier boy is dead.

Go tell my little sister for me she must not weep,
No more around the fireside I'll take her on my knee;
No more I'll sing those little songs to her I used to sing;

60

Her brother is bleeding at the battle of Mill Springs.

I am my father's oldest son to comfort his old age,
My heart is like a little bird a-fluttering in the cage;
But when I heard my name was called a soldier for to be,
I fought for the Union and for liberty.

Listen, comrades, listen, to the girl I speak of now,
If she were only here tonight to ease my aching brow;
But little does she think of me, she walks along and sings,
Her true love is bleeding at the Battle of Mill Springs.

Listen, comrades, listen, to hear him speak again,
The comrades they were listening as he entered his last
farewell;
The stars and stripes, he kissed them, and laid them by his
side,
He gave three cheers for the Union, and prayed before he died.

Now this dreadful battle is the Battle of Mill Springs,
Many a Federal soldier boy lay bleeding in their gore;
Many a Federal soldier boy rose his head and cried,
Their tears shed for the soldier as he dropped his head and
died.[9]

In February of 1862, General Grant captured Forts Henry and
Donelson on the Lower Cumberland and opened the Cumberland
River route to Middle Tennessee. Nashville soon fell to the Union
forces. By June, the North made concerted efforts to extend control
over Cumberland and Monroe counties, Kentucky. Major Jordan and
his Ninth Pennsylvania Cavalry secured Tompkinsville for the Union in
mid-June 1862. A month later the dashing General John Hunt Morgan
and his Confederate raiders invaded Kentucky, after moving northward
from Sparta via Gainesboro and Celina, and routed Jordan's troops.
Morgan moved on northward toward central Kentucky, too adventure-
some to shore up and hold his line of defense.[10]

Oral traditions about General Morgan are numerous in the Upper
Cumberland. One of the favorite stories about Morgan, probably a
migratory legend, tells how he "swaps" plugs or worn-out horses for
fresh mounts with or without the consent of the owner. Because of

his means of acquiring fresh horses, Morgan was described by narrator Arnold Watson as possessing "some of the best horse flesh in the country." Hiram Parrish listened to Watson's account, then recounted his own oral traditional knowledge:

> Some of Morgan's men took a horse from James Ellington, and Ellington went out to get the horse back and went to Morgan. He was going to let him have the horse back, but Mr. Henry Pace (that was Stanley Pace's father, he was one of Morgan's men), and he went to Cousin Jimmy Ellington, and talked him into letting them have the mare.
>
> He said, "Jim, I'll take care of your horse, and we'll bring it back when it's over." Said, "You'll get your horse back."
>
> But that was the last he ever saw of the horse, of course.[11]

George Rush of Cumberland County provided an example of the other types of traditional stories still told about Morgan:

> There was a skirmish there at the Burkesville Ferry. Morgan's men came up from this side of the river and crossed over on one of their raids. And they spent that summer that they stayed on one of their raids, and I'm not sure now which one it was. . . . They stayed in Cumberland County quite a little while that time. As I said a while ago, they rested up their horses and used up all the feed they needed. But they came up on this side of the river and Union soldiers were on the other side—the Burkesville side, the west side of the bank. And that's the time Old Man Ed Smith was shot in the mouth.
>
> My granddaddy said that Smith was on the other side of the river getting him a drink out of the spring, of course, at the edge of the river. As he lay down to drink, one of Morgan's men on this side of the river shot him and the bullet went in under one ear and came out under the other ear. I believe that's the way I heard it. But somebody told me he was shot in the mouth. It might have come out of his mouth, I don't know which.[12]

There were spotty outbursts of successful resistance on the part of Confederate troops under General Braxton Bragg, Colonel Oliver

62

Hamilton, and others in the Upper Cumberland through 1863, all remembered in oral tradition. Nevertheless, the weightier successes were chalked up by Union forces as their numbers gradually choked out the spunky but outmanned rebel forces. All truly significant military activity in the Upper Cumberland, however, belonged to the numerous opposing guerrilla bands after mid-1862. Theirs is an amazing legacy of blood which deserves to be told at some length.

During the war years, the land swarmed with marauding bands of robbers, thieves, cutthroats, and bushwhackers on both sides of the struggle. These guerrillas terrorized the peace-loving citizens of the Upper Cumberland throughout the war, plundering, stealing, and burning while claiming allegiance to the Union or the Confederacy, but giving allegiance only to self-interests and personal indulgence. There was no feeling of safety and security as mothers put their children to bed at night and as fathers sought to hide precious live-stock in canebrakes and in caves away from the renegades who defied the rules of war. They took no prisoners but instead killed those who opposed them. Traditional and secondhand recollections from those strife-ridden years comprise the largest single body of folklore in the Upper Cumberland. The Civil War vitally touched every family in the region in one or more ways, including the contact they all had with the guerrillas. To the last man the guerrillas were renegades and outlaws. Sometimes their names are forgotten and their loyalties unknown; nevertheless, their infamy lives on in the tale and song repertoires of today's residents.

There is no way to identify all the persons murdered during and after the war by these raiders, but their descendants remember. Four generations have passed since then, but there is no forgetting in many families. A resident of Calfkiller Valley in White County, Tennessee, told of one brutality suffered by his wife's family:

> My wife's granddaddy was killed up here in Champ's Hol-low. He had a rail pen, you know, and was living in it—a canebrake. And when he seen the soldiers coming, why, he run, run up the hill and they shot him and broke his leg and tied horses to him and just run all over them fields down there and just broke him all to pieces. And after they done that,

they just spread the cards out on his chest and played cards on him. Sure did![13]

In all of the atrocity stories there is always a victim and an assailant. The victim is generally "innocent," but narrators showed no real signs of pity as they recounted the stories down to the final gory act of slaughter. Descriptions of the assailant's role, in fact, often hinted at hero worship. Confederate raider Champ Ferguson, for example, was audacious enough to decapitate one man and stick a piece of tobacco stem down the dead man's "goozle." Some of the narrators clearly admired this guerrilla who was brave enough to kill and kill again while laughing at law and order. Many who talk about him and the others of his kind seem almost proud that these outlaws injured or killed one or more of their ancestors, a fact which distinguishes them from other persons who cannot personally identify with the protagonists in the narratives.

In spite of the constant threat of danger and death, people were often able to outwit the guerrillas, as revealed in the following oral recollections provided by a narrator whose grandmother reputedly experienced the action firsthand:

> Grandma said they ate up all the food that she had. She said one day that she had a few apples, a little flour, and a little lard. She cooked her apples and was gonna make these little half-moon pies, and it was customary to fry them. But she didn't have the lard to do it so she baked them. The old platter is in there [in the kitchen]. And she said it was rounded up like that with little apple pies. She said, "Now the children will have something to eat when they come in." Said about that time a bunch of soldiers walked in through the kitchen and ate every one of them [laughs].
>
> And she said the horses, she had to keep them locked up somewhere. Said she had one in the house. It stood right out there and she was so afraid it would nicker that she just held her breath until the soldiers were gone away. And said she kept one old one around here that had a sore on its back. Said she'd curry that horse everyday and she curried that scab off its back so it would stay sore [so the guerrillas would not steal

it]. Then she could get a-hold of a little corn, and put one of the boys on that old horse and send him over here to Parker's Mill and have her some meal ground; or if she got a-hold of a little wheat, have her some flour ground.[14]

It is impossible to establish a chronology for such tales, which are said simply to have "taken place during the Civil War." And it is equally impossible to identify by name the renegades involved in the bulk of these stories. The narrators, in fact, seldom know whether the guerrillas originally favored the North or the South. (Perhaps this ignorance reflects the fact that they often operated only for personal gain.) Of the raiders who are identified, Champ Ferguson is the best known of the Confederate lot, despite close competition from Tom Yates of White County, Campbell Morgan of the Jackson-Overton-Fentress County area, George Bates of Wayne County, and Beanie Short of the Cumberland River country in Monroe and Cumberland counties. Ferguson was described by his enemies as a thief, a counterfeiter, a robber, a murderer, and a man of blood, and by his defenders as Morgan's pathfinder, an exemplary citizen, and a respected family man. Feelings in the area today are still divided along these lines.

Born on November 29, 1821, in southeastern Clinton County, on a branch of Spring Creek, Champion Ferguson was married in 1843 to Anne Eliza Smith, who bore him one son. The mother and son died in 1845 during an epidemic. He married Martha Owens of Clinton County in 1848. Their daughter Ann was born in 1849.[15]

Champ was indicted for murder in 1858 in the death of Deputy James Reed, at a camp meeting at Lick Creek Church on Wolf River. Ferguson had sold some hogs to Floyd and Alexander Evans. When the Evanses refused to pay, James Ferguson, Champ's brother, stole their mare and took her to Kentucky. At the camp meeting, the Evans brothers, along with Reed, attempted to whip Champ. At first they threw rocks at him, then attacked him with their fists. Champ whipped out a razor-sharp pocket knife and cut Reed "till he fell." He was on trial for this murder in the circuit court of Fentress County when the Civil War broke out. It is said that Ferguson was promised that the charges would be dropped if he would enlist in the Confederate Army. He became one of the most feared and bloodthirsty men of the Upper Cumberland until his arrest by Union soldiers on May 26, 1865.

Two events in Ferguson's life are offered to expain his actions during the war. A published source attempted to place the blame on a group of Union soldiers who shot and killed Champ's three-year-old son for waving a Confederate flag from the porch as the soldiers passed by. Champ vowed, while holding the dead child in his arms, that he would kill 100 Federals in revenge. (This source cannot be correct, however, since Champ's only known son died in 1845.) The account claimed that Champ had not taken sides in the war until then, although most of his family were Unionists. He learned that the passing soldiers had come from Camp Dick Robinson, a training center for Federal Home Guards located in central Kentucky. Champ "hated every man" who had trained there and murdered several of his own neighbors in search of the man who killed his son.

The other explanation of Champ's motives stems from the time that he was away from home and a group of twelve Unionists forced his wife and daughter to prepare a meal in the nude and then paraded them naked up and down the road.[16] One oral source claimed, "Some Union soldiers come by there and mistreated his wife, raped her and everything." Another noted, "The Yankees come in and made his wife and daughter strip off their clothes and just march up and down the road in front of all the soldiers." Why they did this no one knows, but one published source claimed that the twelve were retaliating against Ferguson's viciousness. Martha Ferguson knew the men and identified them to her husband when he got home. Enraged, he vowed to kill every one of them, one at a time. An oral narrator recalled, "They said that a whole bunch of men took her over, mistreated her. Some people thought it maybe affected his mind. He went crazy. Was a fanatic on killing people."

Whatever the reason behind Champ's bloodletting, his record of murdering, mutilating, and robbing began in late 1861. He took his wife and daughter to Calfkiller Valley and established a farm and home for them there. With a band of followers, he then sought to control much of Clay County, all of Overton and White counties, and the valley portion of Fentress County. His war-long nemesis, Tinker Dave Beaty, a devout Unionist, was running roughshod at that time

66

over what is now Pickett, Fentress, and portions of Overton and Clay counties.

Champ's first wartime murder was a rather telling one—telling, that is, of just how ruthless he was. He shot and killed William Frogg eight miles from Albany on November 1, 1861, while Frogg was bedfast with measles. The murder took place in full view of Frogg's wife and five-month-old son, according to an oral narrator. The wife ran outside in the rain "and just scrooched up against the side of the house and cried." Champ later claimed that Frogg was a Home Guard trained at Camp Dick Robinson, and that Frogg would just as certainly have killed him, given the opportunity.

The second killing attributed to Champ still raises ire in Clinton County. He gunned down Reuben Wood on December 2, 1861, another man trained at Camp Dick Robinson, at his home near Albany. Wood begged for his life, claiming that he had "nursed" Champ as a child. His pleas fell on deaf ears.

Ferguson was charged with killing Alexander Huff, Elijah Koger, four members of the Zachary family, Elam Huddleston, and numerous others in rapid succession. In July of 1862 he allegedly bemoaned the fact that he had killed only thirty-two men. Koger was shot in the back while his eleven-year-old daughter was clinging to him and pleading for his life. He died in his daughter's lap.

Huddleston, a Union guerrilla, lived in an unfinished log house. When he heard Champ and his men approaching, he shot at them from the upstairs window. The attackers set fire to the house; about that time Huddleston was shot and his body plummeted through the joists of the second floor to the floor below. When Huddleston's wife ran to him, a Ferguson gang member shot off one of her fingers.

From the Huddleston place, Champ and his bushwhackers went two or three miles farther and killed two unnamed "bitter enemies" who were sleeping together in a bed. One source stated that Champ entered the room, pulled a knife from his boot, and "fell in a bed with them and commenced cutting them." He killed one on the spot and shot the other as he ran out through the door.

A killing which sparked considerable anger in the region was the slaying of sixteen-year-old Fount Zachary on April 1, 1862, allegedly after the youth, a Union sympathizer, had already surrendered his

67

rifle to Ferguson. Champ shot him, it is claimed, then jumped down off his horse and plunged a knife into the boy's heart. Hellbent on exterminating the Zacharys, Champ killed James Zachary of Byrds-town in May, then murdered Peter and Allen Zachary together in Russell County in January 1863. Reputedly, Champ told the widow of James Zachary that he had killed her husband under a beech tree. If she wanted to bury him, she could; if not, the buzzards could have

John Williams died at the hands of Ferguson, tortured with knives and sharp sticks before being cut to pieces. David Delk was chopped and cut to pieces soon thereafter at the home of Mrs. Alexander Huff in Fentress County.

One of the most poignant of all oral stories connected with the name of Champ Ferguson comes from Clinton County and tells of a dying father who, upon learning that Champ Ferguson had killed his son, asked that the son be brought and laid in bed beside him. The father died during the night. Here is the story:

> Another tale that Grandmother told me, and was the most vivid to me, happened in Duvall Valley, Kentucky. It was near this big spring that Captain Van Duvall, U.S.A., and some other men had gone out about a half hour before sunup.
>
> Captain Duvall's father was L.W. Duvall, and he was a pretty large landowner in Duvall Valley. Captain Duvall's father was in bed sick, and he had called for his son to come home. So he was home. And they didn't have bathrooms at the time. Well, they'd gone out to the spring to wash. I think about three men had gone out from the house to the spring. While they were there, Champ Ferguson and his man came, and he shot Van Duvall and another man.
>
> The thing that was the most vivid to me was that Mr. Duvall was on his death bed. This is why they had called his son home. So when they went in to tell the father that the son was killed, he said, "Well, just bring him in here and lay him here by me." And they brought his body in and laid him down by his father, and the father died some time during the night.
>
> That was the thing that made an impression on me, that he wanted his son laid in bed with him.[17]

With charges such as these lodged against Champ Ferguson, and similar ones against other guerrillas, it is no wonder the Civil War years were a continual nightmare to the highland residents. Colonel Wolford and his Union troops stationed at Burkesville made repeated forays in quest of Ferguson, but Champ and his men always disappeared into the dark seclusion of their mountain bastion.

Champ obtained full revenge on the twelve who had humiliated his wife and daughter with the killing of a Lieutenant Smith. A Union soldier, Smith lay seriously wounded in a hospital bed at Emory and Henry College, Emory, Virginia, in late 1864. An oral narrator observed that Ferguson found the last of the twelve "in a hospital. He just walked right in there and killed him." Smith called Champ by name from his bed and pleaded for his life, saying, "I'm going to die in a few days anyway." Champ told him "that he'd just relieve him of all that suffering," and with that, pointed a gun at Smith and put a minnie ball through his head. Ferguson displayed no remorse over the shooting, stating that Smith had personally executed or ordered executed many of Ferguson's men.[18]

The bloody career of Champ Ferguson came to an end when he was tried by a military court and hanged on October 20, 1865, in Nashville for the murder of fifty-three people. He admitted that the number of victims was much greater than that, but he made a moving speech accounting for his conduct as revenge. His last request was that his body be taken home to Calfkiller Valley for burial. His remains were placed in a cherry casket and hauled to the cemetery in the back of a wagon by his wife and daughter. They buried him and erected a tombstone cut out of the nearby mountainside to mark his resting place. His wife carved on his stone so that all could see that Captain C. Furguson (she misspelled his name) was "married July 23, 1848 to Miss Martha Owens, Clinton County, Kentucky." Martha and Ann Ferguson left soon afterward for Indian Territory, never to be heard from again.[19]

This is not the end of the Champ Ferguson legend. Two printed sources and three oral testimonies, including one from Ferguson's great-grandnephew, claimed that Champ did not die. The story, in brief, is that a ring of soldiers completely encircled the hanging scaffold; then, when the hangman cut the rope, Champ dropped through the scaffold from a loose knot. Soldiers placed him alive and unhurt in the coffin. Together with the casket placed on the back of a waiting wagon, his wife and daughter headed for Oklahoma with their cargo. Once there they began farming and ranching under assumed names. It was reported that Ferguson was later seen in Oklahoma and Missouri, as well as in Fentress and Clinton counties.[20] The explanation offered is that the Union soldiers respected him as a soldier and felt that he should not hang when others equally guilty were paroled, especially since his conviction had achieved the desired exemplary effect on the Southern sympathizers in Nashville.

Of all the rebel guerrillas in the Upper Cumberland, Beanie Short survives in oral tradition with a popularity second only to that of Champ Ferguson. Unlike Ferguson, he has not been immortalized in local published sources, having been mentioned only rarely in print.[21] Further, Short did not range over such a large geographical area as Champ Ferguson; he raided only along the Cumberland River for a few miles above and below the Cumberland-Monroe County line at Black's Ferry, the community in which he was murdered in his sleep in May 1865.

George "Beanie" Short was from the hill country of Monroe County at the lower end of Turkey Neck Bend. When the Civil War erupted, Beanie and his wife were farming in the Spearsville community on Pea Ridge. Like numerous others in that tension-filled era, Short did not know with which side to place his allegiance. After a period of waiting and wondering, Beanie cast his lot with the Confederacy. Oral tradition claims that Beanie was a uniformed soldier for a while but left the army for the life of a robbing, murdering, looting, fleet-footed rebel raider whose interests were vested mainly in himself. Captain Burr Huddleston and other Union bushwhackers from the Burkesville area tracked him for almost four years and finally caught up with him just before the war ended. Some people still search for the gold and silver Beanie Short stole and supposedly buried somewhere on Kettle Creek in Monroe County, and those persons whose families were victimized by him talk readily about those events and times.

One of the best remembered of Short's cruel acts is his killing of

70

Solomon Long, described here by one who heard the account on numerous occasions from his grandfather:

> Walter Huddleston told me one time, Solomon Long was his great-uncle. He said that that was the beginning of Beanie Short's downfall. Solomon Long lost both his legs at the Battle of Shiloh and they discharged him from the army and sent him home. And he said that the only way that—course, back then they didn't have the care that they have now and they didn't have artificial legs like they have now, so he said that the people, when he went to travel about the neighborhood, they'd carry him about on a cot.
>
> Beanie Short came there to Solomon Long's house and started in. Solomon Long had his guns, had his pistols. He was afraid to go in. Solomon Long's wife begged Beanie Short and his men to go on and not harm him. And he told her if she'd get his guns and give him Long's guns, he wouldn't bother him. And she persuaded Long to give his guns up and he did. And they took Long out and got him on a horse, took him up on the hill and shot him. And that enraged all the people round about. So then, a Northern irregular was Captain Huddleston. He made him up a band of men, young and old. Of course, a lot of the younger men were in the army and older men and boys, as young as fifteen, I believe they said, made up his group. That was Allen Huddleston's father.
>
> My granddaddy said when he was in the army . . . he was home one winter night on furlough. . . . That must have been the winter of '64 or '65 because he was just in. . . . And he said that there was snow on the ground and he was down there at his dad's.
>
> Another soldier had come in home with him that had lived right down the road here below [Highway] 449 across the creek. Anderson was in the army with him. He was home on furlough.
>
> And he said that night that he heard a bunch of horsemen coming down that little creek, and he said that he was sure that it was Beanie Short or one of the guerrillas. And, you

71

know, if they could find a Union soldier at home, they'd do him just like they did Old Man Long, and kill him. So he said he went out the back door with his shoes in his hand and he said he came up that hill back of the house in the snow barefoot and he got up on the hill and put his shoes on.

Said he came around to the Andersons' house and came down there and got him out and said they went back up in the hills, stayed out that night and like to froze. Stayed out till the next morning. They slipped back around down there and he slipped on down and saw the horses hitched down there, and eased on down. And it was Old Man Huddleston and his band—they were Union. Said he went back down, and it tickled the Old Man Huddleston because he'd kept them out in the snow all night. . . .

They said that when Solomon Long was killed, Captain Huddleston got his group of men together; they said they couldn't eat nor sleep until they got Beanie Short. But I guess they did, because he also told me this, that Old Man Huddleston was teaching school. And I didn't know there were any schools going on during the war in Cumberland County . . . ; might have been a private school or something. But, anyway, this is the story he told me. And he said that somebody, some woman, I believe, came to school and told Huddleston where Beanie Short was going to be the night he was killed down at Black's Ferry. And he said that Huddleston dismissed his students and told them there'd be no more school until further notice. So he got his group together and they went down there that night. You've heard the story on that.[22]

How Short was tracked down and eventually killed is commonly told in oral circles. Arnold Watson recounted Short's death as follows:

Beanie and his wife lived neighbor to my grandfather, Richard Watson, out on Pea Ridge out here. My grandfather and grandmother, they visited Beanie Short and his wife, Missouri, quite often. And they visited them! And he said that Short seemed to be worried about the war, you know, and

72

all that. And they talked a lot about it, and he couldn't make up his mind which a-way to go, North or South. But finally he decided for the South, and went to the army; and my grandfather opted for the North. He went to the North and the Fifth Kentucky. . . .

Yeah, they were good neighbors; they visited often, my grandmother said. People didn't have no newspapers nor nothing to do at night; they'd visit one another and sit and talk till bedtime. Yeah. And they visited backwards and forwards. But later, when Old Man Beanie, he deserted the Southern army, the word I heard, and come back here and started robbing and killing people.

And that was the beginning of the story. Now, a few years ago, they's some people come down here from Campbellsville and asked me about that story. And I told them about the beginning and the end of Beanie Short. They's places back here on Bear Wallow Ridge; they's a cave out there about White's Bottom on this side of the river that's called the Beanie Short Cave. Big cave where he carried his loot to and hid out, when he wasn't raiding people, see. And the last part of the Beanie Short story, my Grandfather Rainey, A.J. Rainey, took part in it.

He was a young fellow, about sixteen years old at that time. And he was in what they called the Home Guard, had been organized. And it was under Old Captain Burr Huddleston, J.A.B. Huddleston. So they went on the trail of this Beanie Short. Short killed an old man down on Kettle Creek, Old Man Dooley; made him kneel down and shot him in front of his family. Trying to make him give up his money or tell where it was hid, you know.

So they's another old man out on the ridge, Old Man Long, Link Long's daddy. I forget the old man's name, but he'd been in the service, and it was with the North, and he'd had a leg shot off. And he was in the bed, and they come in there and shot him in the bed, with his son in the bed with him, Link Long. That's the story that I hear.

So Old Captain Burr Huddleston, he was head of this Home

Guard. He married my grandfather's sister, Jane, Jane Huddleston. And my grandfather and this Jack Pruitt, we was talking about a while ago in this other case, was scouts for Captain Huddleston. And they trailed Beanie Short down here below Black's Ferry down there and caught up with him. And I've heard my grandfather talk about it. He used to take a little toddy, and he wouldn't talk much till he'd had some of that. So I'd always question him; I was a curious kid, nosy, and I wanted him to tell the story different times.

And he said that they'd been a-going for a week or two.

And they found out where he was sleeping; he's sleeping upstairs down there at a fellow's by the name of Williams. And they told this Williams that if he didn't go up and get their guns, they was going to set the house afire, Old Captain Burr did, and kill him when he come out. And they was a fellow name of Ashlock with them. So this Williams, instead of being burned out, he went up and got the guns. And Grandfather went up. He said he went up behind Old Captain Burr, and he [Burr] shot Beanie Short with a revolver, him in the bed there. . . .

And I asked my grandfather, did he do any shooting? He said, "No." He said this fellow, they jumped and reached for their guns when he shot Beanie Short. And he said this fellow Ashlock that was with Beanie Short jumped up and reached. And he said he took the butt of his gun and smashed him back on the bed. And somebody behind him shot this fellow Ashlock that was with Beanie Short. My grandfather knocked Ashlock down. But Dr. Burr Huddleston used the revolver and he shot Beanie Short, him in the bed.[23]

Allegedly, the blood of Short and his murdered companion, Bill Ashlock, could be viewed on the upstairs floor of the house in which they were killed until the house burned in the early 1960s.[24] Short and Ashlock were taken to a small family graveyard on Kettle Creek and were placed in the same grave, perhaps in the same coffin. For years following his death, Beanie's sister is said to have frequently uttered, "Poor Beanie, he sure left this world in a mighty hard shape."

A lyric song celebrating the exploits of Beanie Short is widely circulated in oral tradition. The verses of the song are extremely fluid as additional stanzas could be improvised on the spot. The song depends for its meaning on the legend, although the seemingly nonsensical verses may indeed serve to perpetuate the legend.

Beanie Short

Old Bean Short,
Never be forgotten;
Way down South,
Picking at the cotton.

Old Bean Short,
Never be forgotten;
Hole in his head,
To hold a bale of cotton.

Old Bean Short,
Never be forgotten;
Buried down South,
With his bones all rotten.[25]

In addition to the Confederate raiders like Champ Ferguson and Beanie Short, Union guerrillas also operated in the Upper Cumberland region. Just as self-serving and ruthless as their rebel counterparts were Boney Pruitt of Cumberland County and Rufus Dowdy and Tinker Dave Beaty of Fentress County. Tinker Dave was, in fact, Champ Ferguson's chief nemesis, and oral legends about him are as plentiful as those about Ferguson; published sources, strangely enough, are rare. From the stories about Beaty's character and actions, he appears to have been as bloodthirsty as Ferguson.

David Beaty was born in Buffalo Cove, Fentress County, in 1823. He died near the home of his youth in 1883. Beaty lived a simple, pastoral life except for the Civil War years when he was the relentless, ferocious captain of a company of local fighters known as Beaty's Independent Scouts. Overton County Judge Jefferson Dillard Goodpasture labeled them "the most desperate set of Federal guerrillas in the Mountain District."[26] Their purpose was to protect their portion of the Upper Cumberland from invasion by the Confederates. Beaty had as many as sixty men in his band on occasion and as few as five at other times. About the time the Independent Scouts were organized, federal troops moved into the Overton-Fentress County area,[27] an act which stimulated Beaty's guerrilla tactics.

One of the first appearances Beaty and his soldiers made was at the home of Amp Poore in Fentress County in early 1861. Poore was seven years old at the time and recalled vividly how forty armed men rode in with chickens tied to their saddles. Beaty ordered Poore's mother to cook the chickens, which had been stolen from various farms along the road, for him and his men. While supper was being prepared, the guerrilla band tied their horses in the yard, went to the barn for hay and corn, fed their mounts lavishly, then proceeded to fill two carts with shucked corn to take along with them the next day.

The soldiers took all of the Poores' horses and cattle except two old bulls. But the incident Amp Poore recalled most bitterly was the killing of Bob, his brindle dog. Bob had been his constant companion since his father and six brothers had gone away to war. (All six brothers were killed during the war, one of them on Wolf River by Beaty's gang.[28])

Beaty's scouts had skirmishes with organized Confederate soldiers and rebel guerrillas throughout the war. These encounters are remembered in oral tradition, but their chronological order has been lost to memory. Will Peavyhouse, descendant of Union sympathizers, recounted the Battle of Buffalo Cove fought between Beaty's men and a band of "thieving Confederates" under Colonel Hughes:

> Colonel Hughes had come in here with a bunch of rebels, of course, a-taking people's cattle and the hogs and the horses and everything, a-driving them off. He stayed up in here and just foraged the country, you know.
>
> Well, Tinker Dave Beaty, he took his men and went over there to stop Hughes. And he did. But he got two men killed, Tom Culver and Jonathan Moody. And they're buried in the cemetery there at my house.
>
> The battles took place—you know where I live. Well, on the other side of where I live from here, a-going up that road, up that blacktop road, right across the cove on the other side

76

of the mountain, over there is where the battle took place.

This Old Colonel Hughes, I reckon he was the one that they come fairly near of getting him. He was on a horse and a fellow shot at him and just as his gun fired, just before, he jerked the horse. Horse threw his head up and the bullet hit the horse in the nose; kept it from killing Colonel Hughes there. So that was the battle that took place there. But they skirmished and fought around there a lot anyway. Tinker, I'll show you where Tinker lived there.[29]

Quinn Davidson, Virgil Beaty, and J.D. Lowrey, all of Pickett County, recalled secondhand accounts of Beaty's visits to the Three Forks of the Wolf and Forbus areas of Fentress and Pickett counties. During these forays Hiram Richardson, John Smith, and Thomas Riley were killed.[30] Reverend A.B. Wright wrote in his *Autobiography* (p. 28) that "Young Riley was taken prisoner and brutally murdered, while begging his captors the privilege of seeing his young wife, who was only one-half mile away, before they killed him. This was denied him. The young wife died soon afterwards of a broken heart." Wright recorded that Beaty's men killed Fountain Frost at Gilreath's Mill in early 1864, while he begged for his life, then cruelly murdered neutralist Jefferson Pile in June near the Three Forks of the Wolf River.

The Wolf Gang, a separate contingent of Beaty's guerrillas, is remembered for the ghastly murder of Jim Raines at his barn in northern Fentress County. They backed Raines up against the barn wall, cut his throat from ear to ear, then proceeded to slash and mutilate his body. After leaving the bloody scene, they moved on to Old Man Bobby Richardson's place on Holbert Creek. Blind, ninety-two, and the father of three Confederate soldiers, Richardson was shot in the front yard along with his dog. They draped the dog over Richardson's body before riding away.[31]

An eighty-nine-year-old resident of Jamestown, Tennessee, whose grandparents were neighbors of Beaty, recalled that her own grandmother had worked for Tinker Dave's wife while he was fighting in the war:

Well, she said if it hadn't been for a bunch of, a big patch of Irish potatoes, they'da just starved to death. She said they

77

would boil them and eat them without salt. They couldn't get salt; everything was so scarce. She said her and Tinker Dave Beaty's wife dug up the dirt in the smokehouse. Back then, they had smokehouses without floors, you know, just dirt floors. They dug that dirt up and they'd boiled it down and would skim the water off and boiled it down and made salt. . . .

She spun and carded and stuff like that, you know, for Mrs. Beaty. I guess if it hadn'ta been for what help she got from Mrs. Beaty, they'da had it a lot harder than what they did.

Her and Mrs. Beaty was working, she said, when a whole bunch of these guerrillas from the other side come in. And, of course, you daresn't open your mouth, you know, whatever they wanted to do. She said that Beatys had a smokehouse full of meat. They'd killed some hogs and said they had a crib full of corn. She said they went to that crib and opened that door and fed their horses. And she said they'd scattered and wasted corn all over the place. And went in the smokehouse, she said, and cut down big chunks of that meat. And they took it out and boiled and eat what they wanted and throwed away the rest of it, she said, just scattered it around all over the place. Said that after they left, her and Mrs. Beaty got out and picked up the [meat], what they could of it, and cleaned it up and fixed it, you know, [to] where they could eat it.

Said that while these soldiers was a-doing all that, said that one of Tinker's boys was a-going across, back and forth on the bluff on the far side of the river, swearing at them and shooting at them. But he couldn't shoot; it was too far, you know, and hit them. But anyway, he was over there, cursing them and shooting at them, she said.[32]

Tinker Dave Beaty spent much of his time during the war looking for Champ Ferguson or being chased by him. When hostilities ceased officially between the South and the North, they continued unabated between Beaty and Ferguson. Champ was a better shot than Dave, and Dave knew it. Beaty went into hiding for a period of time, often seeking refuge in caves, according to narrator Reece Bilbrey. Champ and four or five men later went to a house in Jamestown where Tinker Dave was eating supper. Pretending friendly intentions, they asked Beaty to show them the way to another man's house. Beaty realized en route that they were going to kill him. He jerked his horse around and fled in the opposite direction, but they shot and hit him three times. It is reported that he opened his shirt and showed the unhealed wounds to the court during Champ's trial.[33]

Narrator Quinn Davidson's father told him of being present at Tinker Dave's death and funeral in 1883:

> Dad said that they didn't put a suit of clothes on him, that he wanted to be buried in the old-fashioned way in what's called the winding sheet.* You're rolled in the sheet some way, and the corner of it you roll in some special way; when you viewed him, they brought that over his face. Dad said that's the only man he'd ever seen buried that way and that was his request.
>
> He brought that down, down over his face and turned it back for the people to view him.[34]

Beaty was buried in the family cemetery in Buffalo Cove. A modern stone marks the grave. Quinn Davidson eulogized Beaty with the words, "He wasn't a bad man; he just fought through the war."[35]

When the Civil War ended officially, it was not yet over in the Upper Cumberland. The years following the war were years of strong prejudices and bitter hatreds. The men who fought on opposing sides of the conflict came back home to live together, not knowing how things would be. Most of them adjusted; some could not and moved away. Many former Confederates refused to come back home at all to claim their farms, knowing that death awaited them at the hands of wartime enemies.

Suffering and privation followed the Civil War. Confederate money was worthless, and there was no quick way to get federal money. Stores could not be reopened, and fields that had once produced grain lay fallow. The years of fratricidal strife had broken down the courts, with the result that civil law lost much of its authority. The governor

79

of Tennessee appointed local sheriffs, but they wielded little authority in efforts to destroy the Ku Klux Klan and other organizations that
emerged "to keep the peace."

Some of the wartime guerrilla bands did not disband at all or were
quick to regroup when they saw the "need" of their services. The
Wolf Gang, for example, consisting of Sherwood Pile, James Pile,
Press Hugg, John Overton, a Morgan, and perhaps others, continued
on in northern Fentress County after the war. They so terrorized the
countryside for three years that in June 1868 Tennessee Governor
William G. Brownlow commissioned Clabe Beaty of Fentress County
to organize a company to capture the Wolf Gang.[36]

Some have claimed that Tinker Dave Beaty operated for a year or
more after the war,[37] and Jesse and Frank James reputedly robbed
their way through virtually every county of the Upper Cumberland
from the late 1860s until the early 1870s. Numerous oral legends and
published sources such as county histories attest to the presence of
the James brothers in the Upper Cumberland. Most of the oral stories
about Frank and Jesse James characterize them as unrecognized pas-
sersby, thieves, or Robin Hood types until they had performed their
intended deed and ridden away. One representative story about the
James brothers, told by a black narrator, features a black person as
beneficiary of one of their good deeds:

> Frank and Jesse James come down there [near Gainesboro]
> and spent the night with Old Man Williams. He liked to have
> died when he found out about it.
>
> This man owned a big farm and we lived on this farm. And
> he told me when he found out that that was Jesse and Frank
> James that spent the night at his house, he like to died. . . .
>
> Jesse and them looked at his horses, looked his stock over
> and everything. So that night—they's a colored man bought a
> farm. I don't know how much he paid for it. But he bought
> this place. And this white man was going to throw him out.
> Well, the man had been sick and he couldn't meet his bills
> like he was supposed to. But he'd been sick; he couldn't help
> that, you know.
>
> And so Frank and Jesse James was talking to this man, and

80

this man told them about it, how this man owed him and couldn't pay it. And he was going to take that land away from him; he wasn't going to let him keep it. And he told them about he had some money. They didn't put it in the bank, you know. So he told the James boys where he had his money, didn't know who he was talking to.

So the James brothers stayed all night with him. He [one of the brothers] got up during the night and got the money that the man owed him [Williams]. He went down and give it to this [black] man. Says, "You go pay this place off."

Well, this colored man didn't know who they was, nothing about them.[38]

In view of the horrors they had survived, it is surprising that most of the inhabitants were able to lay aside war-induced animosities as quickly as they did. Or did they? George W. Bell, of Wayne County, for instance, took measures designed to keep his family from forgetting what he went through. His grandson tells it this way:

During the Civil War, the eastern part of Wayne County, which consists of some of McCreary County which was cut off of some of Wayne County, had provisions of soldiers for the Union Army—thirty-five or forty of them. And my father told me when he was an old man; I talked to him about the Civil War. My grandfather, George W. Bell, stated that those who were conscripted in the army during the latter part of the Civil War—every Democrat in that section was put in the Union Army and for that reason came very near joining the Confederate Army but didn't.

And because of a few things like that, he named my father Robert Lee Bell and another one of his boys Stonewall Jackson.[39]

In most parts of the region, the turmoil and discord which followed the Civil War dissipated among the general populace after ten to fifteen years. At last, peaceable men could venture into town on public days without fear of being beaten, knifed, or shot. Former Union and Confederate leaders knew they had to cooperate in law enforcement and in rebuilding churches, schools, and political institutions. Some of the old veterans teamed up in the Pickett County area to request the creation of their own county in 1879. The Union veterans of the Upper Cumberland, who drew twelve to fifteen dollars a month pension, became financial and political powers of the community—ideal "catches" for young widows and single women. During the late years of the nineteenth century, all members of the community observed and attended Old Soldiers Reunions. It was a special treat to listen to these aging fellows recount and boast of their wartime experiences.[40] People in the Upper Cumberland began to pick up the pieces of their lives and build anew.

CHAPTER 3

In the Woods and on the River

By 1870, the tensions brought to the Upper Cumberland by the criss-crossing of opposing armies and renegade bands during the Civil War had subsided. Gone were the treacherous and dastardly deeds of local guerrillas operating under the guise of loyalty to the Union or the Confederacy. The actions of Beanie Short, Champ Ferguson, Tinker Dave Beaty and their ilk were finished; never again would these outlaw raiders raise their heads except in regional folk legendry, which has yet to die out. The people of the Upper Cumberland were ready for progress, ready to merge into the mainstream of regional culture. Ten to twelve arrivals of steamboats every week in Nashville from Burnside, the headwaters of the Upper Cumberland, represented the beginnings of a steamboat empire. During the first years of the postwar period, log rafting was introduced to the area between Carthage and Burnside; after that, residents of the region no longer lived in seclusion from the rest of the country.

Burnside was to become the Upper Cumberland's center for sawed lumber and veneer products and to share equal billing with Carthage as an important crosstie shipping point. Celina, however, was destined to be the regional hub for log rafting. It was located in the heart of an area overgrown with almost impenetrable hardwood forests. These woods held the promise of producing billions of board feet of fine quality lumber, but a way to transport this raw wealth to market was not devised until after the Civil War. There were no real highways and not a single foot of railroad track in the entire region; steamboats could not carry enough of the giant logs to make even the slightest dent in the timber supply.

There were, however, many large creeks—Otter, Sinking, Beaver, Crocus, Meshack, McFarland, Kettle, Mitchell, Iron, Jennings, Brimstone, Flynn, and Defeated, among others—that emptied into the Cumberland or its tributary rivers. When these waterways ran high, saw logs were floated downstream to various points where they could then be combined into rafts and floated on to Nashville.

Timber dominated the economy of the Upper Cumberland from 1870 until 1930. Men with foresight and daring, willing to rob virgin forests of their giant trees and to defy rain-swollen rivers during sub-zero weather, made fortunes and established themselves in the oral repertoires of those who still talk about the river with emotion. Raftsmen, loggers, and lumbermen from the area who won regional and national acclaim included John J. Gore, United States district judge; Benton McMillan, Kentucky-born Tennessee governor and United States congressman; and Cordell Hull, secretary of state under Franklin D. Roosevelt. It is said that on visits to his boyhood home, Mr. Hull liked to reminisce with friends about the days they spent together on the river.[1] Equally famous at the local level and even more celebrated in oral historical traditions are Bob Riley, the Amonetts, the Cummingses, the Hamiltons, the Richs, the Smiths, and the Winninghams, among others.

The importance of logging and rafting activities to the people of the Upper Cumberland cannot be overstated. Money changed hands either in the woods or on the river banks every time a farmer cut a tree to be sold to a timber buyer. Money changed hands again when delivery was made to the big log shippers or processors at Burnside, Celina, Gainesboro, or Carthage. Final sales at major market centers such as Nashville and Cincinnati pumped large sums of money back into the Upper Cumberland region, thus ensuring a continual cycle of economic activities related to the harvesting and marketing of virgin timber.

It would be difficult to estimate how many board feet of timber were stripped from the region or how many millions of dollars the timber industry generated.[2] Since timber was the major natural resource of the area, people looked to the woods for their only reliable source of income. Agricultural crops provided food, but not much hard cash. A former raft pilot on the Obey River summed it up this way: "Well, that's all there was to do around here. There wasn't no factories; there wasn't nothing to do and that's the only way anybody had of getting any money. There was logging, rafting, and running the river. And that was the only sale we had for timber at that time."[3] Some people even gave up steamboat businesses when they realized that more money could be made in rafting and lumbering activities.[4]

With the introduction of rafting, most landowners along the Upper Cumberland and its tributary rivers and creeks relied on agriculture to provide food and on timber to bring in much-needed cash. During springtime, farmers plowed their fields and planted crops. During the summer months they cultivated the crops with single-row plows and chopped weeds from the rows until the crops were almost grown and "laid by." Fall brought about harvesting activities in preparation for winter storage. At convenient intervals during the cultivating and harvesting seasons, and during the winter, the farmers went into the woods to cut saw logs* and to snake* or haul them to the nearest tributary capable of floating single logs or log rafts downstream at high tide to a raft yard.

Many poor hill country farmers owned land near the large creek and river bottom farms, rough land that was heavily forested but scarcely capable of supporting more than a vegetable garden and small patches of row crops. These farmer-loggers spent much of their time in the woods during summer months between 1870 and 1935, cutting logs within their own boundaries or working as loggers for larger landowners or timber buyers. Timber was plentiful; no one hesitated to cut only the best trees or to cut logs from the trunks only up as far as the first limb, leaving the rest of the tree to decay in the woods. Every fall the logs were snaked or hauled out of the woods to the river's edge. Owners received partial payment for their logs from the buyers, who met them with a measuring stick in one hand and a checkbook in the other. Payment received, the farmers allowed the giant logs to be rolled over the steep bluff into the water below.[5]

85

During winter months the poor farmer-loggers and sharecroppers hired themselves out as crewmen to the rafts bound downstream for Celina or Nashville. The daily wages they earned as loggers and raftsmen provided their only means of buying staple items for their families. One narrator noted of both the farmer-loggers and the share-croppers, "That was their living. That was their livelihood."[6]

Prior to 1885 some hardwood along the Upper Cumberland was sawed into lumber and shipped to Nashville by steamboat.[7] Some people claim that sawmilling began mainly between 1870 and 1880, when a few men commenced buying logs in the area around Celina.[8] All of these early lumbermen engaged in rafting activities, but they sawed most of the logs into rough lumber and shipped it by packet to Nashville. While sawmilling likely took place along the Upper Cumberland during those early years, the market served was strictly local. This was because the first sawmills were operated in connection with water-powered grist mills, limiting the speed and thus the output of the saw blades.[9]

Some timber was cut and rafted down the Cumberland before commercial log buyers entered the area.[10] For the most part, however, the grandfathers (or fathers, in some cases)[11] of the oldest living residents witnessed the coming of the rafting era. Rafting or driving individual logs became a serious business on the Cumberland and its tributaries—the Big South Fork, Wolf, Obey, Roaring, and Caney Fork rivers—in the early 1870s. Nashville became internationally prominent as a hardwood processing center by the turn of the century. As early as 1874, an estimated 22,500,000 board feet of saw logs were rafted to Nashville,[12] and by 1900 an unimaginable number of logs had been floated downstream. During fall and spring, when high waters allowed rafting to take place, log rafts on the Cumberland presented quite a spectacle in the vicinity of Nashville; reportedly, they lined the banks of the Cumberland for twenty-five miles upstream from the Nashville wharf.[13]

The Cumberland River was the artery on which the logs were floated to Nashville. An extensive network of smaller rivers and large creeks, all of which had their own logging enterprises, ultimately fed into the Cumberland at Burnside, Celina, Gainesboro, and Carthage, and at other points along its serpentine route. Logs were floated in rafts or driven individually from the far reaches of every tributary river along the Upper Cumberland. Some came from McCreary County, dropping over Cumberland Falls a few miles above Burnside; others were floated northward to Burnside along the Big South Fork from a point near New River. Parmleysville residents, along with their Wayne County neighbors all along the course of the Little South Fork, drove logs to Burnside and sometimes on to Nashville. Celina buyers were supplied by logs which were driven to Lillydale from above York's Mill in the Valley of the Three Forks of the Wolf River. At Lillydale the logs were combined into rafts for the trip to Celina with logs driven out of the East and West Forks of the Obey. Logs driven out of Overton County along the Roaring River were rafted to Gainesboro, and the upper reaches of the Caney Fork River provided logs for Carthage buyers.

It is difficult to identify all of the early log buyers in the Upper Cumberland. The names of some buyers are remembered, however; they are the ones invariably mentioned when the topic of logging and rafting comes up. During the 1890s, when the company of Lieberman, Loveman, and O'Brien of Nashville focused its attention on Clay, Pickett, and Fentress counties, the names of its log buyers came into prominence. Alonzo F. Braswell of Nashville moved to the Tennessee hill country, where he is still recalled with nostalgia. He enlisted the aid of two Pickett countians, Lafayette ("Fate") Parris and Reuben Rich, to help him buy the giant logs. When Braswell retired and returned to Nashville twenty years later, Parris and Rich continued to buy for L.L. and O. and employed Morrison Huddleston of Byrdstown to help them. The company's brand was a circled "L", which was branded into the end of the logs. Parris measured the logs and Rich was recordkeeper.[14] Fate Parris, a man of honest reputation, "would always give a good measure."[15] The poor people of these mountain counties had full confidence in him, for he would give them "every cent for their logs that he was allowed to."[16] Virgil Beaty of Pickett County explained what it took to be a good buyer: "Well, there'd be two men who generally measured the log, one at each end. One of them would get the diameter of the log at one end, and if it was a

Log buyer inspects logs in preparation for purchase in the Big South Fork country. Photo courtesy Mrs. T. B. Grissom, Sr., Burnside, Kentucky.

Crossties being barged on the Cumberland at Burnside, Kentucky. Photo courtesy Bernice Mitchell, Burnside.

89

round log, why, he'd just measure it in a way that'd give about what was in it. And that is what's called a good log man, one who'd give a working man what's right."[17]

The device used to measure the logs and determine how many board feet each one contained was the Cumberland River Rule,* a long measuring stick with a hook at the end that caught under the log. This rule was designed to measure logs in the water rather than on land, as did the Doyle* and Scribner's rules.* The Cumberland River Rule (whose origin is unknown) was used only on the river which gave it its name.[18] Each end of the log was measured, and then an average was taken of the two.[19] The Cumberland River Rule was discontinued during the latter years of the logging era because it had a reputation of being "a buyer's rule, not a seller's rule," and of "just taking your logs."[20] Rich died in 1911, Parris in 1919. Parris was replaced by his son Bill Parris,[21] and by John Donelson of Celina. George Barksdale, also of Celina, was the last buyer with L.L. and O. and remained in this capacity until log buying and rafting came to an end.[22]

Hugh Kyle and Billy Hull are among the earliest known log buyers in the area. Kyle first bought timber around Celina and then worked his way up the Obey. Hull, who lived between the Obey and Wolf Rivers near Byrdstown, first bought timber in that region and gradually worked his way downstream toward Celina. When his children were grown, Hull moved to Celina and later to Carthage. His son, Cordell, bought logs and ran rafts down the Cumberland, but it was another son, Sirnadus ("Nade") Hull who was the real riverman of the family; Nade worked in the industry for years and was widely known for his prowess on the river.[23]

When Hugh Kyle's three sons, Millard, Frank, and Charlie, became adults, they went into business in Celina with their father under the name of Kyle Brothers and engaged in log buying, sawmilling, and rafting activities. Operating under a circled "K" brand, the Kyles covered Monroe and Cumberland counties in Kentucky and Clay, Pickett, Fentress, and Overton counties in Tennessee. Other early log buyers still remembered in the region include Will Overton, who bought logs in the Roaring River section of Jackson County; Phil Goodwin and Roe Todd, big names in White County between 1884 and 1894; and, in Kentucky, Lon Cummings of Clinton County, Cass Ross of Monroe County, and F.F. Smith of Cumberland County.[24]

Ayer and Lord, a crosstie company at Burnside, employed Josh Clark to buy logs on the Cumberland above Burnside, and brothers Willie and Brant Scott to buy downstream from Burnside and southward in the Obey-Wolf country. Jeff Lovell represented Ayer and Lord on Big South Fork and in parts of Pulaski and Wayne counties. Bernice Mitchell, former secretary at Ayer and Lord, wrote to me about Lovell: "Jeff formed his letters as perfectly as any school teacher, but he spelled as it sounded to him. If he hired a horse for a trip, his expense account would have an item for Hoss Har. Later he had car har. If he bought timber from Jerremiah Denney, of Denny, Kentucky, he made the check to Jerre Mar Denny."[25]

Kyle Brothers made a "contract every fall with timber people up and down the Obey." The contract specified the number of logs and called for delivery at Celina. The Kyles often advanced timber cutters up to $250 to defray expenses of cutting and transporting logs to the river and rafting them when the winter tide* came.[26] Most of the contracts were written; some of them were not. For the most part, contracts were not really necessary, for in the words of Hugh Kyle, grandson of the founder, "if the Obey people made a contract, they'd usually fill it."

Log owners throughout the area received 50 percent payment for the logs at the water's edge. The balance was paid when the logs were delivered at such regional centers as Burnside, Celina, Gainesboro, Carthage, or Nashville, depending on the contract.[27] Logs lost in the river en route because of receding waters or a broken boom* were lost to the seller and buyer alike: the farmer kept the down payment but received nothing else.[28] Successful delivery of the logs put cash in the farmer's pockets, cash which was vitally necessary in the spring when he had to buy seed and fertilizer for the new crops.

Contrary to popular belief, some cheating did occur between log owners and log buyers. Kyle admitted that if a log had a knot on it, the knot was usually submerged when the raft was constructed for shipment to Nashville. He added that "hollow logs with two good ends" were turned down so that the cavity was submerged.[29] On at least one occasion, Kyle himself was deceived by a dishonest Cumberland

91

County logger who sold him a giant walnut log for the rather astronomical figure of $75.00. The original owner had mortised a hole in it, then cut a plug and wedged it into the giant cavity. When the log was taken on to Nashville, it failed to produce a single board foot of lumber.[30]

Log piracy was not uncommon and, like mortising a hole, was a penitentiary offense in both Kentucky and Tennessee.[31] On occasion, thieves went to log yards where logs were awaiting rafting, sawed off the ends containing the brands or hewed off the brand with an axe. The "new owner's" brand then was affixed.[32] It was far easier and less risky, however, for log pirates to go down the river and find logs stranded in brush or on the banks where receding water had left them marooned. Unbranded logs found in this manner were open game, even though some people were not above removing a log brand.[33] Stray logs* were rechanneled and driven or rafted to Burnside, Lillydale, East Port, Celina, Carthage, and other raft assembly points to be sold for cash. Raftsmen often caught stray logs and pinned them into regular rafts en route downstream.[34]

Amos Stone, who lived on the Cumberland just above Celina, made considerable money during the winter months by means of the activity known as drifting,* that is, catching loose logs that came floating down the Cumberland. He received twenty-five cents a log from the owners of branded logs. Often, the log owners were the Kyles of Celina, who came to Stone's place to claim their logs and pay his fee. Stone collected the logs from his boat with a rope which he used to check the flow of the logs and to bring them under control. On occasion, Stone caught entire raft tiers* that had broken away from the main raft. His widow recalled the time a log boom broke at Burnside, releasing logs in such abundance that they were "almost thick enough to walk on." She remembered another time that the giant eddy near Stone's Landing shifted its position and came in close enough to the bank that her husband could stand on the bank and bring in countless spinning logs by means of a spike pole.* He chain-dogged* them one by one as he pulled them in.[35]

Preparations for large-scale logging activities were made during late fall when farming activities were at a standstill. Mules and oxen were shod and groomed. Tools and equipment were collected and readied for heavy use. Cooking utensils and food were loaded into wagons along with the tools and equipment, and men and animals departed for the woods, the steers plodding along behind mule-drawn wagons. Cabins were built at the campsite for the men to live in, and barns or lean-tos were built for animal shelter.

Logs were transported from the woods to the river by means of mules or oxen. Some logs were snaked while others were hauled (from as far away as forty-five miles) on log wagons with wide-gauge rims or carted on two-wheel, ox-drawn carts. While this was one of the most picturesque parts of logging operations, it was also a neces-sary one because motor vehicles had not yet made their way into the rugged terrain of the Upper Cumberland. Steers, more surefooted than mules, were used in very rough places. "They were calm and didn't get excited," commented Arnold Watson. "They weren't as easy hurt as mules or horses in the woods," he continued. Steers were also much stronger and more easily cared for. They were stubborn creatures to train, however; green steers soon learned to "twist the yoke," that is, move away from each other at their tail ends and twist their necks in such a manner that the yoke ended up underneath their necks. Good steer trainers knew to tie the steers' tails together to prevent this catastrophe. They also knew when and how to apply the steer whip, a leather lash about eight feet long tied to a two and one-half foot hickory handle.

Uncle Bud Spears of Clay County was one of the finest steer drivers in the business. Reputedly, he had only to point to an opening and the steers would go through it. His acumen was so impressive that Spears' foreman, Hugh Kyle, requested that he be carried to his grave overlooking the Cumberland at Celina on a log wagon pulled by a yoke of oxen driven by Uncle Bud.[36]

Some logging operations were large enough to merit construction of tram roads* or pole roads* from the river or railhead to the logging camps. Long, slim, flat poles were connected in a linear fashion with metal pins, extending in parallel lines about eight feet apart, like a railroad line. Pole cars, drawn by mules and manned by a muledriver and a brakeman, hauled the logs to the railhead, to the banks of the river where they were rolled into the water and rafted, or to a nearby sawmill. This was done in virtually all counties of the Upper

93

Cumberland, but the practice was most common in Fentress, Overton, and Pickett counties, and perhaps Wayne County.[37] Some tram roads were constructed of two-by-four-foot metal rails, but the log car was still drawn by mules.

Once the logs were on the bluff overlooking the stream, they were rolled into the water along a cleared path (called a chute*) fifty to one hundred yards wide. The logs often tumbled end over end into the stream below. Logs which fell broadside into the water splashed a spray skyward more than one hundred feet. Many logs were split and damaged during the "bluffing"* process.[38] Elvin Byrd of Clinton County remembered watching the chuting procedure:

> A lot of them hauled logs to the top of the hill and yarded them on top of the bluff and scooted them over the bluff; rolled them over this big log chute, see, and let them go into the river. And they'd catch them down there at the river—put a boom across the river so it'd catch the logs when they come across, when the water was low.
>
> That was up here at the Elder Bottom. The Elder Log Bluff they called it. This was just a small boom to get enough logs to make the raft, see. If they didn't catch them, some of them would wash on out. I've seen rafts stay there for two, three weeks before they got ready to go—put together, all tied up. And have them fastened to the bank till it'd come a big tide. When it'd come a tide, they'd take the rafts out, see.
>
> My granddaddy [Jack Booher] was one of the very first ones to raft logs down the Wolf.
>
> One time down about the bluff down there, a big log had lodged against a tree. He went down in under this log chute to break these logs loose with a cant hook.* And so there's twenty-five to thirty logs lodged there. Every one of them rolled over him! He was down in that gully where they'd been a-scooting over. He laid down in this ditch and let them all roll over him, and down the hill.
>
> I lived on the river there. I've seen logs come over that bluff a-changing ends—big logs would hit on their ends and just keep tumbling end over end.[39]

94

At periods of high tide, logs were driven individually down the small creeks which comprised the headwaters of the Big South Fork, Wolf, Obey, Roaring, and Caney Fork rivers. It was necessary to drive logs in single file along the extreme upper reaches of these rivers, as their shallow depths and tortuous channels precluded the shipment of logs in rafts. Driving logs was risky business but great sport. Some of the mountain lumberjacks were skilled in leaping from log to log as they sought to keep them in the middle of the stream channel. Others rode in boats as they accompanied their logs on their trip downstream.

Sarah Jane Koger and Ona Barton talked about men driving logs on Caney Creek, a small stream which fed into the upper Wolf. "They would cut these logs back on the mountain and would drag them to the edge of the creek," Mrs. Koger said. "Caney Creek used to be as big as Wolf River. When it would come a big rain and they'd get a flood in the creek, they'd go push them in the creek and they would go on down. The dam at Gilreath's Mill would catch them. . . ."

"And push them out of Caney Creek into Wolf River," interrupted Mrs. Barton, "And then Wolf River went into Obey and then Obey into the—"

"—Cumberland," Mrs. Koger went on. "People who cut and ran logs down Caney were John and Bill Koger, Jim Crabtree. . . ."

Mrs. Barton then recalled, "These Parris boys would come. They had a branding hammer. My Uncle Sam Dishman worked at running logs. He said the cold water would settle to the bottom, and that it would be so cold on the feet. They'd have on boots, you know.

"I've seen those big rafts tied up on Obey [at Gunther Hill Ferry]," she went on, "but I never did see them floating."

Willie Rich of Pickett County told about log driving on the Obey:

> Here's what they'd do. They'd go and yard them on the river bank—maybe several hundred, maybe a thousand. There'd be different yards. They'd go and measure these and they'd pay them 50 percent down on them. Them poplar [logs], I guess they paid them all down. But they didn't deliver them. They'd roll them in there [the stream bed] and when the river would get up, why, they'd go on down. They'd catch them at the boom, put them in there where they'd take care of them.

And then the spring of the year, some of them would wash up on islands and places, you know. They'd just be a-laying there. Well, there'd be a bunch of men go down the river with cant hooks and one thing and another, crowbars, and they'd roll all these logs over in the current where the next rise comes and takes them all down, so they wouldn't be laying there.[40]

Logs were driven northward on the Big South Fork from Morgan County, Tennessee, to its junction with the Little South Fork, which originates in southern Wayne County above Mt. Pisgah. Logs (as well as crossties and staves*) were individually floated out of the Mt. Pisgah headwaters down to where they were sometimes tied into blocks* (small rafts). Mary Littrell of Albany recalled seeing the waters of Little South Fork "black with logs and staves." There were mill dams along the Little South Fork, according to former Judge Ira Bell, "but in times of flood the rafts would go over them. Sometimes the river would rise twenty-five to thirty feet at Parmleysville and you couldn't tell there was any dam there." Thus, logs frequently were rafted from Parmleysville.

Logs driven loose were trapped and held in check by log booms in several locations: at or near Burnside on the Cumberland, at Lillydale on the Wolf and Obey, at East Port on the Obey where the East and West Forks converge, at Celina on the Obey, at Gainesboro on the Roaring, and at Carthage on the Caney Fork. A log boom was composed of a log trail,* which was a narrow platform or catwalk extending along the stream bank for a considerable distance, and a swing,* which was a floating log rope with one end permanently anchored to the opposite bank. When looped across the river and secured to the trail, the free end ensnared the logs floating downstream. A large log boom operation also had a headwork,* where the loggers stayed when not walking the trail to check on logs,[41] and a mechanical winch for holding the swing in place, called a crab.*[42]

The log float* or boom was made from yellow poplar logs about twenty-four inches in diameter. Holes were drilled through the diameter of the logs large enough to accommodate a metal chain with finger-size links. The chain ran from one log to another holding them in place and creating a floating log chain.[43]

One of the largest log booms belonged to Chicago Veneer Company, a lumber and veneer outfit which took over the holdings of Rodes-Junk Lumber Company in 1904. Their boom was located at Tateville above Burnside and was over two miles long. Here the veneer logs were selected and sent on down to Burnside; the other logs were sawed into lumber on the spot. At the boom were located boom houses for sleeping and feeding the loggers.[44]

At Celina, the Lieberman, Loveman, and O'Brien log boom was located about three-quarters of a mile up the Obey River. It was anchored to trees on opposite sides of the river. A winch was used to wind in the wire cable located on the whip end of the log swing. When in boom position, the log float would extend straight across the river, with only a slight sag in the middle. The L.L. and O. boom could accumulate about three thousand logs before having to raft the logs to Nashville. The company also operated log booms on the Obey and Wolf rivers at Lillydale.[45] When the log boom was not in place in Celina, where the Obey met the Cumberland, it is said that raftsmen from the Wolf and Obey rivers would leap from their rafts and swim ashore rather than face the "big river."

When the logs were placed into position for rafting, floater logs* (ones which floated partially submerged in the water, including poplar, cucumber, ash, lin, and other lightweight timber species) were alternated with sinker logs* (hardwoods such as walnut, white oak, red oak, and black oak) until the raft was completed.[46] Occasionally a big sinker required two floaters on each side, while one large floater sometimes carried four sinkers. Some rafts sank because not enough floaters were included in their composition or because the crew failed to keep mud from accumulating on the raft.[47] All sixteen-foot logs were placed at the bow of the raft; next came the fourteen-foot logs, the twelve-foot ones, and the ten-foot ones. This arrangement of the logs tapered the raft from front to back, causing it to handle more easily as it moved downstream. The tapered shape also helped to keep the stern from striking rocks, bluffs, and stumps in the river bends.[48]

At Miller's Mill on the Wolf and at East Port on the Obey, blocks containing forty to fifty logs were assembled just below the log chute, a flume* which permitted logs to pass over the top of the dam. Log traffic from the Wolf and the Obey converged at Lillydale, where blocks containing up to one hundred logs often were pinned together for the final phase of the journey downstream to Celina.[49]

Miller's Mill was the only mill dam on the Wolf River possessing a log chute. The chute there was a twenty-foot-wide wooden trench, a millrace, through which the water passed across the dam into the river below.[50] When a tide came, the chute was opened, the gates were raised, and large logs passed through. They were caught in a boom below the dam, then tied together and rafted from there to Lillydale and Celina in groups of three or four floats. Small logs were tied together into blocks above the dam at Ike Lee Bluff, Elder Log Bluff, and the Sally Tompkins Place at the mouth of Spring Creek[51] and went through the chute intact. A double float* could go through the chute at Miller's Mill if the logs in it were tied together securely with hickory whaling.*[52]

As the bow started through the chute, the raftsmen ran back to the stern of the raft and grabbed hold of a rope which extended across most of the raft. The men held onto the rope as the bow went under; as the stern settled into the water, they darted forward again. In the late nineteenth century, Ed Tompkins of Clinton County regularly took small rafts through the chute while the other raftsmen waited on the shore. He was adept at moving about the raft as it traveled through the chute. "Hell, he wouldn't even get his feet wet!" recounted one narrator.[53] John I. Cummings, who also had taken rafts over the dam many times in more recent years, exclaimed, "Good God! Hell, I'd get wet from my knees to my chest!" Cummings described the procedure in some detail:

> Well, we'd get down there and we'd pull the raft over on the side next to the chute which was on the far side of the river. And we'd tie a fifty- or sixty-foot cable from one end of that raft to the other.
>
> And we had a wire loop of about eighteen inches. When we started over that dam, we'd hold to that till the front end started over. And we had a twenty-four-foot paddle on that

thing—an oar* we called it. It was a poplar mortised out with about a sixteen-inch board in it—two inches at one end tapered off to a half-inch at the other end. That was what we called our paddle we guided them rafts with. And we'd loop that thing over there, and just as quick as the raft went over that dam, it would hit the bottom and then it would come up. Then we'd have to grab a oar and go to pulling over to the left to keep it from hitting some trees on this side.

Most money I ever made in my life, one morning—my daddy lived right down there about 1,000 yards or so. I was about sixteen years old. Jack Booher come over there one morning. It was down pretty close to zero. Jack done that for a living most of the time [ran rafts]. He was the pilot.* And my daddy was a pilot. My brother-in-law was.

And we went up there to that dam, they'd run them rafts down to there and pulled in to the bank. Then we'd ride them over [the dam] for about 1,000 yards, straighten them up. And they'd set us off and we'd run back up there. We rode twenty-two rafts over that in one day!

We'd just take the rafts; they'd set the crews in on a boat and set us out. We'd run back up there about 800 yards and get on another one. I made twenty-two dollars [a dollar a raft] in one day. I felt like a millionaire!

They didn't want to. It was cold weather and they didn't want to ride over and get cold. And some of them was afraid to go over.[54]

Assembled rafts could remain tied up to the banks of the Wolf for two to three weeks awaiting a raft tide. They were turned loose at the opportune moment regardless of the time of day. Elvin Byrd, who grew up within earshot of Wolf River, recalled the sound coming from the rafts:

When they [the raftsmen] left the raft landing, they'd holler. Every farm had a boat, and the farmer would go to the bank and tie the boat up or put it in a little slough. If he didn't, the raft would come down, tear the boat loose, and take it on

99

down the river. You could hear the trees breaking down if the raft didn't hit the main channel. They'd run into timber and drag trees down, tear rafts apart, and tear logs loose from the raft.

They'd go down of a night lots of times. They'd have a big log-heap fire on the raft. You could see the firelight coming down the river for a long way.

They used to get in the canebrakes, and would cut themselves a lot of river cane. Get that on them rafts and make guns out of them. Put them in a fire; worse than firecrackers popping! They'd do that just for the sound of it. They'd just pile that fire full of them, like a brush pile.

You'd be surprised how fast a raft would run when it got a long stretch where it could really go. But, now, you had to really take it slow around these bends.[55]

A former resident of Willow Grove, a once-proud Obey River community, wrote how as a child he watched rafts and raftsmen on the river:

I remember watching the log rafts drift down the river on the way to market. There were from two to six men on each raft, depending on the number of logs fastened together. Raftsmen talked around a small fire on the raft while watching for shore lines and obstacles in the water. They would guide the raft around, using homemade oars.

It was a thrill to hear their voices come down the stream, watch the raft pass by slowly, and then float around the bend of the river.[56]

The East Port community was the center of rafting on the upper Obey, since it was there that rafts from the east and west forks met. The raftsmen who could pilot a raft out of the east and west forks above East Port—with their sharp bends, dangerous curves, jutting rocks, and tides that occasionally ran above the treetops—were a breed unto themselves, it was claimed;[57] everyone admired but no one envied them, and few pilots on the main course of the Obey could emulate them.

100

Crews were changed at East Port for the final trip down river to Lillydale and Celina. During the heyday of rafting, around 1905, men and boys from nearby communities in Fentress and Overton counties came to East Port to seek employment as raftsmen. As many as 150 were there on any given day during rafting season, hoping to get the nod from raft pilots.[58]

People who lived along the river could sense when the water was high enough for rafting, according to W.K. Irvin, a lifelong resident of Creelsboro. It was fairly easy for the river rats* to predict the crest of the waters in accordance with folk standards. Their estimates were based on how wet the ground already was, especially if there was any snow on the ground in the headwater country.[59] If rain fell on the Cumberland above Cumberland Falls, on the Big South Fork at New River, or on the Little South Fork at Parmleysville, then some Burnside "experts" would multiply the amount of rainfall by four and predict a Burnside tide within six inches of the final crest.[60] A "tide" meant that the rivers were swollen enough to run or raft logs on; it also meant a flood in Burnside on numerous occasions. Store owners, however, would never remove merchandise from shelves above the flood level predicted by folk prognosticators.[61]

At Creelsboro, residents gauged the size of the tide by certain markings on trees at the edge of the river.[62] In Celina, the Kyles predicted the tide on the basis of the amount of rain caught in a straight-sided milk pail. Hugh Kyle's black cook once caused considerable consternation when she used the bucket to get well water and left a large quantity of water in it. Upon seeing the water, Kyle yelled for everybody to get to the river before the rafts were washed away. Another method Kyle used to predict tides was to watch a certain bluff. There was a raft tide when the water "ran white over the bluff." When government gauges were installed on the Cumberland at Celina, much of the guesswork went out of predicting high water in that area.[63]

Loggers on the Wolf chopped notches on trees or tied a red cloth around certain trees to gauge the water level.[64] It generally took a two days' rain or thaw from a big snow at the headwaters of the Wolf to cause the water to reach the markers.[65] It was necessary to exercise caution to keep the rafts above the low-water line, for big rocks lined

101

the channel of the Wolf in many spots. "The Wolf River was really rough when it was up," commented an observer. "I've seen waves ten foot high on it. It was a steep river and rocky."[66] On the East Fork of the Obey at the mouth of Poplar Cove Creek, there was a big rock appropriately called the Tide Rock. When the water got up over that rock, it was time to run the rafts to East Port.[67] Many times tides above Lillydale and East Port ran out before the Obey River got high enough to raft on. When this happened, a group of men channeled* the logs by rolling them from the banks and swampy areas back into the stream channel so they would float down the river on the next tide.[68]

Raftsmen encountered danger at every tuck* and turn in the Cumberland's tributaries. The men had to be alert at all times, watching for dead water, sand bars, broken treetops, bluffs, or jutting rocks. Many rafts of logs and crossties en route to Burnside on the Big South Fork were ripped apart on a legendary big rock called "Old Yaller." So deadly was its constant threat that the rock was finally dynamited out of the stream channel in 1931.[69]

Residents of the Wolf River area tell personal and traditional stories of disasters encountered at Old Skonch, a big rock in the stream channel. Losses of logs against Old Skonch became so numerous that rafting activities on the Wolf above Miller's Mill came to a standstill. The presence of the rock, coupled with several grist mill dams, made rafting on the Wolf above Lillydale a virtual impossibility.[70] For these reasons, logs from the Upper Wolf had to be floated individually.

The rocks posing the greatest threat on the Obey were Tide Rock, Granny Rock, and Drum's Back Rock, which received its name from its close resemblance to the drum fish. Will Peavyhouse recalled a near-disastrous personal rafting encounter with these rocks in the Obey stream channel:

> Well, the water would get so low in the summertime that you couldn't raft. When the fall rains begin to come and the river's up, you could raft, but then you had to wait for the coming of tides. Down the river here, just above the mouth of Poplar Cove Creek, there was a big rock they called the Tide Rock. When the water got hold of that raft, up over that rock,

102

you could run a raft. People everywhere had some mark for the water to get to when they could run a raft.

Some would start from the mouth of Big Piney, they called it. There was a creek up there called Big Piney Creek. It ran into the river. They'd raft the rafts there and start the rafts there. That's as far up as I recall now. They may have come out a little further above that, I don't know. Then all along down the river, down to just a few miles above East Port, they banked them. And run them down there. Sometimes, now, the river would get real big and out of banks, and you couldn't run a raft then. It was dangerous to you. If you tried to run them, you couldn't even do it; they'd get in bushes with you and everything. I've gone down on some rafts like that. There's a big rock down there they call the Granny Rock. That's on down there where the lake is now—Dale Hollow Lake. And they had to keep the raft off the Granny Rock, to keep from hitting it.

And I went down on a raft one time and they couldn't keep off the Granny Rock, to keep from hitting it. It went right square over it, the Granny Rock, and we went right on over it. On below there was a rock they call Drum's Back Rock. Looked like the back of a drum fish. I was on a raft once that hit Drum's Back, knocked the stern oar down. We had to go on down with one oar.

Yeah, there's all kinds of dangers and things on there. I was on one raft one time that hit Crab Bluff and tore all to pieces, just all to pieces. There wasn't no logs left together, hardly at all. My father was a pilot and I was a-pulling on the stern oar at that time. I was just a boy. He took another boy on the raft, under age, which was the wrong thing to do. Oh, it wasn't against the law, but if you got the boy drowned, you could've been sued for damages. Under twenty-one years old. See, then a man wasn't a man of his own until he was twenty-one years old.

Well, we got down there and we didn't have enough men, couldn't keep the raft off of Crab Bluff. It hit Crab Bluff and tore up! Well, one of these men, just as soon as it struck, he jumped off and swam out. It was a cold day; we'd had a big rain and it quit raining, turned cold, and it was snowing a little blue snow. Well, this is awfully cold. And I got back up to the stern oar, thought I'd pick up that stern oar and see if I can do anything with it and it was about to knock me off the raft and I jumped off and swam out. I come out right at the roots of a big sycamore tree. I was a high swimmer; I was a good swimmer. I didn't even get the top of my shoulders wet, but I was wet all over everywhere else, except my head.

Well, then, another fellow over there, he jumped off the raft and he went down feet first, plumb under; then he come up, but he swam out. Everybody but my daddy and this boy. I hollered at my father, "Get off there, Dad! Get off there!" He said, "I'm not going to get off until I get this boy off." And the boy had a raincoat on. But he jumped off and swam out with that raincoat on. They all got off but my daddy. He was on the raft. And I kept following. And something happened and two logs spread apart and he fell down between these two logs plumb up under his arms. But he got out and got the raft put back together. The dangerest thing I ever saw. And the raft went on down to what they call Sugar Camp Island.

They was all wet; wet and cold. And he was a good swimmer, my father was; and I was too—raised on the river down here. So we went back walking up the river to find a way to get across up there, and we found an old dinky boat up there, an old canoe. He got in that canoe and crossed the river and he went on home. And the other men went on home. And I had an uncle lived up on Crab [Creek]. And I went up there, and I was so cold and wet and everything. I went up there and stayed a week before I went on home.[71]

Rivermen still talk about the dangers involved in being knocked into the river by an oar stem;* about feet, legs, hands, and even whole bodies which were crushed to a pulp between the raft and the sheer face of a protruding bluff; about long, violent, crooked streaks of lightning which reached down on turbulent waters to claim the life of a raftsman; and about men whose hair reputedly turned gray as they fought the river in a state somewhere between life and death. Will Peavyhouse shared an incident from personal experience in which a young man in his twenties turned gray during a near-disastrous rafting accident. His account indicates that stranded rafts and their crews sometimes were ignored by passing raftsmen:

> The other time I was telling you about, our pilot stuck the raft on Crab Island. Other rafts would pass us, one after another, and we'd holler to them, 'cause we were stuck there, to throw us a rope or let us throw them a rope. Dick Wright, he come along on a big raft; he was a pilot himself, Dick was. And he was afraid of losing his logs and getting tore up. He come along and he wouldn't even look at us; no, he wouldn't even offer to help us at all.
>
> I saw my brother a-coming, so a raft was coming, and my brother was on there and I knew in reason, they'd help us if they could. But they couldn't do anything for us.
>
> Grandpa Coker was another pilot. He come along on a raft and we throwed him the rope and he got it under the whaling but never could tie it. And he went on. Everybody was passing us. Wasn't a thing for us to do but chop that raft in two; part of it was stuck on the island, the other floated off. We floated on down past Indian Creek, went around Sugar Camp Island, went on around Crab, then tied the raft up there and went up to Crab and stayed all night. Come back next morning, got us another oar, unstuck the other half, and then took all the logs on the East Port.
>
> I never got hurt or pretty near getting drowned. I was a good swimmer. One man here by the name of Bob Beatty—his daddy's name was John Benton Beatty and they called him Bob Benton. Well, he got knocked off the raft and raft run over him. Got knocked off the bow and the raft went over him and his father was on the raft and so everybody thought he was gone. His father just turned around and tied him to it and just put him down, hunkered him down on the raft. Said directly he popped up behind the raft. And somebody dragged and pulled him in.

105

Said it wasn't but a little while, his hair [turned] just as white; wasn't gray-headed, he was a young man just in his twenties. Just turned gray-headed right now.[72]

A gripping account of death on the river was recounted with emotion by John I. Cummings, who recalled a personal experience from his teenage years on the Wolf. He and his father were taking a raft down river near Sulphur Creek when they saw a stranded raft with two men on board:

We went to them. One of them was dead, and the other was just barely breathing. We got him out first. Went back and got the other one. . . .

And they'd [fallen down] walking a figure eight. If you make a figure eight you won't get drunk and [fall down and freeze to death]. If you go one way in a circle, you will. They had that bark wore off them white oak and poplar logs where they'd walked all night to keep from freezing to death.

One of them froze. I don't know whether the other one did or not. We took him out. They [other rescuers] had a covered wagon there and a big fire; had bed blankets and everything. And we took the live one out. There's one old man there. He said, "I've brought a quart of moonshine whiskey." They just jerked the buttons off the freezing man's clothes and stripped him off. The old man went to bathing him in that whiskey. Had it milk warm, and he was a-breathing pretty good when we took the dead one out.

They was from East Port, Tennessee. I forget their names. I was about seventeen. They'd hit what they called a tow head in there and they couldn't see that night. Anyhow, it got up on them and their raft stuck there. They was just two men on that raft.[73]

Logs were rafted from Carthage, Gainesboro, Celina, Burkesville, Burnside, and other key spots along the Upper Cumberland, especially at the mouths of major creeks that emptied into the Cumberland. Celina, Gainesboro, and Carthage in particular were the big regional rafting centers, as each received logs from the Obey-Wolf,

Roaring, and Caney Fork hinterlands respectively, and conveyed them on to Nashville in large log flotillas. At these towns and other sites along the Cumberland, raft assembly was a sight which local people grew accustomed to seeing.

Celina lay in the heart of the region's timber belt and was closely identified with logging and rafting from 1870 to 1930. There, the Kyles first tied their logs into blocks (single rafts), then secured the blocks into drifts,* three blocks (or tiers) wide and three deep. A single tier for a Cumberland River drift was approximately 280 feet in length, and it usually took three or four men an entire day to build. Three tiers were tied together at the bow and stern by means of long logs that were lapped between tiers to make a connection through overlapping whalings. Along the length of the tiers, fastenings were made with chaindogs and hand-whittled wooden pins. A padway* of planks was laid for the hands to walk on while steering the drifts down river.[74] A typical drift contained up to 2,000 logs and about 300,000 board feet of lumber.[75]

When properly constructed, Cumberland River drifts had a minimum of flexibility and expandability. This was a must for easy handling and durability. No pilot wanted to have to take off an entire day en route to patch up a raft. The size of the rafts was governed by the size of the seven locks built by the United States Army Corps of Engineers on the Cumberland between Celina and Nashville. These locks were 52 feet wide and 300 feet long; the rafts were built accordingly.[76] Prior to the construction of the locks, most rafts exceeded 300 feet in length.[77] The Kyles alone had fifteen to twenty Cumberland River drifts moving down the river at any given time during the rafting season.

The Kyles kept raftsmen on call at all times, any one of whom could put a raft together. Most of the time the company employed about one hundred men from the Celina-Byrdstown-Livingston area. Up to half of those men who rode the Kyle rafts to Nashville were from the Obey-Wolf country, who had brought blocks down from Boatland and Lillydale. It is said that, in all, there were over one hundred men who piloted rafts from Celina to Nashville.[78] The raft pilot, who generally stood on the stern,[79] had to know his river at every stage of water, at every bend and shoal. He had to know the location of swift water, treacherous eddies, and shoals. In short, he had to envision a mental picture of the entire stretch of river. The pilot also had to be able to spot sand bars building up below the surface of the water, and he had to know where to look for waterlogged tree trunks and other snares that might incapacitate or destroy a raft. Will Peavyhouse described a pilot on the job:

> Whenever they got ready to go, they'd get all the men on the raft—the men on the bow and on the stern, and then the pilot would untie the ropes there and pull the rope in. And he'd say to the men on the bow, "Now turn your bow out," and they'd pull down in the river.
>
> Course, he'd say, "Pull your stern out." We pulled it out in the river and then she's going down the river, down a-floating. And when we come to a curve or a bluff, why, if she's on the right-hand side, he'd say, "Turn your bow over the left." Well, they'd pull the bow over that way. And if the stern was warping around toward the bluff, he'd say, "Ease your bow, ease your stern." And when we come to another place, they'd tell them to pull the bow to the right or left, whichever it was. And if they'd get in a hard place and just about hit the bluff, you ought to hear that old pilot a-hollering. You never heard no Free Will Baptist preacher make any more fuss than he would: "Tell them to get her out of there, boys, right quick!"[80]

Hugh Kyle described the role of a good raft pilot: "He's the man who knew how to do jobs easy and not work his men to death pulling on the oars." Taking the rafts down the river was no easy task, for pilots not only had to anticipate hazards well in advance but also had to exercise great self-control and not get excited easily.[81]

A story, likely a migratory legend, about an excitable pilot drifted out of the Obey country:

> There was a place up here on Obey where they tore up lots of rafts. It was at a sharp bend in the river where the water was swift. . . . The pilot was standing on the bow when he became scared. Well, said he was hollering to the boys, "Hold her out, she's going to hit the bluff!"

108

Everytime he'd holler, he'd jump up. Said he got so excited and just kept hollering for them to hold the raft.

Finally, the whole raft ran out from under him and he jumped right in the river![82]

The average raft on the Cumberland was manned by a crew of six men, one of whom was the pilot and another of whom doubled as cook. They manned the oars at all times to swing the drifts around the horseshoe bends of the river. A trip from Greasy Creek to Nashville took about ten days, from Burkesville eight to nine days, from Meshack Creek about eight days;[83] from Celina it took seven days and about four from Carthage.[84] But every now and then, given the right pilot and plenty of water and moonlight, the trip could be cut almost in half.[85]

Bill Bybee of Cumberland County was known for taking rafts on through to Nashville on moonlit nights. He knew the river extremely well but took no unnecessary chances. His system of taking soundings was described by Hiram Parrish of Burkesville:

He said he'd get out on the front of a raft—he'd know pretty well where he was—and knock two rocks together and it'd echo from the bluff; he'd tell how close he was to the bluff by the echo. And another way he'd tell, said sometimes he'd throw a whole sack of potatoes away, go down there and every once in a while he'd throw a potato toward the bank and if he heard a splash in the water, why, he was all right. If he didn't, why, he'd pull out. That's some of the stories that were told.[86]

Bob Riley, along with Cordell Hull, was one of the first raft pilots to make the run from Celina to Nashville. He grew up at Fox Springs, a rural community located just below the mouth of Mitchell Creek on Obey River. In early partnership with Hull and later on his own, Riley made a small fortune from his logging and rafting enterprise. Riley is said to have been one of the finest raft pilots to run the Cumberland. Part of the legendary aura surrounding his name may stem from the claims that he was an expert forager. This local hero was chief actor in a cycle of stories told about him, some of which are migratory legends. One of them tells how he conned a farm woman out of a fine turkey:

109

Bob's raft had been torn apart near the bank and was being repaired for the further trip. He spied a large flock of turkeys in a farm yard, and he paddled to the bank, as every raft had a boat tied to the raft.

He singled out a goodly-sized gobbler, and began chasing him around the farm yard. The wife of the house, hearing the commotion, came out and demanded an explanation: "Why are you chasing my turkey?"

Bob answered very quickly in a tearful voice and told of their plight of hunger. They had brought the turkey from Celina and aimed to eat him, "but this morning he picked the knot untied and joined your flock. Won't you please help us catch him?"

The lady gladly helped him catch one of her turkeys. So the turkey was cooked. The hungry raftsmen had a feast.

On the next trip down the river, Bob stopped and explained to her the truth about the turkey and more than paid her the worth of the turkey.[87]

According to another story, Riley

once killed a calf found on the river bank, and put rubber boots on its hind legs and a rain slicker over the rest of it. When the owner saw him and came down to investigate, Uncle Bob told him not to come aboard, for his brother had just died with smallpox. Pointing to the calf in foul weather gear, he said, "There he lays now." Uncle Bob began to sob, and the owner of the calf began to run, not wanting any contact with the contaminated body.[88]

Similar stories were told about other Cumberland River raftsmen. One of them was a black man, Bob Allen, who was also involved in a turkey theft:

They had a shanty* on them and you could lay in that at night; pillow of straw, and they'd take quilts. And cook on that. And lots of times they'd tie up, maybe slip out and steal a turkey or something. Uncle Bob Allen, colored man, stole several turkeys down here. Cooked them up. They was going on down the river, you know. I think Uncle Bob was the cook. I don't think he went and got the turkey, but some of the other hands brought the turkey on and picked him, and Uncle Bob cooked him. They had him in court. And they got Uncle Bob up as a witness to prove that Uncle Bob, that he cooked the turkey.

And he says, "Well, I cooked fowl."

Says, "What kinda fowl was you cooking?" Says, "It was turkey, wasn't it?"

"I don't know. They were fowl; they were picked. I didn't see the feathers; they was picked. I was cooking meat. I was cooking fowl!"

They kept teasing him, pinning down on him. Finally he says, "I said fowl! It could of been a hummingbird!"[89]

Although there are humorous stories about the raft pilots, that is not the vein in which most of them are remembered. Toughness had its place in the order of things, too, especially when the raftsmen were confronted by steamboat captains who wanted to hog the river channel. When verbal assaults at the steamboat captains failed, it was occasionally necessary for raft pilots to fire rifle shots above the packet cabins to persuade the boat captains to make room for the rafts.

In the following conversation, Cumberland countians John Stone, a retired steamboat watchman and mate, and Hiram Parrish mention some of the encounters between the boatsmen and the raftsmen.

Hiram Parrish recalled, "Well, I did hear one time that a boat got close enough to where the boat was coming right up on the raft. Bob Parrish, who was raft pilot, run out and took his axe and stuck it in the hull."

Stone replied, "I don't know about that, but I was on a boat once when we hit one all right, but it was in fog."

Parrish went on, "And I think Bob Parrish throwed a big piece of whaling into a wheel one time because the boat got too close to him."

"He thought that they wasn't doing him right," explained Stone. "And they might not have been! I don't know."

"I think it was a Nashville boat," said Parrish.

111

Stone continued, "But I do know that Carley Smith, because Carley worked for Red Gulf Cedar Company here for years. Of course, he was on rafts, and went with them, and may have run them, I don't know."

"Yeah, he was a raft pilot," Parrish confirmed.

"Now he was really nice to them," Stone said. "I've seen him stop way before he got to them and back up and float along and wait for all them waves."

Stone went on to explain the difficulty raftsmen had in navigating in the wake of steamboats:

> A boat made a lot of waves! And especially if the raft was over here in this curve. I've seen waves go as high as that door there up on that bluff. In straight water they didn't go that high. They'd slosh up two foot on the banks. I've seen them, boy, see a raft; naturally, they never was on the point side, unless they was fighting to try to hold them there. And going around this bend, they's always a bluff. And when a boat passed them, they couldn't pull with them oars. Them waves would go clear across the raft on that bend side, and that's where they passed them unless it was straight. But they passed them in all kinds of places. And when they was in them curves like that, it was hard on them. And sometimes, they'd drag, lose logs, and they'd have to work! I never was on a boat when it tore one up. But I've been on one when I've seen men on them in the water waist high, and they's trying to take care of their oars.[90]

Hugh Kyle claimed that the boat and raft pilots got along pretty well: "The steamboats would slow up most of the time. Sometimes the boats would shake them up a little, but not much. Lots of times there'd be a raft stuck, and them boats would cut their motors back for the rafts. I knew all those old steamboat pilots."[91]

Life aboard a raft was not comfortable, and it certainly was not easy. The raftsmen would alternate between being wet, cold, and dirty and being hot, sweaty, and dirty; their drinking water generally came from the muddy Cumberland itself.[92] In the middle of the raft was a rather large lean-to, usually called a *shanty*, where the men took turns sleeping on beds of straw and where the cook prepared the food on a mud fireplace, a rock grate, or a small stove.[93]

In winter, whiskey was taken as a stimulant and as a blood warmer. Sometimes, the men dipped too heavily into the jar. Elvin Byrd recalled, "Most of the fellows who went down on them rafts drunk whiskey all the time. Take them a gallon of whiskey with them, and they'd drink whiskey along as they went down. Some would get drunk. I guess a lot would fall off when they's drunk."[94]

Although many rafting trips were made during wintry weather, the raftsmen normally did not bundle up in heavy clothing. They had to be able to step quickly during emergencies and to swim out of the river following a raft break-up.* Nor did they always wear coats; when they did, the coats generally were worn underneath overalls so that "if the raft tore up and I had to swim, I wouldn't have that coat flopping around."[95] John I. Cummings recalled, "We just had a suit of underwear and overalls and just a common coat. We wore low-cut shoes called brogans. You'd fill the soles full of them great big carpet head tacks so you wouldn't run them over and wear them out. I have seen a few people go down with the knee-high gum boots, but most hardly ever wore them."

Sub-zero temperatures often froze the wet overalls to the men's bodies. A crackling noise could be heard as the men walked from the raft to an office or a house. Ayer and Lord personnel in Burnside prepared a roaring fire in the office's cast-iron stove when they were expecting the arrival of rafts bearing bone-chilled men. Bernice Mitchell recalled that

> their regular procedure was to hand us the foreman's ticket, showing the number of ties, the contractor's name, how much to pay the runners* and deduct from our settlement, and then sit by the stove to remove their shoes and socks. They would wring as much water as possible from those woolen socks and warm them a little before putting them on to start the long walk back up the river. The heat soon caused steam to rise from the wet overalls and socks, and the odor was not like roses![96]

113

In the spring, when temperatures moderated, raftsmen often went without shirts and shoes. A former raftsman on the West Fork of Obey recalled: "At the mouth of Buffalo Cove Creek we would see the rafts coming out from up here, and these men on there bare-headed and no shirts on. They wasn't very common then. People would think they were hillbillies. But they's just big, strong men, tough and not afraid."[97]

Raftsmen were respected by all who came into contact with them, whether at Burnside, East Port, Celina, or Nashville. They were "just good, honest, hard-working people," many of whom were sharecroppers during farming season and river rats during rafting tides.[98] They were considered to be among the finest people in the community.[99]

The Wolf River raftsmen often stayed overnight at Mouth of Wolf in the home of James Scott, a log dealer who purchased many logs from the area's farmers.[100] Overnight lodging also was obtained from Old Man Jim Gamel, who lived atop a bluff on the south bank of the river, about 1,000 yards downstream from the Scott place. Gamel was a heavy drinker, according to one narrator, but "an awful good old man. We'd get up the next morning and have ham meat and biscuits. He'd wrap us up a little snack in a shoe box for dinner."[101]

Two big log houses positioned end to end served as a hotel further downstream at Lillydale, where the Wolf joined the Obey. Several rooms both upstairs and down were set aside for raftsmen. There were six to eight beds in each room; only one person slept in a bed. Blacks cooked the meals and waited on the raftsmen.[102]

In Celina, the raft crews from the Obey and Wolf were treated as hardworking men and were given hotel accommodations, if available. Even when all the beds were rented, however, they were not turned away; they lay on the floor and slept on the bare planks. John I. Cummings recalled that at Celina they were "treated as nice as if we was home. They was an old fellow there by the name of Bill Napier. He kept raft hands; wouldn't turn nobody away! He'd say, 'Boys, I can feed you, but I can't bed you. You'll just have to do the best you can.'"[103]

In Celina, raftsmen also stayed at the New Central Hotel, operated by Bill Dale, and the Riverside Hotel, operated by T.L. Meadows and a Mr. Denton, an old steamboat pilot. All places served food in abundance, but Mr. Denton took in only as many as he could bed down. Sometimes the raftsmen got drunk, but there were few drunks who worked the river. Some were big spenders; others saved virtually every cent they earned. Almost all the men were honest and trustworthy, faithful to their promises and work assignments.[104]

When they arrived at their destinations, the men passed the time in groups of twenty-five to thirty, telling big tales and reliving their rafting exploits.[105] They were not above practical jokes, even on the hotel proprietors. Take, for example, the night that a bunch of Obey River raftsmen loosened the tin stove pipe running through their room and inserted into it a pair of river-sogged overalls. Mr. Napier, the proprietor, spent the remainder of the night and part of the next morning trying to rid the lobby of smoke and to determine the reason the flue would not draw.[106]

Raftsmen returning home went all the way back up the river from Nashville by steamboat or rode the Tennessee Central to Carthage and caught the packet.* Others rode the rails back to Glasgow, Kentucky, or to Algood, Tennessee, where they struck out across the country on foot for home.[107] It was possible to ride a packet up river to Celina for about two dollars deck fare, bed and food excluded.[108] But many raftsmen preferred to walk rather than squander a portion of their hard-earned money on needless luxury.[109] Thus, with a small supply of cheese and other easily carried foods, they began the three-to seven-day trip home, the time depending on where they lived.[110] Raftsmen from as far away as the Little South Fork area of Wayne County generally walked from Nashville.[111] They followed a well-traveled path from Celina to Clinton County, crossing Pea Ridge by way of Spearstown, where the weary travelers generally ate a meal and rested before heading for the Forks of the Wolf at Lillydale. They expected to be across the ford there by nine o'clock the evening of the fourth or fifth day.[112] From that point they fanned outward into most of the rafting communities along the state line.[113]

John I. Cummings remembered the return trip to southern Clinton County this way:

> We used to go down the river and walk back from Celina. That's the only way we had of coming back. Come through

115

Captain Bob Meadows, one of the foremost upper river pilots, from Nashville and Lee's Landing. Photo courtesy Katherine Cassetty, Whitleyville, Tennessee.

116

Narrator John I. Cummings of Clinton County, Kentucky, recalling his early days as a farmer and raft pilot on the Wolf River for the author, (*right*), 1976.

117

Pea Ridge that way. Come to the mouth of the Wolf down here and come across there where Miller's Mill used to be. Zet Tompkins, Aunt Sally Tompkins's girl, if there's a light in the house, we could give a big nigger whoop,* she'd come out and answer. We'd say, "Come set us across the river." She'd set us across the river about eight or nine o'clock many a night. She could handle a boat just like a man.[114]

By 1915, the giant trees within reasonable distance of the rivers were gone and the boom days were over.[115] The Nashville market dried up by 1931 as economic depression gripped the region and the nation. That same year the Kyles of Celina closed the doors of their Nashville operation. By the early 1940s all log rafting ceased on the Upper Cumberland.[116]

Crossties as well as logs, however, claimed the attention of many men and several tie companies throughout most of the lumber-rafting era. The crosstie market was based on timber that was considered too small for good saw logs. The big tie companies were operating out of Burnside by the early 1880s, deriving their raw materials from the hinterland served by the Big and Little South Forks in McCreary, Pulaski, and Wayne counties. Oak, walnut, and poplar crossties there, as well as elsewhere in the region, were hewn out with a broadax by individual farmers, then hauled to the river and rafted in a manner similar to rafting logs. Chaindogs and raft pins were utilized, but sixty-penny nails* could also be successfully employed to fasten the whaling to the crossties.[117]

Burnside and Carthage were the two centers for buying, processing, and shipping crossties, barrel staves,* handles, heading,* spokes, golf clubs, and other timber products. Generally the ties from Russell, Wayne, and Clinton counties were barged up the Cumberland to Burnside, while Carthage received all the ties on the Cumberland southward from Cumberland County and from dealers along the Wolf, Obey, and Caney Fork rivers. Among the names associated with the tie and stave industry, none loom as important in folk memory as Ayer and Lord Tie Company and Ches-Wyman Cooperage Company. With operations in Burnside and Carthage, Ayer and Lord attempted to buy nearly all the ties the region afforded.[118] Ches-

118

Wyman of Louisville, "the largest cooperage company in the world," had branches in Nashville and Carthage and at one time received staves from seventy-two mills.[119] Buyers for these two companies, including Ayer and Lord's Jeff Lovell, who became legendary in the South Fork country, criss-crossed the region many times. They still left enough timber for several other corporate names to become prominent over the years, including the Tennessee Stave and Lumber Company at Oneida, Tennessee, which bought heavily in the upper Wolf region; Davis, Hicks, and Green, which exploited the upper reaches of the East and West Forks of the Obey;[120] Grissom-Rakestraw Lumber Company;[121] Hardwood Products Company and Crouch and Spurrier in Livingston; Cumberland Lumber Company in Sparta; Turner-Day-Woolworth Handle Company, a Nashville-based outfit that ranged throughout the hill country and established mills in Byrdstown, Albany, Tompkinsville, and other places in the Upper Cumberland; the J.B. Witson Company of Cookeville, with a branch office in Carthage; the Welch Stave and Heading Company with headquarters in Monterey;[122] and the B and B Lumber Company of Jamestown, Tennessee.[123]

There is no way to measure the positive impact of these timber companies on the region's economy. The volume of their operations was staggering. J.D. Lowrey, who worked as buyer for Ches-Wyman Cooperage Company, observed that the company had one million staves stacked at Carthage at one time. Arnold Watson noted that, collectively, the crosstie and stave companies produced millions of items from Upper Cumberland lumber. The economic benefits of the industry were not limited to the timber owners but extended to those hired to process the lumber as well. Watson remembered that Ches-Wyman paid ten cents an hour for ten hours of actual labor at a time when salaried jobs were rare in Cumberland County. To earn this, the men pulled crosscut saws six days a week and never took off time to eat lunch. At the end of the week, they were paid in silver. "Those guys went around with six silver dollars in their pockets, rattling them. They thought they was rich."[124]

Others made money hauling stave bolts* from the stave yards to the nearest railroad shipping center or steamboat landing or to local cooperage plants. E.R. Gaskin told how his father employed neighbors to haul stave timber in wagons and then shipped it by boat to Burnside:

> They'd haul them to Somerset and load them in railroad cars. Haul them by wagon to Somerset.
>
> One fall my daddy had a stave yard cut and they was drying. He got ready to move them to market. He said, "I'm going to open the market up." Usually, they'd vie for who would get to haul. They'd haul for $2.50 a day, and furnish their team and a man and their wagon. Said, "I'm going to open this haul up. I'm going to let every neighbor and everybody that wants to haul to come in here and haul."
>
> And I saw almost a hundred wagons line up there and load those staves and start to Columbia, Kentucky, with them. That was kind of a halfway house. Wagons would then come from Campbellsville to Columbia and pick them up and take them on in to the plant at Campbellsville.
>
> We shipped a lot of staves, my daddy did, when he was operating there on Melson Ridge. It's on the edge of Adair County; come out from Columbia there. That section of the country has not changed like it has around Russell Springs. It still has a lot of old log houses; pretty much like it used to be. Well, out at the end of Melson Ridge where it runs out there at Creelsboro, I've been there when we used Creelsboro Landing to ship our stuff by barge. We'd ship up the river to Burnside, and there they'd load it in box cars.
>
> I've seen fifty, sixty wagons at Creelsboro with lumber and logs. The Irvins were the biggest merchants. People came there from all over the country. They sold caskets, wagons, buggies. Kept them parked outside.
>
> We had a yard of staves there at Creelsboro, my daddy did. They were stacked on the river bank ready for loading out. And they came a tide in the river. Dad heard it was rising fast and he went down there to see if we could get some help to move the stock back away from the river bank. By the time we got there, the river was raising so! I rode a little sorrel mare. She was a dandy. And he rode a big old bay horse that he

got from Jim Cravens. And we rode out there into those staves and saw the river coming [rising]. There was nothing we could do. We rode back just a little ways and we stopped and turned around on a little high place and watched those staves. The river would get up almost to the top of them, and they'd just jump up like a cork and start floating down the river, scatter out, you know.

He lost that yard of staves [in 1916], and we started back to the store—Irvin's Store. And they was a slough* or a low place up the river and it had gotten full of water. It happened while we was on that high place watching them staves. When we came back through there, that was deep enough to swim that horse I was on. And Daddy's horse got tangled up in a bunch of barbed wire or something that had washed down in there, and I thought it was going to drown him and the horse both. That happened right there at Creelsboro.

Then we had a yard of staves to wash away at Helm, Kentucky, right below Wolf Creek bridge, now it is. Twice he lost all that he had. But that was common on the river.

My dad was always a small stave operator, but he was one of the biggest in Russell County. He owned his own mills, but the mills wasn't much, you know.[125]

Dolph Humbles of Somerset had the first bucking mill* in the area; others soon followed his lead, and small fortunes were made in the production of barrel staves. Paramount in this regard were the Luttrells and Gaskins of Russell County, who established bucking mills just after the turn of the century. A bucking mill was powered by a horse which pulled a long tongue in circular fashion much like a cane mill. The mill contained two sharp blades which trimmed and shaped the stave timber into market-ready barrel staves. It was a slow operation and one man could feed the staves into the mill. The large piles of wood shavings were utilized as cooking wood for kitchen stoves.[126]

Staves of white oak cut along the Cumberland furnished the wood for Kentucky bourbon barrels and for wine and oil casks in Spain. Even cedar grown in the area has its own claim to fame. Many of the old cedar rail fences, built mainly by Kentucky and Tennessee pioneers, were torn down about 1910 to furnish the world's principal supply of wooden pencils.[127] Burnside mills were important in this regard.

The first sawmills in the region were powered by water,[128] and they mainly produced custom-sawed lumber and barrels. The first barrels, kegs, and hogsheads were used as containers for storing and shipping home-grown products. Steampowered band mills* (mills whose saws went around in an unbroken band) became big industry in the Upper Cumberland about the turn of the century, while rafting was still very active. From 1905 to 1920 it was common practice to construct onsite sawmills whose saws were either band or circular. In the words of Benjamin Edmunds of Russell County: "Those old sawmills had two saws; one above and the main big saw was down below. They would have to run both of those saws on some of the logs, they was so large, to cut through. They had to have two saws. They didn't have band saws. We don't have timber like that now. Listen, it's poles you take to the mill now!"[129]

Some of the Tennessee milling camps shipped lumber on rail cars which traveled into the rugged terrain along the spur tracks from the main line. Lumber from other camps was shipped by steamboat or by mule-drawn wagons, the only modes of transportation known in the more isolated Kentucky portion of the Upper Cumberland. Charlie Burtram recalled how he outmaneuvered sixty or more wagons loaded with lumber outbound from a sawmill in Frost Hollow of southern Wayne County:

> There was a string of wagons as long as from here to that house out yonder, you might say. And the front one stuck, you know, with a load of lumber [laughter].
>
> Well, there I was with four old mules; couldn't get by and I had to be at Bethesda at a certain time, you know. So Charlie Pears, old Doc's boy, he said, "I'll fix it so you can get through." Well, he took a big cardboard and put on the front "U.S. Mail" and on the back "U.S. Mail" on the wagon bed. And I was going on down there at Hidalgo, pulling that hill and I see two Negroes. They had a load of lumber, going on, and I was catching up with them. And there's one a-riding on,

122

a-looking back at me. And I seen him read that "U.S. Mail." I can tell by the working of his mouth, you know. And he told that other fellow, and, boy, here he pulled out just quick as he could. And whenever they seen that, they'd get out of my way. Them was good old days!

There were over sixty wagons loaded with lumber. They's from everywhere.[130]

Most sawmilling camps were populated exclusively by men, and only sparsely at that. Men ate, slept, fought, laughed, cried, and murdered each other under rough, frontier-like conditions. Recorded recollections and oral traditions present vivid descriptions of all facets of life in these mill encampments. They are not pleasant by any means. E.R. Gaskin offered the following description of life in a Kentucky lumber camp about 1920:

I can remember when my daddy sent me off down to Harvey's Ridge to wind up a set of lumber. I was nearly grown. He gave me a pair of horses. One of them was blind. And two other fellows drove the young mules. They all was laughing at me. They said Old Blindie would break his neck. That horse was never down one single time! He'd feel his way with them feet, and he stood up and he'd pull; it was a sight in the world!

We took a can of Karo syrup and some corn meal and a little flour and plenty of potatoes and beans. And there was a stove already in the shack where he'd sawed the yard of lumber out. And he'd just sent down there to move it [the timber]; it had set there and dried. That was on Harvey Ridge on the edge of Adair County. And Mother wrapped us up two great big balls of butter. It was awful dry and dusty that fall. I got breakfast ready while they'd feed of a morning, curry the team and harness them, and get ready to leave with a load of lumber.

Benny Wade said one morning, "Come on, sit down and eat here while it's hot." Said, "You can't eat it when it gets cold." I said, "Let me peel this butter." It had laid there in the dust in that old lumber yard and dust had got in there and settled on it and I had to peel it![131]

123

Among the mill camps that permitted women was the one at Cooktown, a community located near Crawford in Overton County, consisting of over 600 lumbermen and their families; and the camps run by Spencer Koger in eastern Fentress County. Koger's camps had boarding houses for the men. If families were present, they generally lived in railroad boxcars. "Bad women" sometimes drifted into camp and the men fought over them, "but they weren't worth fighting over."[132] Koger had eighteen teams of mules which demanded the services of several drivers. Logs were cut and snaked to the tram roads where they were loaded on railroad cars by means of large cranes mounted on the cars. When one site was logged over, the entire operation was moved to a new location.

Most of the big sawmilling companies moved out of the Upper Cumberland after the virgin tracts of timber had been depleted. In a 1931 editorial bearing the heading, "Jamestown Sees Dawn of Era of Prosperity," the Jamestown, Tennessee, *Banner* summed up the plight and a proposed remedy: "There are thousands of acres of cut-over lands for sale in Fentress County. . . . A strong effort will be made to attract farmers from other sections, especially German and Scandinavian farmers of the North, to these lands. A great deal of land can be bought for ten dollars an acre." An influx never materialized, not even a trickle.

After the demise of large-scale sawmilling in the area, small milling operations moved in to do the mopping up. Sawmilling camps were scuttled during the 1920s in favor of smaller, readily portable sawmills. These units were called peckerwood mills* because it was said that a woodpecker could peck out more sawdust in a day than one of these mills could saw. Eventually, most peckerwood sawmilling reverted to much larger stationary units which operated on the same sites for several years. In 1937, for instance, Grissom-Rakestraw of Burnside had the largest lumber concentration yard in the United States in a nonmetropolitan area;[133] in the 1960s, when it was sold to Hamer Hardwood Manufacturers, it was the largest producer of lumber in the Upper Cumberland. With the transfer of Grissom-Rakestraw to a nonlumber producer, saw lumber leadership was assumed by the Stearns Coal and Lumber Company, a McCreary

124

Peckerwood mills like this one in Metcalfe County, Kentucky, are virtually nonexistent on the contemporary landscape. Photograph 1978 by the author.

125

County outfit that is now much larger than Grissom-Rakestraw was when it was sold.

Today, a few peckerwood mills are still found across the region. Gibson Lumber Company of Breeding, Kentucky, which is no longer a small operation but uses the slogan "The World's Largest Peckerwood Mill," is located in the rugged hill country of southern Adair County along the Cumberland County border. It is a family venture operated since 1963 by two brothers, Walter and Charles "Soap" Gibson. Their father was a veneer log buyer, so the brothers had heard "wood talk"* all their lives.[134] This is the case with virtually all of the other sawmills in the region: they are family-owned, folk enterprises. Most of these mills are rather large commercial operations, home-owned and operated by natives of the region. The equipment is generally run completely by electricity, and a large fleet of trucks hauls logs from the woods to the mill. They do, nonetheless, advertise for delivery of logs to the mill as well as for boundaries of standing timber.

In conclusion, the coming of modern sawmills and other mills producing specialized wood products signaled the end of rafting logs and crossties on the river as a way of life.[135] The advent of sawmilling was inextricably linked with improved road construction, which came to the Upper Cumberland chiefly because of governmental action to lift the country out of the throes of economic depression. The improvement of roads meant the arrival of yet another modern force: heavy-duty, gasoline-powered trucks. These machines phased out rafting but gave additional impetus to logging activities in general. It was a far simpler matter to move portable sawmills to a boundary of timber than it was to cut the logs, haul them to the river, tie them into rafts, and then wait for a flood tide to float the rafts to market. Timber sawed by the numerous large mills which sprang up throughout the Upper Cumberland could be loaded by hand onto trucks or mule-drawn lumber wagons and then hauled overland to rail centers for shipment to processing centers at Burnside, Cookeville, Carthage, or Nashville. The timber supply, though diminished in quality, was still abundant in the 1930s and 1940s, and it was more accessible to market than ever.[136] That situation continues to the present; pockets of virgin timber and plenty of good second growth serve as the basis for folk industries of significant magnitude—significant when weighed against other facets of the region's economy.

The key to understanding the timber industry of the Upper Cumberland lies in the term *home-owned*. While Northern entrepreneurs were grabbing up large acreages of forest lands and mineral leases in the Appalachian South for a mere fraction of their actual worth, the people of the Upper Cumberland, in the main, remained in charge of their own economic destiny. This hardwood timber belt thus developed rather differently from neighboring regions. The people of the Upper Cumberland controlled their own hardwood industry throughout the rafting era from 1870 to the 1930s; they continue this pattern at the present time by maintaining ownership and management of the area's sawmills. The timber industry continues to be a folk industry dominated by native farmer-loggers and modest milling operators. In the words of Steven A. Schulman, "It is impossible to separate the logging industry of the Cumberland from the folklife of the area, because of the involvement of the [local] people in the business."[137] To study the timber industry of the Upper Cumberland is to study the folklife of the area.

CHAPTER 4

A Steamboat Empire

Since its first settlement, the Upper Cumberland region—a diversified geographical area of fertile bottom land and rugged hills, plagued with threats of isolation and resulting economic peril—has been at the mercy of the evolution of transportation. This statement is true of practically any area of the nation; the Upper Cumberland, however, is unique in that its chief means of transportation shifted from ox-cart to flatboat, thence to steamboat, and finally to motor truck. The railroad affected the region to some extent but was never integral to the hinterland communities. Changes in modes of transportation always were gradual. Each new method had to pass a test of reliability before it was accepted totally by the residents of the area. People still reminisce fondly of the steamboating days, but they also recall the days when an inland town could be reached only by wagon. Most residents of the Upper Cumberland agree that those are indeed only times to *remember*, not to be relived.

During the late eighteenth and early nineteenth centuries, the Upper Cumberland was accessible only on horseback, by horse- and ox-drawn vehicles, and by occasional river craft which could haul cargo only one way—downstream. Toward the end of the 1700s, flatboats and keelboats were used to transport surplus agricultural and animal products to New Orleans. The advent of the steamboat on the Upper Cumberland in 1828 brought the area in closer contact with the outside world, not only supplying a dependable means of exporting produce and receiving merchandise but also providing reliable passenger service to and from the region. The steamboat, which augmented flatboats and log rafts, was itself supplemented by the railroad, which linked certain local waterways and roads to form a patchwork system of transportation connecting the Upper Cumberland with other parts of the Upper South and the Midwest. Although the railroad was responsible for the demise of steamboating in other parts of the country, the convergence of these two methods of transportation at Burnside in 1880 proved advantageous to the Upper Cumberland area.

In the second quarter of the twentieth century, improved highway systems were developed in the Upper Cumberland region, creating still more efficient methods of travel and trade. Dependence on water transportation ceased altogether. Gone were the days when a train crossed a Cumberland River trestle at Burnside and the passengers could look below to see a steamboat shrouded with black smoke, pushing barges up river. Yet because the river dominated commerce and transportation in the region from the late 1780s until 1930, the Cumberland River remained the central element in regional consciousness. Many people associated with the river have become legendary in the minds of the present residents of the Upper Cumberland area. Oral stories about them reflect a close affinity with the river and the human dramas enacted upon its waters.

In the late eighteenth and early nineteenth centuries, when travel was limited essentially to ox-cart and horse-drawn wagon, residents had little contact with the outside world; for example, mail was delivered once a week by a carrier on horseback.[1] Those settlers who had cleared lands and established productive farms during the twenty-year span from 1790 to 1810 needed a dependable means of transportation to get their surplus goods to market. There were no large towns in the Upper Cumberland area; in fact, in the year 1800, Nashville, which later grew into national prominence, was a small town hardly deserving of the title of trading center. The closest major trading point downstream was New Orleans.

Sometime between the years 1795 and 1804 settlers of the Upper

129

Cumberland area began to view the river as a means of transporting produce to New Orleans, at that time a booming commercial center serving both ocean and river traffic. Prior to this time only trappers and fishermen navigated the river, taking their furs and fish down river to market, but now farmers began constructing flatboats from timber cut on the homestead.[2] Edward Cason of Jackson County, Tennessee, and James Stone and Ambrose Peterman of Clay County were among the first men in the Upper Cumberland to construct boats to transport their wares on the long trip to New Orleans.[3] Flatboats were built as far up the Cumberland as Laurel River, just below Cumberland Falls in Whitley County. They were also constructed on the Wolf River near Byrdstown and floated down river to the Cumberland.[4] These craft navigated the Obey River as well, which was later important in the timber and lumber industry. Boatland, a community on the East Fork of the Obey River, was so named because flatboats were built there.

By the end of the eighteenth century, commerce on the Cumberland was flourishing. Much of the land along the Cumberland River was settled between 1798 and 1799, and soon items such as whiskey, chickens, corn, cattle, hogs, bacon, apples, tar, turpentine, saltpeter, cotton, tallow, and beeswax were produced for export from the area.[5] In 1800, an inspection station for flour, hemp, and tobacco was established in Pulaski County.

A flatboat was fairly simple in construction. It was similar to a barge, flat-bottomed and rectangular in shape. The sides were raised about four and one-half feet above water, and the entire boat measured from ten to fifteen feet wide and fifty to seventy-five feet in length. A shanty was built on one end of the boat and used for sleeping and eating quarters. The men on the boat slept inside the shanty on straw, old quilts, and blankets. They ate fatback, cornbread, and whatever game they could shoot along the river. The boat was steered by a board fastened to a long pole and steadied by oars on each side.[6] A flatboat required a crew of five to twenty men to steer it and guide it away from dangerous shoals, as the trip to New Orleans was not an easy one. Farmers often built a flatboat large enough to carry the products of several farms. Together they took the boat to New Orleans, sold the cargo and the boat, and walked back home.

130

Gladys Stone of Celina included most of these facets of early river navigation in her oral traditional recollections of the flatboats which her husband's grandfather took down river to New Orleans:

> He made flatboats and put his hogs and what corn he had on it, and run it to New Orleans. And it took him three months to go from here to New Orleans on the river, and that's the way they got their money to pay their taxes and buy their salt to salt their meat.
>
> They'd feed their hogs as they went along. And they would be fat by the time they got there. And what corn they had left, they'd sell it. I've got the little trunk that he brought the money back in from New Orleans. Put it in a tow sack and put it on his back and walked back.
>
> I think there was several boats would go together. It might be that they combined part of it, but there was several boats would go along together. When they'd come to a shallow place, you know, they'd help each other over those shoals. *
>
> He made several trips and his last trip he caught cholera and died in a little while after he came back home. He died terrible young.[7]

Arnold Watson of southern Cumberland County told of the trips his great-grandfather took to New Orleans, testifying to the longevity of oral historical traditions in the Upper Cumberland:

> Now, back in the days before rafting was popular much, people shipped stuff by flatboat; that was before the days of steamboats. They'd build flatboats. My great-grandfather lived in Willis Bottom; John Willis, this place was named after him.
>
> So they built a flatboat every year, and loaded it; took it down the river to New Orleans, see. And he had some boys that he'd send on this flatboat. They'd take turkeys and wheat and corn and everything down the river in this flatboat; and they'd sell all these products in New Orleans and then they'd walk back. And my grandmother's brother, they say, helped Willis.

131

People were superstitious back in that day. He made nineteen trips to New Orleans, but he never would go the twentieth trip. He claimed that nobody ever got back from the twentieth trip. They was a place down on the river somewhere, Natchez Trace, where they had to come up and through a gap in a hill. And there's where the most of them got stuck [held] up. Everybody coming back this way had money, see, when they'd sold all that. And a lot of them got killed and robbed, see. They come up the Natchez Trace, they called it.[8]

Flatboats were a common sight on the Upper Cumberland as late as 1880. The advent of the steamboat, however, heralded a new era in the growth and development of the Upper Cumberland region. The steamboat made possible the shipment of goods into the region on a regular basis and likewise afforded passenger service to and from the river towns.

The first steamboat on the Cumberland River, the "General Jackson," tied up at Nashville on March 11, 1818. Carthage was not reached until the late 1820s, however, and it was not until 1833 that steamboats crossed the state line into Kentucky. In January of that year, the "Rambler" landed at Burkesville and the "Tom Yeatman" reached Creelsboro in Russell County.[9] The "Jefferson," a steamboat piloted by E.S. Burge, went all the way up river to Point Isabel (later renamed Burnside) in April 1833.[10] The head of navigation on the Upper Cumberland for the next one hundred years would be Burnside, a frontier town located 208 nautical miles above Carthage. Treacherous shoals at that point made steamboat travel further upstream impossible.

Steamboating was responsible for the growth of many towns along the river. Carthage, Gainesboro, Butler's Landing, Burkesville, and Burnside all flourished during the early years of river transportation and developed into the first regional trading centers. The feasibility of shipping gave rise to the wide distribution of home-grown products and increased demand for manufactured goods. For example, businessmen with foresight in Burkesville, sensing a demand for river traffic, built the first steamboat ever to be constructed in the Upper

132

Cumberland area. The boat, built in 1834, was christened "Burkesville" and hauled many loads of timber, farm products, and merchandise to points along the river throughout its many years of service.[11]

In 1850, ten to twelve steamboats from the Upper and Lower Cumberland arrived at and departed from Nashville during a typical week.[12] Boats traveled the Upper Cumberland with frequency during this period, although their schedules were unreliable. On March 19, 1872, the *Nashville Republican Banner* reported: "Expected: The 'Ella Hughes' from the Upper Cumberland." It was three days later before Nashvillians read: "Arrival: The 'Ella Hughes' from the Upper Cumberland with 1,000 sacks of corn and 79 hogsheads of tobacco, 13 for Louisville and 66 for New Orleans."[13] A merchant in dire need of goods simply learned to be patient with the steamboat schedules, as did the produce company owners who shipped poultry and hogs by boat.

The Civil War brought fear and concern to the merchants and steamboat line owners alike in the area from Carthage to Burnside, and it temporarily dampened the activities of this steamboat empire. Both the Union and Confederacy used the Lower Cumberland west of Nashville to maintain their supplies and reinforce their troops. Gunboats also ran the river, often firing at innocent people on shore who reportedly fired back at the boats. The first appearance of gunboats on the Upper Cumberland is said to have been in 1864, when General Grant ordered that supplies be sent by riverboats to Point Isabel where General Ambrose Burnside was stationed. Eleven gunboats were dispatched on the mission.[14] Oral sources claim that three shots were fired into Confederate Colonel Oliver Hamilton's house near Celina by the Yankee gunboats. In addition, it is commonly held that shots fired from the gunboats caused the burning of Celina.[15]

Tinsley Bottom, a prosperous river community comprising about 2,000 acres of land in Jackson and Clay Counties, was one of the many areas ravaged by war. Kibbie Gardenhire, who was seven years old at the time the war broke out, years later wrote of it in her memoirs. Despite the fact that the Gardenhire house was eventually plundered by Yankee soldiers, she cited numerous examples of Yankee benevolence to the people of the Bottom. She told also of her father's capture and later release by the Federal troops:

133

The Yankees marched on; part of the line passed through our yard. They took my father prisoner and took him to the big road. While he was there, one of the soldiers came down from a house and said, "Somebody shot at us from that house. We got to burn it up; we ought to burn up this whole country." The Captain said, "You are mad now; that course won't do." He asked my father some questions, then said, "I see you are truthful, go home and keep your family in and keep them from being shot."[16]

The war-torn region between Carthage and Burnside was served by the steamboat only intermittently throughout the war years. Fewer steamboats plied the river at this time, and many of them were army supply boats. Thus, shipment of livestock, produce, and timber from the Upper Cumberland declined to a virtual standstill. Fortunately, with the ending of the Civil War, river traffic and trade resumed their normal course. Steamboats were once again constructed by local men who desired to cash in on the demand for river traffic. John Balis Anderson, for example, with the help of several relatives, built the hull of a steamboat out of hand-hewn timber at the mouth of Greasy Creek in Russell County. He then floated the hull to Nashville where it was outfitted by the Lovell brothers about 1873. This boat, the "Arch P. Green," was a familiar sight on the Upper Cumberland for many years.[17]

The number of steamboats on the Upper Cumberland increased by the 1880s as production and trade flourished. Steamboats loaded with produce from Upper Cumberland towns carried the commodities upstream to Burnside or downstream to Carthage and Nashville, all major points served by the railroad. Boats left Nashville for the Upper Cumberland with cargoes of dry goods, dress material, shoes, fruit, wagons, buggies, cement, and fertilizer.[18] The steamboats also carried goods ordered from mail order houses, such as Sears, Roebuck and Company. Several prefabricated houses were also purchased from the latter and shipped up river, piece by piece, via steamboat.[19] The merchants in hinterland villages were glad to receive goods via the river; that was more convenient than hauling them by wagon from the few railroad towns located on the periphery of the region.[20]

134

At one time, in fact, the heartland of the area was seventy-five miles from the nearest railroad. Jefferson Dillard Goodpasture of Overton County wrote in 1897 of the dilemma of the Tennessee section of the region: "The child born here fifty years ago was taught to expect a railroad . . . before he reached his majority, and in his turn held out the same delusive hope to his own children. Many of [the area's] ambitious young men sought honor and wealth in more inviting fields."[21]

The situation was not different for area residents forty years later. An apocryphal story perfectly illustrates the point. In 1936, the Tompkinsville high school football team, in its first year of varsity competition, traveled to Baxter, Tennessee, to play tiny Baxter Institute. During the course of the game, a railroad engine and two box cars passed by within sight of the players. The Tompkinsville players, who presumably had never seen a train before, stopped playing and watched in amazement and bewilderment as it rolled out of sight, unaware that the Baxter team was running a touchdown play while they stood gawking. "What *was* that thing?" one of the Tompkinsville players asked. "I don't know," replied Captain Darrell Carter, "but if it comes through here sideways, it'll wipe out the whole town!"[22]

Aside from Burnside and Carthage, which were served by both rail and water, the Upper Cumberland was almost totally dependent upon the river for shipping and transportation well into the twentieth century. Yet concurrent with the development of steamboating on the Cumberland was the construction of overland roads and traces* which served stagecoach lines and mule trains. These forms of transportation and commerce acted as connectors for water and rail transportation systems as well as joining individual farmsteads and small villages with regional trading and marketing centers.

Most local wagon and mule trains emanated from Nashville and Louisville. Prior to the coming of railroads to towns located on the margins of the Upper Cumberland, freight wagons drawn by horses or mules regularly traveled between the major boat landings on the Cumberland and the emerging towns located several miles into the hinterland. For example, mule-drawn freight wagons regularly traveled between Burkesville and Lebanon, Kentucky, by way of

Columbia (located on the northern edge of the Upper Cumberland) and Campbellsville, a small town twenty miles to the north served by a railroad.[23] A still larger venture was organized in 1881 by Fate Gunnels of Pickett County. His drayage of mule-drawn wagons, which numbered as many as one hundred at some points, carried area farm products to Nashville to exchange for farm implements, sugar, coffee, and dry goods. Each trip took approximately ten days to complete, since the wagons stopped in Livingston, Cookeville, Carthage, and Lebanon, Tennessee, to serve merchants and individuals of the area.[24] Mule and ox teams made regular runs from Tompkinsville to Louisville through Glasgow in the days prior to the construction of the Louisville-Nashville branch line into Glasgow, and regular freight runs* were established from Tompkinsville to Glasgow after the coming of the railroad in 1870. Rufe McPherson and Booth Peterman traveled this route weekly, hauling freight with mule-drawn wagons.[25] Joshua K. Baxter was involved in transporting freight from Glasgow to Hestand, although he actually was located closer to McMillan's Landing on the river. Preferring a more dependable schedule than that afforded by the steamboats, Baxter loaded his wagon with farm produce, took it to Glasgow, and there exchanged it for merchandise for his store at Hestand.[26]

Stagecoach lines were established in the first half of the nineteenth century in many sections of the region. As early as 1834, a stage line ran weekly from Sparta through Gainesboro and Tompkinsville to Glasgow; a line also ran from Sparta through Carthage to Gallatin, Tennessee, twice a week.[27] Several years prior to the Civil War, a stagecoach line was established between Somerset and Stanford, the county seats of Pulaski and Lincoln counties respectively. The stage made a one-way trip daily, usually traveling the distance of thirty-six miles in about ten hours.[28] Prior to 1868, when rail service was introduced into Horse Cave, a stage line was formed connecting Burkesville, Edmonton, and Horse Cave. This line tapped into the Louisville and Nashville Turnpike. After the railroad spur to Glasgow was completed in 1870, the terminal point of the Burkesville stage was changed to Glasgow.[29]

The Burkesville-Glasgow stage line is vividly recalled by several

136

sources. R.P. Bledsett of Glasgow provided the following personal observation:

> The road from Burkesville to Glasgow was just an ungraded mud road full of holes, except in wet weather when they were filled with water. The distance was forty miles, and it was impossible to drive with a wagon. So they used high-wheeled stagecoaches. They carried the mail on the Glasgow-Burkesville road for ten post offices, including Glasgow, Eighty-Eight, Summer Shade, Marrowbone, Waterview, and Grider. In the dry season the route would be operated with four horses; when it turned wet and during the winter six horses were used. Halfway, twenty miles from Glasgow, the stage from Glasgow and the one from Burkesville met. This was at Beaumont [Metcalfe County]. At that point there was a roadhouse where passengers and drivers had dinner.[30]

The stages left Glasgow and Burkesville at eight in the morning and arrived at their destinations at seven-thirty in the evening, thus taking all day to negotiate the forty miles and to serve the ten post offices. The fare was ten cents per mile, or four dollars the entire distance one way. When the waters were high, the operators required an additional charge.[31]

Shorter stage lines ran between some of the towns in Kentucky and Tennessee. A coach ran between Burkesville and Albany, a distance of twenty-two miles. As early as 1893 a stage line ran between Columbia and Campbellsville. Two stages ran daily on this route, furnishing mail, express, and passenger service.[32]

The Monticello-Burnside stages traveled over good, turnpike-like roads. Charles H. Burton was the owner of the line, whose coaches made six trips daily between Monticello and Burnside (a distance of twenty-two miles one way). Mrs. T.B. Grissom, Sr. of Burnside recalled her childhood fascination with the stage: "As a child, when my father drove one, I would ride halfway down and meet the other one and come back with him just for entertainment. That was like going to New York, Cincinnati, or to the zoo someplace."[33]

The demise of stage lines in the Upper Cumberland area was a natural one in the course of the history of transportation. In 1913, the last horse-drawn stage which ran from Burkesville to Glasgow was replaced by a speedwagon.* "It had high wheels and solid rubber tires and a chain drive. A passenger model, it had seats in it just like a spring wagon."[34] The Monticello-Burnside stage ceased operation in 1915 for similar reasons. The advent of motor trucks and cars into the Upper Cumberland drove out the last vestiges of outmoded overland transportation even before it signaled the demise of the river boats. Because hauling goods by wagon and traveling by stage were slow, arduous, and expensive, it is little wonder that the river and the boats which traveled upon it were vital components in the area's transportation network for so many years.

Oral testimonials gathered from across the Upper Cumberland affirm the importance of steamboat traffic in the social and economic life of the region. Landon Anderson of Celina offered this commentary:

> The river was the only way Gainesboro had of getting their merchandise for a long, long time. We didn't have any roads out of here; the closest railroad was twenty miles away and we depended wholly and solely on boats. Sometimes, before Christmas, if it was a droughty season and we didn't have any rain, we didn't have steamboats; and if we didn't have steamboats, we didn't have any Christmas. And we would really worry about that. Of course, all of the little ones watched for the clouds.[35]

John Stone, himself a former boatman, talked about Albany's reliance on the packet steamers:

> The only reason that steamboats went was because of no roads through this country. There wasn't no other ways of transportation. But it was some tough going, now! They'd unload—Albany had three landings: South Burkesville, Whetstone Landing, and Winfrey's Landing. If one road would get so bad that they couldn't haul over it with teams, they'd have their freight shipped to another one. It was awful! It'd take four mules—four good mules and a wagon—and it

138

took four good ones for them to take a ton at a load. They'd come down here in twenty or twenty-five wagons; make two trips a week hauling stuff to Albany. It would take them all day to get here with their produce and stuff to the warehouse; next morning they'd load up and it'd take them all day to get back to Albany.[36]

The Upper Cumberland was dotted with river landings where boats regularly stopped to exchange merchandise and produce. In 1925 there were 121 major river landings between Burnside and Carthage. The multiplicity of landings made steamboating extremely slow, for the boats were required to stop wherever there was cargo to take on or dispense. It was not uncommon for a boat to dock for unloading cargo in the evening and, because of repeated stops during the night, be only six miles nearer its destination the following morning. A typical run from Burnside to Lee's Landing, a distance of 326 miles round trip,[37] took approximately ninety-six hours to complete.

Boats bound up river for Burnside often carried cargoes for the George P. Taylor Company, a local wholesale produce company with branch warehouses in Albany, Celina, and Gainesboro. Former steamboat pilot Escar O. Coe recalled the nature of the cargo hauled on the boats:

> They carried everything that a farmer would use, or a merchant would sell in a country store. We made two trips a week. Would leave Burnside on Saturday night, go to Lee's Landing, Tennessee, and arrive back at Burnside on Wednesday morning. We'd bring egg cases down for people to put eggs in to ship back to the George P. Taylor Company. And bales of wire, roofing and nails, and all kinds of hardware and groceries shipped to merchants.
>
> We'd pick up produce, chickens, eggs, livestock, lumber, staves, and what-have-you that you could load on a boat.[38]

Burnside was one of the two upper river towns served by both steamboat and railroad, the other being Carthage. General Ambrose Burnside, who had commanded Union troops stationed on Bunker Hill at Burnside, saw the need for a railroad in that locale and was

139

instrumental in establishing both freight and passenger service in Burnside in 1880. The Cincinnati, New Orleans, and Texas Pacific line (CNO & TP)[39] served the area, and George P. Taylor was by no means the sole shipper of produce from Burnside. Other Burnside businesses to take advantage of shipping by both boat and rail included the Cumberland Grocery Company, R.J. Smith Grocery Company, Bauer Cooperage Company, Chicago Veneer Company (later called the Burnside Veneer Company), Buffalo Tie Company, Ayer and Lord Tie Company, F&O Cedar Works, Drake Brothers Lumber Company, and the Kentucky Lumber Company.[40]

As the shipment of farm products and timber increased along the river, certain towns and landings along the Cumberland became established as points for obtaining specific types of cargo. In an almanac published at the end of the nineteenth century, Tom Scott gave this account of Burkesville:

> As a lumber and stock shipping point, Burkesville cannot be excelled by any town of its size in the state. Enjoying as she does, a favored position on the river, she has become a point of transfer between the lower and upper river line of the steamers, which places her in touch with the Nashville market for lumber, and Cincinnati and Louisville markets for livestock and produce; furnishing her a good market for the former, a competitive market for the latter.[41]

Hugh Kyle, a former warehouse owner in Celina, recalled the role Celina played as a river landing: "At one time Celina was one of the biggest chicken markets in the country. People would sell their crop of chickens off in the spring of the year. I loaded a boat here with chickens and would have to wait for another boat to put more chickens on it. These chickens all went north; they went to Burnside."[42] Kenneth Massey, whose father was president of the Burnside and Burkesville Transportation Company, recalled seeing coops containing chickens "stacked up beyond the pilothouse.*"[43]

Mill Springs Landing in Wayne County was noted for shipping flour. D.E. Roberts and Son owned and operated a large roller mill there which produced flour and grain. Fall Creek, a landing twelve miles south of Mill Springs, also was noted for the shipment of flour;

Rankin and Stokes operated a roller mill there close to the river bank.[44]

Many landings were used primarily for the shipment of livestock or timber. Robertsport, Bart Ramsey's, Stokes' and Indian Creek were just four of the landings above Burkesville which were important livestock shippers; from these points, hogs and cattle were shipped to Nashville. Landings involved chiefly with the shipment of timber included Norman's, Indian Creek, Helm, South Burkesville, Bear Creek, and Bluff Landing. Some landings, such as Winfrey's Ferry, had several functions. At such a place, the steamboat picked up livestock and put off merchandise for the merchants served by the landing.[45]

Most of the important river landings served at least one nearby general store. Creelsboro Landing, for example, was noted for receiving merchandise for the J.D. Irvin General Store. Irvin's store was one of the most important in Russell County. Irvin ordered literally "carloads of goods," which he kept on inventory at his store.[46] He sold an average of one hundred pairs of shoes daily between 1900 and 1925, and he kept an inventory of 5,000 pairs of shoes, all of which he received via steamboat.[47] Arat Landing, below Burkesville, served William Smith and Son at Leslie, one of the largest general stores in the Upper Cumberland.

Landings at larger towns were, of course, important for both shipping and receiving. Burkesville was an important landing that handled merchandise for several stores in town as well as the whole Marrowbone Valley to the west. Boats unloaded dry goods, groceries, hardware, and wire at Burkesville Landing and picked up poultry to be taken to George P. Taylor's at Burnside. Other farm products hauled by wagon from hill country villages as far away as Edmonton, county seat of Metcalfe County, were shipped out of Burkesville or from Bluff Landing by boat. Greasy Creek Landing served the towns of Jamestown and Russell Springs and thus was important for both shipping and receiving. Martinsburg Landing served the Pea Ridge, Peytonsburg, and Kettle Creek communities.[48] Butler's Landing, north of Gainesboro, was important in that it served communities such as Sparta, Monterey, Cookeville, Hilham, Allons, and Livingston until the coming of the railroad during the early years of the twentieth century.[49]

141

All significant landings had warehouses where goods were stored until merchants and traders came to claim them. The Celina warehouse was typical. It was operated by Hugh Kyle who was responsible for transferring goods to merchants from as far away as Byrdstown and Jamestown, Tennessee, as they arrived at the dock, sometimes with several mule-drawn wagons. Kyle's warehouse was franchised, thus ensuring him rights to the warehouse business for two miles up and down the river from Celina. Franchising was a common practice on the Upper Cumberland.[50]

Ferd Williams operated the store at McMillan's Landing in Monroe County for several years, and his brother Cloyd Williams operated the warehouse there. Merchandise consigned to Tompkinsville, Hestand, Rock Bridge, and other eastern Monroe County communities was stored in the warehouses until the merchants could come to get it. Edith Williams recalled watching the unloading of the merchandise from the boat: "The boat would unload on the bank side down there, and sometimes when the river would get up you could haul [the merchandise] in the house on a sled. Sometimes he'd [Cloyd Williams] have to haul it up the bank, and mud on the bank would be almost knee deep on the mules."[51]

In addition to the major landings which lined the Cumberland, virtually every farmer who owned property bordering the river had a private landing. If a farmer had a quantity of corn or tobacco he wished to sell, he would flag down a passing steamboat by waving his hands and yelling out. The boat would then dock and pick up his products. Similarly, if a farmer or farm wife ordered goods from a firm that shipped by steamboat, the boat would stop to deliver them. Lena Howell Martin of Jackson County recalled the time her little girl signaled for a boat to land, and how she ran in fright as the boat began blowing for a landing:

> When my second girl was four or five years old, they were out playing. Says, "There's a steamboat coming; we want it to land. Let's flag it down." And so she went to waving and flagging down, and he went to blowing for the landing. It scared her nearly to death!
>
> The house wasn't underpinned to the ground back there,

and she went back there and crawled under the floor. But I had ordered a bed for her and they were putting the bed off here. She thought she'd flagged the boat down.[52]

A native of the fertile river bottom country in northern Wayne County told of her experience with an unscheduled steamboat landing:

> They landed there once at our landing. We didn't have but a road there. They just landed there. We asked them if they could land there for us to get off there. They said "Yes," and they did.
>
> I know when they put out that gangplank that you walk on, they didn't get up close to get all the way up to the bank. They told all the fellows to jump, jump in the river, pull on it. They jumped in the river and pulled it in. We got off there. It's a wonder they landed there. I knew the pilot at that time. He was awful nice. We never asked them to land there again.[53]

To give an idea of the number of landings on the river, Lewis Goff named seven landings located in White's Bottom, a farming community bordering approximately eight miles of the Cumberland River just above Salt Lick Bend: Oliver's, Shirt's, Daughtery's, Parmley's, Goff's, Murley's, and Galloway's.[54] Some of these farm landings shipped enough produce and timber to be considered important by the river men. When this number of farm landings in White's Bottom is combined with those in adjacent Salt Lick Bend—which included Tobin's, Wright's Point, Wilburn Bar, Cary's Ferry, Arat, Cloyd's, Bluff, Mud Camp, Glasscock Branch, Judio, and Black's Ferry—one need not wonder why the boats moved so slowly during periods of heavy farm production.

In addition to affording an inexpensive means of transporting cargo, the river also offered a viable mode of travel for the residents in the Upper Cumberland area. Wagons or stagecoaches were uncomfortable and slow. The steamboat was more attractive to travelers, as it was a kind of hotel on water. Steamboats nonetheless afforded a rather slow means of travel as they stopped frequently to load and unload cargo. Travelers planning to board trains in Nashville for the

143

western states often allowed for such delays on steamboats bound downstream. Kenneth Massey of Burnside told the story of a man walking along the river on crutches. Massey's father, who was the steamboat pilot, happened to see him, stopped his boat, and asked the man if he wanted a ride. The man replied, "No, thank you, Captain, I'm in a hurry."[55]

Passengers could choose two types of passage on the steamboat. People riding a short distance or a rafting crew which had completed a run to Nashville or New Orleans usually chose deck passage. They were not entitled to the accommodations of a stateroom* but they could eat in the boat's dining room, where the meals were rather good. Prior to 1920, deck passage could be purchased for $1.50 to $2.00 for the entire run from Nashville to Burnside, and meals cost 25 cents. Travelers preferring more extravagant accommodations purchased tickets for cabin passage. About 1920, prices for fares and meals increased. The trip from Burkesville to Burnside cost $2.75 for deck passage, meals were 75 cents and baths cost 50 cents.[56]

Few children or adults ever lost their excitement over the coming of a steamboat. People came to the river from miles around to watch the boat approach the dock, with its picturesque white rails and the black smoke billowing from the stacks. The flurry of the roustabouts and the deck hands as they prepared for landing, the captain's orders shouted above the cussing of the crewmen, the precision in positioning and lowering the gangplank—all were part of the excitement of steamboating. By the time the steamboat had docked, the bank was lined with men and women, both young and old, black and white. Songs were composed about steamboats and their arrivals at towns and other landings. One such song was sung by roustabouts:

> Me and my wife,
> And seven chillun,
> Is a-gwine to take a ride
> On the "Benton McMillan."

Each steamboat had a distinctive whistle, and those who were accustomed to the arrivals of steamboats could tell which boat was docking by the sound of the whistle. Oral sources agree that the "Dunbar" and the "Rowena" had the most pleasing whistles of any

144

boats on the river; the "Jo Horton Fall" had the softest-pitched whistle, one which nevertheless covered great distances.[57] Most of the whistles could be heard up to fifteen miles away from the river.

Arnold Watson, who grew up several miles from the river at Kettle in Cumberland County, said that the boat whistles could be heard "if the wind was right." He then gave a traditional account of his family's reactions to hearing the now-legendary wildcat whistle mounted on one of the boats:

> Way back yonder, clear as I can remember, there was a boat come up the river and had a wildcat whistle on it; scared people to death! I don't know what kind of whistle it was, but it screamed.
>
> Now I don't know what boat it was on. It was at least a hundred years ago when my mother heard it. She was a small girl, and she and her older brother got in bed with my grandmother and covered their heads up.
>
> The way these steamboats would echo up these valleys, you'd hear the whistle, then you'd see the boat and see the steam fume come up to whistle. But you'd count a good deal before you'd hear it. And after it'd stop, you'd count more before the sound would leave.[58]

The wildcat whistle is known in local black tradition also. Luida Ellington Williams, born in Cumberland County in 1878 to former slave parents, explained why the wildcat whistle was outlawed:

> They was one steamboat that had a wildcat whistle on it. It used to come down the river and it scared everybody in the world to death! Why, that thing hollered, and nobody didn't know what it was. They never thought about it being a whistle on a boat. Didn't know what it was.
>
> It passed once or twice with that wildcat whistle blowing. And they made them stop that. Told them they'd better not blow that whistle nary nother time; told them what they'd do for them. And they quit it, too!
>
> Some white fellow had a great big pretty mule—the biggest, finest mule he had. And that whistle blowed and that mule

broke and run to the house. And this man thought that mule was a-whistling and making that racket, and went to the door and shot his mule.

And they stopped that boat from blowing that whistle.[59]

Whistles were not the only distinctive characteristics of the Upper Cumberland boats. They differed in size and style and were known by the pilots for their maneuverability on the river. Some of the boats were equipped with powerful engines and were able to push sizable cargoes on barges. Most of the upper river boats were smaller than the ones which plied the river below Nashville. The "Rowena" was a typical upper river boat. Measuring 160 feet by 28 feet, it had ample room for cargo and passengers. A former pilot of the "Rowena" stated that it was "the easiest handling boat in my time, and it had fairly good speed."[60]

The steamboats which plied the waters of the Upper Cumberland often were owned by large transportation companies. A.R. Massey, along with Dave Heath, G.S. Dick, and C.W. Cole, owned the Burnside and Burkesville Transportation Company of Burnside, which probably handled more tonnage during the six- to seven-month navigation period than any other steamboat company in the South at the turn of the century. This company began in 1888 as a steamboating concern. Instead of using steam power, some of the B and B boats of this period were powered by two horses turning a capstan.* Dave Heath and John Coomer became legendary as old-time B and B boat pilots. By 1894 the company had expanded its transportation interests to the railroad system; it built the Burnside and Cumberland River Railroad, which was a line in Burnside running from the river landing on Big South Fork to the various stores, factories, and mills in Burnside before merging with the mainline tracks of the Queen and Crescent Railroad. By 1904 the company operated three packet steamboats, the "Warren," "Burkesville," and "Rowena," as well as the towing steamer "Albany," which handled the big timber barges. The boats departed for points downstream from the Burnside landing after the arrival of passengers and freight on the Queen and Crescent Railroad. In the same year, however, the transportation company sold

146

the B&CR Railroad to the Cincinnati, New Orleans, and Texas Pacific Railroad, which had recently purchased the Queen and Crescent.[61]

Another transportation company headquartered in Burnside was the Cumberland Transportation Company. This company had started as an offshoot of the Cumberland Grocery Company of Somerset, and it owned small, gasoline-powered boats that were used in connection with their grocery business. In 1911 or 1912 the company purchased the "G.W. Nixon." Two years later the "Patrol" was purchased and in 1916, W.J. Davidson, president of the company, had the "Burnside" built. In 1917, the Cumberland Transportation Company bought out the Massey line, whose holdings now included two steamboats (the "Rowena" and the "Celina"), a towboat ("Raymond"), twenty-six barges, and several wharf boats.[62] The company was purchased for $40,000. With the acquisition of this line, the Cumberland Transportation Company became the strongest company on the upper river and one of the largest in the South.[63]

Nashville boats on the Upper Cumberland were permitted to run from Nashville to Greasy Creek Landing in Russell County; Burnside boats were franchised to go as far downstream as Carthage. Thus, the landings between Carthage and Greasy Creek were open to either set of boats. Most Burnside boats preferred to turn around at Lee's Landing, just south of Gainesboro. The Cumberland Transportation Company tried running a boat to Carthage during the latter years of the steamboat era, but the venture was not financially successful. The pilot of that boat was Bridges Montgomery of Rome, a river landing fifteen miles below Carthage. Montgomery had previously been a Lower Cumberland pilot.[64]

The "Bob Dudley," the "Dunbar," and the "Jo Horton Fall" were the largest boats on the upper river during the last years of steamboating. Lewis Goff, who lived all his life in the bottom lands along the Cumberland, stated, "There used to be a big steamboat come up here by the name of 'Bob Dudley.' And I've seen fourteen barges hooked onto that; he'd come down this hollow and shoot down, why, it was the most powerful thing you'd ever seen! It went up the river just a-plowing that water and loaded with everything!"[65] Another source recalled the tremendous power of the "Albany," first a packet for the

The ferry at Turkey Neck Bend, Monroe County, Kentucky, is one of two ferries still operating on the Upper Cumberland between Carthage and Burnside. Photograph 1977 by the author.

148

The steamer "Patrol" at Burnside Kentucky. Photograph courtesy Mrs. T. B. Grissom, Sr., Burnside.

149

B and B line and later made into a towboat: "I've watched it go down the river many a time, pushing eight or ten barges loaded with lumber, logs, or crossties."[66]

Steamboats that hauled livestock had a loading chute in the deck. The "Dunbar" was one such boat. "The gangplank was wide enough to run a wagon on it. They had gates, and when they were going to load a load of livestock, they'd either bring a seine or a bunch of sticks out and they'd make a pen on the banks. They would get the stock down in a pen and work them on down into the boat."[67]

Of the three largest boats, the "Jo Horton Fall" was considered the largest and most palatial boat on the upper river. It hauled cargo during the days when shipping was in great demand. Later, when river traffic declined, the "Jo Horton Fall" was used as an excursion boat.[68]

Steamboats plied the Upper Cumberland easily during the tide seasons (late spring and late fall); service was generally interrupted during summer months. This was especially true before Lock 21 was constructed in 1915 thirty miles below Burnside, creating a pool of water between the treacherous shoals there and Burnside.[69]

Garnet Walker of Monticello testified to the importance of the construction of Lock 21: "The steamboats had always gone down the Cumberland River, but they couldn't come all the way up to Burnside except when it had come a big rain. They built in 1915 Lock 21, which pushed or raised the river then to the level that a boat could reach Burnside."[70]

The importance of Lock 21 notwithstanding, Kenneth Massey noted that the lock did have its drawbacks: "Sometimes the water would get to a certain height during flooding and stop; you couldn't get through the lock, and the water wasn't high enough for you to go over the lock."[71]

Winter provided the best months for steamboating, as the river was highest during that time of year. The upper river, which was considerably more narrow and twisting than the lower portion of the river, was difficult to navigate when the tide was low. Steamboat pilots had to be particularly careful to watch for shoals, bars, and protruding stumps if they ventured up river on a low tide. When the river got too low for steamboats, gasoline boats out of Carthage delivered goods to merchants along the upper reaches of the river. John Stone recalled a

150

spot known as Wild Goose, near Rowena, which caused problems for many boats traveling the Kentucky stretch of the Cumberland:

> Wild Goose up here caused more hours put in there than any one place on the Cumberland River. That's a shoals up there. Beaver Creek runs into the river there and boats would get stuck there. But they'd pull them through. It was a gravel bottom. They had a big cable. It took eight men to pull that, keep it in the water. You had to keep it outside the timber, of course, and they'd take a round and turn it around this tree, and a round and turn it around that one, about a dozen of them big trees so it couldn't pull it out rootwise.[72]

Bill Town, located on the Tennessee side, was singled out as a bad stretch on the river by former pilot Claude Hackett of Gainesboro:

> Bill Town, between Brooks Ferry and Gainesboro Landing, was a hard place to make. They's more fall on the river between Brooks Ferry and Gainesboro than any other place on the river.
>
> It was very easy to go aground there, and we used to get aground there every once in a while. No sinkings, though; we'd always manage to get off. But we have stayed there two or three days at a time!
>
> Lots of time we had to shin crack* them off. It's done with a rope and a pole—turnstuds, you see. Pull them. Hook the rope to a tree. Tie it on a tree, and they had a capstan engine on the bow of the boat; lots of times we could pull off. Sometimes that wouldn't work; they'd have to raise it with spars out of the water.[73]

Navigating a steamboat on the Upper Cumberland required great skill and acumen on the part of the pilot and crew. Even the best of the pilots hit an unseen shoals or bar at some point in their steamboating careers. John Stone recalled an incident which, although humorous, could have proven disastrous and even fatal. This account depicts some of the difficulties in navigating after dark. Stone was steering the boat up river past Celina, working the shift opposite the pilot Joe Claunch:

151

When we went down that night, we took on a bunch of freight, produce and so on, that was going up the river, so we wouldn't have to land late at night as we come back.

And I'd been steering all night for the other pilot. And Joe come on duty down below Celina a few miles. River was up pretty high! Not out of banks, but a real big river. Well, he just come in and laid down. Said, "Well, you've got her. We don't have to land at Celina."

Now Joe loved to make time. As big a thing as a steamboat, you wouldn't think it would save time, but they's a lot of difference in plying right at the middle of the river or catching these eddies* and dragging the brush. Some people don't like the idea, but Joe did. And he told me, "Now hold her in close." He wanted to get in for some reason. Said, "Drag them bushes."

And the river was up. See, them headlights, you'd have one on each side if the river was low and you was running in the bed of the river. But when it was up, that was all you needed to see was that water. And keep it in there close.

And I had them lights cut around short, you know, and was dragging them willows and bushes along there. Well, I passed Celina! I seen that! But right above Celina, I touched the far side and I jerked that headlight over there. It was a narrow, and there was a log raft tied up and a gasoline boat over here. Big sycamores hanging out, and I couldn't figure it, for I knowed I just passed Celina. I reached around and got ahold of the bell, but I didn't pull it. I walked over to the other side and looked out the window, and there was the bank. I walked back over here and there was that bank, and she's wide open!

And Joe was the easiest man to wake I ever seen! If you barely pecked on his door, he'd jump out on the floor. He's the easiest fellow; kinda nervous. And directly he raised up, "Where are you at?"

I said, "Right above Celina."

He said, "Stop!"

I rung the bell. He commenced laughing, "Kinda backwards, ain't you, old boy!"

He sorta hollered up through the pipe. He hollered up there and asked me where I'd started! And I was going up Obey's River! [The Obey joins the Cumberland at Celina.] I'd failed to see it! My headlight was cut so short around that I hadn't seen it. Boy, it's a wonder that I hadn't drug that point over there, ain't it?

Well, we backed it out in the river. Joe said, "Now don't go up Kettle Creek [the next major tributary]!"[74]

Former pilots and others associated with the river recall races and tales of races between some of the steamboats. Some of the pilots were known to "hot-rod" their boats on a long run. One oral source recalled the excitement and danger involved. "We had a few steamboat races that burned up all the lard and meat and everything to make more steam," he recalled. "Sometimes they'd adjust the safety valve to where it was dangerous."[75]

A race between the "Harley" and the "Hardison" was immortalized in song. This stanza of the song remains in tradition:

The Harley and the Hardison had a race,
The Harley threw water in the Hardison's face.

Oral tradition has it that every time one boat passed another, the deck hands passed a small brass cannon to the leading boat as a sort of trophy.[76]

Accidents on the river occasionally claimed the lives of one or more of the boatmen. Escar Coe recalled losing "several people along the river":

We lost one boy here from Cumberland County that was missing. His name is Milton. And nobody ever knew he was—when we got to Burnside, you see, those boys could all rest—they had crews there to load and unload the boat—until they'd get ready to start back down the river. They had liberty to go to town or be anywhere they wanted to, or to lay around back in the engine room or what-have-you, and rest and sleep.

And so this boy was missing and we never did know what ever happened to him; don't know if he was ever found along the river.

153

And we lost a boy that lives down below Celina. I believe his name is Sutton. About Robertsport there came a pretty high tide, and he was found way down the river somewhere. Found him several weeks afterwards.

And we lost a boy off of a boat that I was on up here at Winfrey's Ferry. He just deliberately walked off the wrong side of the boat, you know. I woke him up to come out to load. We were loading on the starboard side; he just walked off the port right into the river. High water. My wife was on the boat; she heard him screaming. My brother was the engineer; he heard the screams and he run out to see, and then just as he went by, why, he just tipped his finger. Couldn't reach him to pull him out. And he was found out here at Scott's Island just above Burkesville, about a month later.[77]

Willie Rich of Pickett County described an accidental death which occurred on the Obey River while staves were being loaded on a barge towed by the "C.M. Pate" or the "Dick Clyde":

Ches-Wyman Stave Company made the heading, and they'd haul it to a high bluff, and they'd fix chutes and these steamboats, they'd bring barges up there. They'd be sixty feet long and thirty feet wide. They'd anchor these barges down under the chute. A man would carry the stave to these chutes and they'd go in these barges. They'd have two or more chutes. Two men on the barge would go up there and start stacking them in. Well, then they'd go to putting in the lower rails. And just keep on that way until we got the barge full. There's a fellow right down here below Byrdstown, a fellow by the name of Hill Holt, got killed. A fellow went and put some staves in the wrong chute, you know; it hit him here in the head and killed him.[78]

Life aboard the Upper Cumberland boats was hard, the work rigorous and demanding. There was always time for raw and sometimes crude humor, however, as attested to in stories still told of those days. And there was time for drinking, rowdiness, fights, and—sometimes—killing on the river. The deaths of two steamboat captains in

154

two separate incidents stand out in contemporary oral legendry about life on the river.

One of the steamboat pilots who died as the result of a shooting was Captain Tom Ryman, Jr., part owner in the famous Ryman Lines in Nashville, and son of Tom Ryman, builder of the Ryman Auditorium which was to become famous as the home of the Grand Ole Opry. "Little Tom" was widely recognized as a skilled river boat pilot. A flamboyant skipper of the "Jo Horton Fall" in his early forties at the time of his death on June 1, 1915, Ryman was shot on his boat at the Hartsville landing by Captain Wilson Montgomery.[79] The other pilot who fell victim to violence on the river was L.T. Armstrong, the respected pilot of the "P.D. Staggs," who met death at the hands of the Williams brothers of Celina.

Of those who worked and lived close to the river, none parallels the notoriety of McClure and Joe Williams. Raised just above Celina on their father's farm, the brothers knew the hard work involved in farming and are reputed to have been good workers. Clure and Joe, however, were noted more for their rowdiness and drunkenness than anything else. They were also skilled raftsmen and frequently ran log rafts from Celina to Nashville. Following one rafting trip to Nashville, the brothers booked deck passage on the "P.D. Staggs" for the return trip to Celina. Loaded with whiskey, one or both of the Williams boys got into an argument with Captain Armstrong, who likely threatened to put them off the boat. Captain Armstrong was killed February 2, 1895, not far above Nashville. Public opinion holds that it was probably Clure who did the killing, and some versions of the ballad written to commemorate the event note that

> Clure jumped into the river and begin to swim;
> Says, "Goodbye Joe Williams, I'll see you again."[80]

The following is the version of the song sung by Richard Akin of Keno, in Barren County, Kentucky, on April 4, 1960:

> *"Clure and Joe Williams"*
> If you don't believe John Dabney's dead,
> Look at whatta hole in Dabney's head,
> Ho babe.

155

Well, I killed that bully in Celiny town,
Ho babe,
Killed that bully in Celiny town,
A-quit his drinking and a-ramblin-around.
Ho babe.

Shot Milt Williams at the storehouse do',
Shot Milt Williams with a forty-four.
You may dodge from do' to do',
But you can't dodge my forty-four.

Shot Joe Williams at the farmer's gate,
Shot Joe Williams with a thirty-eight.
You may dodge from gate to gate,
But you know you can't dodge a thirty-eight.

Frank Harlan and Clure Williams had a fight,
Frank shot Clure with a forty-five.[81]

Soon after the killing, both Joe and Clure met with death themselves. Joe was killed near Celina on November 2, 1895, in a gun duel with Clay County Deputy Sheriff Ed Parrott. Clure was gunned down October 8, 1896, in a battle with Deputy Sheriff Frank Harlan in Tompkinsville.

Steamboating on the upper river proved profitable even during the 1910s, when the lower river was suffering economically because of the advent of railroad spur lines and improved roads. The steamboat business did not decline on the upper river until about 1920, by which time steamboating had already died out elsewhere in the country. The railroad, a major factor in the demise of lower river traffic, was not a significant cause for decline in upper river traffic on the Cumberland. Railroads had their effect, of course, but hard-surfaced roads were chiefly responsible for the ending of boating on the Upper Cumberland.

J.E. Leslie, a former Monroe County newspaper publisher and historian, claimed that railroads and trucking jointly lessened his county's dependence on river traffic:

For about three quarters of a century, steamboats ran the Cumberland River regularly and handled 90 percent of the freight traffic of the central and eastern parts of Monroe County. During these years, Nashville was the chief merchandise market for this section. When the Glasgow branch railroad was completed and began operation in 1870, it brought this territory in touch with the Louisville market. Trade began gradually to drift toward Louisville and this reduced the traffic between this section and Nashville. As the years moved on, Nashville freight coming into this section was routed [by rail] by way of Glasgow. With the coming of motor trucks, the transportation system of this territory was changed again, and 90 percent of the shipping into and out of this territory is [now] handled by motor trucks.[82]

Trucking, introduced about the end of World War I, brought about a change in the transportation system in other counties of the Upper Cumberland as well. According to several oral sources, trucking was the major reason steamboats went out of business.[83] Trucks made it possible for farmers to haul their products to market and sell them the same day. Trucking thus brought about improvement in the living conditions along the river and the adjoining hill country. A Wayne Countian observed, "Steamboats would still be running, I suppose, if it hadn't been for the invention of trucks and improved roads."[84]

The first jitney* services, carrying passengers by car to towns formerly served by stage lines, trickled into the region between 1912 and 1915 but did not have a serious impact until shortly before World War I. Individuals in the area began purchasing automobiles around 1910; however, they had to contend with bad roads and hazardous conditions. It was virtually impossible for automobiles to travel on the hard-surfaced roads of the area, which had been constructed as boat landing roads designed to carry mule-drawn freight wagons. The large crushed stones played havoc with the rubber tires on the cars.[85]

One narrator recalled the novelty of the first automobile road in Russell County:

> Somebody contracted to build a stretch of smooth road from Russell Springs to Jamestown, a five-mile stretch there;

some old fellow by the name of Harris brought teams there, hired teams and wagons, and hauled gravel out of the creek up there. And people would come for miles in their T-models and ride up and down that five miles. Had to push them all the way down there to get to ride on that five miles![86]

From 1915 on there was an increasing concern for road improvements, although funds were limited. Communities of the Upper Cumberland required male residents to work on community road crews* for six days each year. If a man preferred to furnish his mules and wagon, his required road work time was reduced from six to two days. In some counties, road crews were composed of county prisoners.[87]

In the early 1920s, both Kentucky and Tennessee used funds acquired from gasoline and auto license taxes for the improvement of roads. This move by the legislatures provided for full-time construction crews and equipment; thus improvements were rapid during this decade. Funding for grading and graveling additional roads was provided in the 1930s by the federal government. These were usually rural "farm to market" roads from the county seat to outlying communities in the county. The Works Project Administration provided funding in 1934 to continue work on these roads and to begin construction of a few state roads connecting towns within the region.

Changes in transportation meant not only that one means of transportation replaced another; a way of life changed also. The river landings had grown during the days of steamboating and people looked to the river for their economic stability. The stores which flourished during the river days lost business when roads were built. "Trucks and roads began to close steamboating; that closed down a lot of these country stores," according to Escar Coe. Will Scott of Monroe County attested to this fact also. A resident of the river area, Scott observed that "You can't get nothing like you could when the boats run."[88] Improved roads reached into the mountain hamlets of the Upper Cumberland, making these communities more accessible. But while stores and businesses in outlying towns and villages grew, the river landings, once frequented by hill and river people alike, faded into obscurity as victims of progress.

In a last-ditch attempt to recapture the declining boat business,

158

transportation companies began booster trips* on the Upper Cumberland. These steamboat companies invited merchants to ride the boats to Nashville where they could view and purchase merchandise to be shipped up river to their respective business concerns.[89] Sometimes the shippers came up river from Nashville and passed out souvenirs from their companies. This attempt to promote business was similar to the tactics of the railroad companies in earlier times. Officials of the railroad would often give away cigars and calling cards at major shipping points along the route. Booster trips were not common practice, however, and were discontinued before steamboating came to an end. The booster trips did not yield enough increase in tonnage to make them worthwhile.[90]

Another unsuccessful attempt to offset the decline of steamboat trade was initiated in the early part of the twentieth century and flourished from 1915 to 1925. This was the *excursion trip*, designed to attract human cargo. There were two types of excursions on the upper river: short runs and long runs. A short run was usually not an advertised trip. People from one town or community would fill the boat, and the excursion would be completed in one day. The cost of a round-trip excursion from Burkesville to Celina, for example, was about two or three dollars. A longer excursion trip usually was advertised. The boat stopped at several towns along the way to pick up more passengers. These excursions seldom proved quiet and relaxing, as excursion boats were known for their party-like atmosphere. There was an orchestra, dancing, and an abundance of food and drink. Before long, arguments broke out, and it was up to the crew to quiet down the people who had had a little too much to drink. Excursions became a popular pastime,[91] at least to those who purchased fare, and steamboats continued to host them until the boats ceased operation. James F. Butler of Cumberland County went on several of the excursions:

> Well, I've been on several excursions on steamboats. Once about 150 of us got on here at Cloyd's Landing, and we went down the river on the excursion and we's gone, I think, a day and night. And they had an awful time! They danced on that boat from the time they got on and was still a-dancing when they got off!
>
> And they had one of those self-playing pianos; had records.

159

All you had to do was turn the thing on and it done the playing, and we had a terrible time on that boat. I never did try to dance, but I watched lots of it.

And there's several of them got drinking pretty heavy on there. And one old fellow wanted—we eat on the boat and they come around and they asked him what he wanted to drink. He told them he wanted milk. And this waiter told him, says, "We don't have milk on the boat." "Well," he said, "just give me a glass of water," he said, "if your cows is all dry." And it sounded pretty funny. He was kind of drinking, you know, and he thought the cows was all dry, because they didn't have no milk.[92]

A century of river travel left a dozen or so boats in the watery depths of the Upper Cumberland.[93] Oral tradition identified twelve of those packets. The first in oral memory to go down was the "John W. Hart." Shortly before the end of the nineteenth century, it sank off Holloman's Landing above Greenville in Jackson County when a floating log ripped a hole in her bow. The "I.T. Rhea" went down near Brook's Ferry near Fort Blount in Jackson County after striking a rock bluff during a violent windstorm. The boat's skipper, it is said, was an experienced pilot. One oral narrator knew the "truth," however, behind the sinking that day: "Let me tell you the story I've heard on that. The Captain was in love with a girl at Celina. And they'd been on an excursion, and she gave him the door when she got off in Celina. And they was all drinking. He got drunk and tried to straighten the river out and he run into the bluff down here in the wind. The woman that told me that was on the boat! Lilly Brown."[94]

The sinking of the old "Burnside" ("Burnside #1") is the most legendary of all the mishaps. On a cold winter's day in 1899, the boat hit the bank (or a sycamore tree) with a resounding bump during an ill-fated landing attempt at McMillan's Landing, located between Celina and Burkesville. Oral sources reported that a thirty-gallon barrel of engine oil fell off the platform and exploded on a pot-bellied coal stove. The boat burned, claiming the life of a crewman known as "Cat Eye." The hull of the boat was visible near the landing for many years.[95] The "Crescent," which was "one of the oldest boats on the river and had the wheel on the side of the boat," supposedly sank at old Bart Landing above Lock 21.[96]

The "Henry Harley" sank in 1906 at Buffalo Landing, between Granville and Carthage, after hitting a big rock while backing in during landing; the "Bob Dudley" perished at the Nashville wharf just before World War I; and the "H.G. Hill" went down at Wooddale Beach in the early 1920s. The last boats on the Upper Cumberland to be lost during active service likely were the "Creelsboro," which sank below Lock 21; the "Patrol," which "hung up and dried out" and went under at Harmon's Creek; and the first "Albany," which sank at Burnside.

The last three boats ever to run the river were claimed by its waters after steamboating on the Cumberland had already run its course. The new "City of Burnside" sank at Burnside but, according to reliable sources, was later raised and sold for lumber.[97] Both the "Rowena" and the "Celina" sank while being towed downstream. They had been in dock at Burnside for two or three years after the dissolution of the transportation companies. When the new owners of the boats, Porter Dunbar and Paul Dunbar, ordered them towed down the river, the vessels were in no condition to make the trip. The "Celina" fell apart and went down at Indian Creek in 1933; the "Rowena" was stranded by low water at Greasy Creek and sank a few months later.

The original purpose of the steamboat was to provide the fastest, most convenient, and most economical method of transportation available. In their heyday, the steamboats admirably achieved this goal. When roads and trucking began to provide a more viable alternative to steamboating, however, business on the river dwindled until by the end of the 1920s it had ceased altogether. A Russell countian[98] recalled using the stranded "Celina" and "Rowena" as fishing stations in 1933 just before they went under, and he remembered that the old boilers of the "Patrol" could still be seen protruding out of the river's depths until the rising waters of newly impounded Lake Cumberland claimed them in the late 1940s and forever sealed from view these artifactual reminders of a vanished way of life.

161

CHAPTER 5

A Changing Way of Life

Customs and institutions do not undergo radical changes. Traditions have a way of overlapping time boundaries. Many of the older, traditional ways of thinking and acting that had their origins in an earlier period are often a very viable and vigorous voice of the present. Conditions and places *do* change, however, and social forces such as school consolidation, flood control reservoirs, and garment factories can be identified and studied for the effects they have on traditional facets of social and cultural institutions. By understanding the causes and effects of change, one can better understand the changing nature of folk traditions.

It is difficult to ascertain when the old days ended in the Upper Cumberland and modern times began. Improved road construction came to the area between 1900 and 1930, along with banks, silent-film movie houses, and telephone systems such as the very early crank-box system in Monroe County which ran from Tompkinsville to Summer Shade via Rock Bridge. Numerous humorous stories are told about residents of the region who were unaccustomed to these new technologies and who usually came away from encounters with them looking rather foolish. The following secondhand account, provided by Sarah Jane Koger of Jamestown, Tennessee, recounts the reaction of a ten-year-old girl to a new telephone in the local store:

There was a telephone only in Jamestown, Travisville, and Albany, Kentucky, when I was growing up around the turn of the century. The telephone was in the Travisville store. I never will forget my brother Jim. He was a mischievous person and was all the time trying to find something to laugh about. And he was at the store one time. And Old Aunt Lizzie Reneau had her granddaughter with her. She was a great big girl, ten or eleven years old. And she didn't know what a telephone was.

And Jim said he was setting there, and the phone rang. The storekeeper went and answered it. And said that girl grabbed her grandmother by the arm and was just shaking the life out of her. Said, "Granny, Granny, look up yonder. That damned old fool is a-talking to the wall."[1]

Technological improvements notwithstanding, the years 1900 to 1930 did not herald a new age, for most facets of the old way of life persisted. No changes of a basic nature occurred in agricultural practices, and steamboating and logging were in their prime during the first two decades of the twentieth century. The most logical date to assign to the emergence of the Upper Cumberland into so-called mainstream society is approximately 1930, with the coming of the Great Depression. That event signaled the final end of steamboating and rafting in the area and brought home from northern industrial cities young men who, during the late 1920s, had migrated from the Upper Cumberland to find employment. During the 1930s and early 1940s, the region's agricultural practices took on a new look. Burley replaced dark tobacco, better varieties of corn and hay were introduced, and a few tractors with steel cleats were purchased. It was also during the 1930s that continuing floods on the area's rivers stimulated local and federal action which eventually led to the construction of flood control reservoirs and, subsequently, to less expensive electric rates and to the introduction of labor-saving domestic devices. These were some of the forces of social and cultural change, easy to describe retrospectively in generalities but fraught with trauma for the individuals who experienced them. Where there was a positive good, there was an accompanying disruptive factor that often led to the break-up of families and the end of a way of life.

163

Once a center of community life, the country store often now stands decaying from disuse. Boles, Monroe County, Kentucky. Photograph 1978 by the author.

Country stores such as this one owned and managed by Bertha Key of Hanging Limb, Tennessee, are where local residents gather to share news and talk of earlier days. Photograph 1979 by Debbie Gibson.

165

There was no real industry in the area from the days of settlement until after 1950. From 1910 to 1930, migration to northern cities such as Detroit, Toledo, Akron, Cincinnati, Dayton, Indianapolis, Muncie, and Chicago offered an attractive solution to the economic plight of the people of the Upper Cumberland. Some families went west to Oklahoma, Texas, Arizona, and California; others left for the fertile farming zones of Illinois, Indiana, Ohio, and Michigan. Such agricultural migrations occurred in the main between 1860 and 1900, although some movement took place in the present century.

"Indiana Letters," "Illinois Letters," "California Letters," and the like from migrants were regular features in several newspapers of the Upper Cumberland from 1920 to 1950. For example, a former Monroe countian in Muncie wrote a weekly letter for publication in *The Tompkinsville News*, telling about the doings of other transplanted natives in that area, commenting nostalgically, and asking about conditions back home.

Factory work in the North afforded good job opportunities during the 1920s, and local "taxis" from the Upper Cumberland made weekly trips hauling passengers to and from their work there. Some of the taxis were Overland touring automobiles; others were constructed by welding portions of two cars together. Willie Montell, a Monroe County native, recalled several weekend trips by taxi to and from Toledo during 1928 and 1929. The vehicles he rode in were operated by Dudley Collins and Bedford Johnson of the Oak Grove and Moss communities in Tennessee. Due to poor roads and crowded conditions in the vehicles, such trips were long and strenuous.[2]

Like other migrants from the Upper Cumberland who held industrial employment, Montell lost his job abruptly when the Great Depression hit in late 1929. Most of the migrant workers then returned home and made what preparations they could for the uncertain days ahead. Some of them had already witnessed bread lines forming in the northern cities they left behind; everything considered, they felt that their prospects for survival were better back home on the farm. Hopes were shattered, however, during the season-long drought in 1930, when a much-needed good harvest did not materialize.[3]

166

The often romanticized process of quilting actually involves long hours of solitude for Flossie Williams. She quilts in her north central Monroe County, Kentucky, home on quilting frames used in her family for three generations. Photograph 1979 by Debbie Gibson.

167

When the men in the family are busy with other jobs, women take over the daily chores. Shown here is Lennie King of Cumberland County, Kentucky, who manages the family farm while her husband works as a long-distance truck driver. Photograph 1979 by Debbie Gibson.

168

There was never enough money for most families during the Depression. They relied on tobacco crops to bring in cash, but tobacco sales during the early 1930s often netted less than ten dollars for a year's work. Many families supplemented their income by trapping fur-bearing animals. Quentin Perdew of Clinton County provided the following description of this activity:

> Another thing I remember about the Depression is hunting. Hides were relatively high during the Depression and the mountain people made extra income from [selling] the hides of animals.
>
> My brothers and I survived during the Depression on hides for spending money. You would have to be a certain age before you could join certain activities of the family. I can remember my first time going possum hunting in the fall. We always had a good possum dog, and possum hides were relatively easy to take and easy to dry and so forth.
>
> On this particular night, I was probably seven years old, and they agreed to let me go possum hunting with them. But the youngest had to carry the possum sack. They'd put a pole over a possum's head and pull his tail till its neck popped and then throw him in the sack. And the least one always got the job of carrying the sack. They was breaking him in to let him go. On this night I was walking along carrying the possum sack. It was easy as long as the possum sack was empty, but along about nine o'clock they treed the first possum. And they shook this possum out of that tree. (Most of the time, they'd go up a small tree.)
>
> By the time they shook it out of the tree, one of the other dogs had treed on down below. And they just grabbed the possum and threw it in the sack—he was sulled [playing dead], and they went to the other tree. We shook the other possum out. And by that time the dog had treed somewhere else, and they just grabbed the possum when he hit the ground sulled, throwed him in the sack, and took off.
>
> The dogs were just treeing in a circle around us. And the dogs had treed six or seven times. One of them [brothers] got

169

Between Livingston and Byrdstown, Tennessee, is a grim reminder of death on the highway. Photograph 1976 by the author.

170

In southern Cumberland County, Kentucky, grandfather and grandson skin this animal for its pelt. Photograph 1972 by David Sutherland.

171

hold of one of the smaller possums and said, "I'll swear that looks like the possum the dogs treed a while ago!" And he looked in the sack and I only had two possums in the sack! They'd treed about seven times, but they'd treed the same two possums all along. I'd got a sack with a hole in it, and they'd crawled out this hole![4]

Possum were plentiful, but it was often necessary to place them in pens and feed them in order to produce marketable hides. Possum meat, cooked with sweet potatoes and served with cornbread, was standard fare for many families two or three times a week.

To help provide money for personal and family comforts, many young men went each fall to the Corn Belt states to pull and shuck corn for a period of eight to twelve weeks.[5] Men still talk about these trips, describing the progressive farms there, the competitions they entered into daily to see which man could pull the most corn, and the pranks they played on each other. The wife of one of these men told of the time her husband's traveling companion ate a live grasshopper rather than announce the creature's presence to those at the table with him:

> Willie had gone to Illinois with Arthur Rasner to shuck corn. They went four or five times up there during the early years of the Depression. Had to to get a little extra money. Anyway, Willie said they were at the dinner table one day; they had lettuce to go along with the meal. Said he noticed Arthur not eating, and he just watched him to see what was wrong. Said in a minute Arthur fished that grasshopper out of that lettuce, took his knife and cut it into two pieces. Said he ate that live grasshopper![6]

Although money was scarce in the Upper Cumberland during the 1930s, not many people went hungry for any length of time, for the agrarian economy reverted during those years to subsistence-level production and consumption. Clothes, of course, were needed, but, as Ben Edmunds of Russell Springs stated, "Overalls were cheap. We could buy a good pair for fifty cents, and a couple of pairs lasted all year."[7] People bartered eggs and chickens at the local general store for items that were absolutely essential; otherwise, they provided for their needs at home. For example, children either played with home-made toys and playthings or did without them. A few fortunate families bought battery-powered radio sets between 1935 and 1940, but often the radios remained silent when the original battery died or a tube failed.

A few families in each county were unable to make it through the early Depression years without help from neighbors. For these people, "it was a terrible time. Nobody has ever seen a time like it," commented a man who personally experienced such hardships. He claimed that "when you tell about it, people won't believe you!" One old man in Fentress County reportedly wrote to a senator in Washington and "told him that all he'd had to live on for the last six months was potato peelings and hickory nuts. The senator wrote back and wanted to know who ate the potatoes."[8]

Overdue bills mounted month by month. Many people lost their homes because they could not pay off their mortgages; tenants were generally in arrears with their rent. Critically needed surgery was often postponed—generally until it was too late. A deadly "bloody flux" hit the area in 1934, and natural disasters such as floods, fires, and tornadoes kept the people in the Upper Cumberland in a state of anguish through the thirties.

A Clinton County native provided a graphic, personal description of the Depression. Humor, joy, pathos, and a mother's will to succeed at any cost are all a part of his testimony:

> I grew up with seven brothers back during the Depression. The days were rough and lot of times the nights was rough because most of the time the housing was very poor.
>
> We lived in a big two-story house. We had a fairly good house for this day and time. It was a large two-story house with a double fireplace; that was all the heat we had downstairs. Upstairs there was no heat at all. The gables of the house had about a four-inch hole at the eave of the house. In the wintertime, I slept upstairs with my brothers. When it would come blowing snow, lots of mornings I'd wake up and shake the snow off my bed.

173

Mrs. Ona Barton lives in the house that her great-great-grandfather built before 1817 in Tennessee's Upper Cumberland. Photograph 1979 by Debbie Gibson.

174

Mrs. Barton's life style is much like that of her forebears who raised and harvested or gathered their food wild. Photograph 1979 by Debbie Gibson.

175

Each year, Mrs. Ona Barton raises a garden and uses the vegetables year-round. Here she shells beans for canning. Photograph 1979 by Debbie Gibson.

In her kitchen, Mrs. Barton continues to prepare food in a traditional manner.
Photograph by Debbie Gibson.

177

My mother had lots of homemade quilts, and lot of times we'd have as many as ten or eleven of them on us on real cold nights. If it was zero outside, it was about zero on the inside. The only fire you had was in the fireplace, and back then you let the fire go out about eight o'clock of a night as you went to bed.

You could always tell a family that had children, especially if they had a two-story house back in those days because there was no bathrooms. The bathroom was the woods, or the hen-house, or the barn, or something. Very few families even had outside toilets.

And you got up of a night and it was too cold to go outside; so most of the time when the kids slept upstairs, they'd use a window. And when they would pee out of the window (most of the time the house was weatherboarded and painted), you could go by the house and all the paint would be off below the window in these two-story houses, or it had turned yellow, if they had children.

Times was hard during the Depression. I know one time we was hunting dryland fish. We called it that—some type of mushroom. Only come up in the spring of the year when peach and apple trees are in full bloom. They only stay up for a week or ten days. They were a specialty because it was something different from the beans and potatoes you was used to.

We got out one year and found a couple of two-and-a-half-gallon waterbuckets full of these mushrooms. We came up on this old woman; she had a little one-room shack. She lived with her husband and had two, three kids, but he was always drunk. He was a-laying across the bed passed out.

At this time, Roosevelt had already started the relief, [as] they called it back then. They didn't call it commodities; just called it relief. My father had been a proud businessman before he'd went busted, and he wouldn't accept it. We just had to survive the best way we could.

This woman, she looked at these dryland fish and she said, "What would you take for one of the buckets of mushrooms?" Said, "You can't eat both buckets."

And so my brothers being brought up like they was—they was older—they drove a hard bargain. She had all this relief

Every Wednesday Mrs. Barton joins other local women at the Chanute Community Center to quilt. The quilts are sold and the profit used for club activities. Photograph 1979 by Debbie Gibson.

179

Mrs. Barton places flowers on her husband's grave. Because she is unable to get to the grave regularly, she uses plastic flowers—this time yellow and white to observe Easter. Photograph 1979 by Debbie Gibson.

180

Writing in her journal is the final task of each day for Ona Barton. She records birthdays, deaths, and weather along with highlights such as trips or visitors. Photograph 1979 by Debbie Gibson.

stuff. And at that time we didn't have any flour. And they was putting out relief flour, meal, and butter and prunes. And he got just a little of all of it. She was getting more than she needed. And she had cheese, too. He got two, three boxes of cheese, and a couple of pounds of pure butter. And he got a ten-pound bag of yellow meal. (We always had white meal, and the relief people got yellow meal.) He got the yellow meal, mainly to see what it was like. He'd always been used to white meal. And he got a twenty-five-pound bag of flour.

We come carrying all these things back in home about dark. I remember my mother praising him for the good trade he had made. He'd traded a bucket of dryland fish for all this stuff.

We was all real little and things was going really bad along about 1930 or '31, right at the height of the Depression. My father sold his tobacco that year. He always grew two or three acres of tobacco. And he sold his tobacco, and the warehouse where he sold it sent him a bill for twenty-seven cents. The crop liked [lacked] twenty-seven cents paying for the floor charge, and that after working in the tobacco all year long.

So my mother said she went in and set down and cried. She had five children at this time, and she knew that they was going to have a hard time making it through the winter. She said she'd cry awhile and she'd pray awhile. (She was a Christian and a church-goer). She said that it come to her mind that she'd watched her father make whiskey, when it was legal, for the government. And she knew how to make whiskey. And she said, "I know a person that has a still with a copper already set up and everything."

So she went to this person who had the still. (I really think her father had made the still, although he was dead at the time.) In the meantime, she told the Lord, "If You don't want my kids to have clothes and shoes, You have him to turn me down and not let me have the still. But if You want my kids to have something to eat and shoes on their feet, if he lets me have the still, I'm going to take it that You want me to make the whiskey."

And so she went and asked the man, and he said, "Yeah, I'll be glad to let you have it."

182

So she put the still in a wagon and put a little hay around it and brought it home and set it up below the house. It wasn't over twenty or thirty feet from the house. I can remember where the still set because they was always a joke after that that "that's where we put the still."

She made (and my father helped her). And they took the corn and they made whiskey. They made one run. She said she promised the Lord that she'd only make one run of whiskey; that's enough to buy her children shoes and clothes during the winter.

And so she made one run of whiskey, and it was eight gallons. And she took this eight gallons of whiskey and sold it for four dollars a gallon, and sold it all to one man. The man's name was ———; lived in Wayne County.

My father and mother never did make any after this. But my father had made it before. He was twenty-six or twenty-seven at the time, and Mother was twenty-three or twenty-four. And she sold this whiskey for thirty-two dollars. She said the whiskey that they made and sold for thirty-two dollars was more money than they had worked out in the three years before.

I talked to her the other day, and she said that it had been almost sixty years since she made her first and last batch of whiskey, and said she'd stayed true to the Lord, that she never made another batch of whiskey since then. But said it did cause her to survive with five kids through the winter.[9]

During the depths of the Depression, the Works Project Administration and the Civilian Conservation Corps provided jobs for men and teenage boys. Locally, WPA was said to stand for "We Piddle Around"; in actuality, this agency built roads, school buildings, and public service buildings and accomplished much of value throughout the area.

As the 1930s came to a close, World War II stimulated the economy of the Upper Cumberland. Farm prices rose, and families benefited accordingly. Younger members of the family were given enough money each Saturday to purchase a ticket to a Western movie, a bag of popcorn, a hamburger, and a soft drink—a total cost of approximately

35 cents in most county seats through the early 1940s. Parents often accompanied the children to watch Western film heroes Tom Mix, Hopalong Cassady, Buck Jones, Roy Rogers, Ken Maynard, and a host of others. Maynard was especially popular in the theaters of the Upper Cumberland, for he was a native of Monroe County and had married a Tompkinsville woman.

Most of the region's young men and women left the area soon after the United States entered the war in late 1941. The women who left went to work in war-related industries in the North; a few of them entered military service. Ruth McCreary of Tompkinsville was a member of the WAAC and was killed while stationed in Germany. The young men were inducted into one or another branch of the military and went off to war. A few disabled men worked in northern munitions plants and other war-time industrial plants; fewer yet were professed pacifists. One young Monroe countian preferred a life of ostracism and confinement in a Pennsylvania concentration camp to fighting, and another took his own life rather than go to war.

World War II was the great cultural watershed in the lifestyles of Upper Cumberland residents. The region suffered many battlefield casualties, but the majority of the soldiers made it home safely, with new ideas about life and living. Many of the civilian employees in war-related industries also came home when the war was over, but an equal number stayed on in their new homes up north. Some of those who came back from foreign battlefields to Pickett, Overton, Clay, and Clinton counties found no home as they had remembered it; the old homeplace of memory was now in a watery grave at the bottom of newly impounded Dale Hollow Reservoir.

Among the most significant agents for change were the flood control reservoirs confined by the dams constructed by the Army Corps of Engineers. These projects forced mass evacuation of 150-year-old homesites, but they made low-cost electric power available to all of the area's residents. With this potential came labor-saving tools, kitchen appliances, electric radios and, by the early 1950s, television sets. All of these introduced rapid and radical changes in the area's lifestyles.

The first of the giant dams, Dale Hollow, was constructed on the Obey River about three miles above Celina, a town that had been inundated by flood waters more times than the people remember. For

184

too long, one of the residents' greatest fears had been the danger of floods, with the attendant deaths and property and crop damage. The destructive floods of 1926, 1929, and 1937 finally stirred the residents to action. Dale Hollow Dam, which impounds the Obey and Wolf rivers, was completed in 1943. Yet Celina, like other towns and villages farther up the Cumberland, was still not safe from the Cumberland's floods. Two devastating floods hit Burkesville, Celina, Gainesboro, and Carthage in 1946 and 1949. The long-awaited Wolf Creek Dam, located in Russell County, was completed in 1950. There have been no floods on the Upper Cumberland above Carthage since then.[10] Center Hill Dam, located near the Smith-Putnam-Dekalb counties line, impounds the waters of Caney Fork River several miles above Carthage, and Cordell Hull Lock and Dam, located above Carthage on the Cumberland and completed in 1974, backs up the Cumberland all the way to Celina. The historic Cumberland River and its once-wild tributaries are now bottled up by a network of dams, comprising what is essentially one continual lake from Carthage to Burnside.

The fear of natural flooding is past.[11] Now some people worry about a broken dam. Such a catastrophe is a real possibility, for Wolf Creek Dam cracked several years ago, and repeated repairs have failed. Area residents feel that the fresh concrete which has been pumped in almost daily for several years is disappearing into giant underground caverns and chasms.

Although the dams have been beneficial to the region, there is no way to measure the intense grief and mental anguish of the unfortunate families who were forced from their homes. All of the Wolf and Obey River Valley farm lands—and consequently, all of Pickett County's good arable lands—were inundated by Dale Hollow Lake, and one out of four persons in that county was moved from land that had been handed down from one generation to the next since before Tennessee was a state.[12] Willow Grove, a thriving Clay County town of three hundred residents which possessed its own grade and high schools through the 1930s, perished completely. Former residents gather annually in Celina for the Willow Grove Homecoming and talk about the old days. They vow orally and in local newspaper columns that their children and grandchildren will know about the Willow Grove of their memories. Mrs. W.T. Cherry wrote this piece

185

of protest poetry in the mid-1940s, shortly after the building of Dale
Hollow Dam:

> A lovely little village nestled at
>   the foot of the mountains,
> With friendship flowing every-
>   where, like bubbling fountains.
> It was loved by all who dwelt
>   thereabouts—young and old,
> The Dale Hollow Dam drove
>   them out in the rain and cold.
>
> We thought having our men folks
>   to go to war was all that we
>   could stand,
> Then came the building of the
>   dam and the taking of our good
>   land;
> The village was home of two
>   of the best doctors in the na-
>   tion,
> But nothing could they pre-
>   scribe for our Willow Grove's
>   salvation.
>
> Our grief would not be so great
>   if there was a purpose to
>   suffice
> But we know it has turned out
>   to be just a "Fisherman's
>   Paradise."
> I'll admit fishing is a good
>   sport and they are very deli-
>   cious to eat,
> But still the life we enjoyed
>   up there was mighty hard to
>   beat.

We are fond of our new friends
   we have found both here and
   there,
But there's something about
   Willow Grove people you can't
   find anywhere;
The village folks were spoken of
   by others as being very
   clannish,
There's no doubt we could speak
   for ourselves as a Miles
   Standish.

The good people of Willow Grove
   are scattered both far and
   near,
It was hard to say good-bye to
   their old homes and friends so
   dear;
Sometimes, I find myself wish-
   ing this could only be a dream,
If the same thing happened to
   you, wouldn't you get off the
   beam?

We loved our school, churches,
   post office, stores and "the
   station,"
To us, it was the best little
   community in the entire nation;
Of course, it was only natural
   for me to love best the drug
   store,
That was papa's place of business in the good old days of
   yore.

The basketball teams, as you
　　well know, were always quite
　　above par,
With coaches Apperson, Cher-
　　ry, "Foxy," "Jelly," Wat-
　　kins, and let's mention Carr;
We must truthfully confess the
　　tournaments don't seem all the
　　same.
If other teams do not win the
　　trophies now, Willow Grove
　　is not to blame.

We were proud of Johnson
　　Bluff, the Harvey Knob, and
　　Cold Spring Hollow,
In all undertakings, we had good
　　leaders and the rest willing to
　　follow;
This section was made up of
　　some of the best farms in the
　　County of Clay.
But, dear folks, "stop, look,
　　listen," and think where Willow
　　Grove is today![13]

　　The people of Burnside, the historically important town at the head
of navigation, had more time to plan their strategy for combating the
Army Corps of Engineers. The Corps originally planned to relocate the
several hundred people of Burnside in nearby towns and rural communities, but the intensely loyal citizens of Burnside demanded the
town's existence be continued at a new site.[14] The engineers yielded
to their demands and relocated the town on the heights overlooking
the old town.

　　Generating turbines were installed at Dale Hollow in 1947 and
1948 to produce low-cost electricity supplied through the Tennessee
Valley Authority power system. Generating facilities were later installed at the other three dams in the Upper Cumberland. Low elec-

tric rates were responsible for the increased use of electricity and the introduction of "luxury living" into the area. With refrigeration readily available, it was no longer neessary to practice traditional foodways such as canning and curing. Broadcasting the music of Hank Snow, Roy Acuff, Ernest Tubb, and Eddy Arnold, the radio disc jockeys of Nashville and Louisville greatly influenced musical tastes and changed traditional music habits, so that the singing of old-time ballads and songs at gatherings gradually passed from the regional scene. Television altered family visitation patterns. New and better roads, which came in spite of strong efforts to halt their construction, changed bartering and buying habits. By the early 1950s, the Upper Cumberland had become a part of mainstream society.

The modern trend was reflected in certain changes in traditional agricultural practices as well. Cooperative marketing associations were formed to encourage production of strawberries, cucumbers, bell peppers, tomatoes, and fruits. Local farmers produced specialty crops for dealers in Celina, Cookeville, Monticello, and elsewhere. Some farmers raised broiler chickens while others moved more and more toward the dairy industry. Agricultural specialization pumped more money into the rural economy and was sufficient to create a noticeable shift away from general farming practices by the mid-1950s.

Because of the availability of cheap electricity and a large female labor force, and in the absence of labor unions across the region, garment factories were built in every county seat town and sizable village. Factories and towns alike prospered. Individual families also benefited from the heretofore unknown luxury of a payroll check on a regular and sustained basis. Some families moved from the country to town so that the wife and mother would not have to drive upward of thirty miles each way to and from work. Fathers often served as babysitters or worked in town at low-paying, part-time jobs. A few men found factory employment with their wives. Most farm families who lived closer to town stayed on the homeplace, believing that the commuting distance was worth it. Such families continued to farm as well, although on a reduced basis. For them, agriculture supplemented family incomes derived from garment factory payrolls.

Pay checks had often been a part of townspeople's pattern of living, for men worked at sawmills, ax handle factories, or other local industries which owed their existence to the region's natural resources. Now, however, urban residents also experienced a change in their lifestyles as women went to work outside the home.

Garment factories alone, however, could not resolve the high unemployment situation in the Upper Cumberland. Most counties of the region presently have no more than about 1,000 persons employed in all types of industry, and that figure represents an increase of at least 100 percent since 1960.[15] In November, 1975, the Upper Cumberland Tennessee area's official labor force report estimated an unemployment rate across the region of 9.9 percent.[16] A Celina newspaper in 1970 bemoaned the constant loss of population through emigration, chiefly to the industrial North, and maintained that "more industrial jobs must come for Clay County to grow."[17]

In the 1960s, a new type of marketing involving chain-controlled supermarkets and quick-order restaurants exerted economic pressure on some local businesses, such as groceries and family-operated restaurants. Most of the older business establishments involved in goods and services survived, however. These local enterprises, often owned and managed by the children and grandchildren of their founders, were firmly implanted in their communities, and their customers seldom left them.

The old river towns of Burnside, Celina, Gainesboro, and Carthage became tourist meccas because of their proximity to recreational lakes. Motels, gift shops, and gasoline stations built to serve tourists attest to the new orientation of these four towns; Albany and Jamestown, Kentucky, also are centers for tourist trade near Wolf Creek and Dale Hollow dams. The inland towns of Columbia, Edmonton, and Tompkinsville in Kentucky and Jamestown, Byrdstown, and Monterey in Tennessee have retained more of the old flavor of the Upper Cumberland. They, along with five other more rapidly growing inland towns—Monticello, Livingston, Sparta, Crossville, and Cookeville—have kept "King Lumber" on the economic throne. At least thirty saw mills are located within a thirty-mile radius around each of these eleven towns, and there are timber-related industries within the same areas. There is no foreseeable shortage of timber of the present quality anywhere in the region.

To reiterate, World War II was the great agent for social change for the people and traditions of the Upper Cumberland. Persons who went into military service and war-time industries were socialized according to standards and tastes previously unknown to them and to the people they left behind. Those who returned to the region were the chief instigators in its emergence into mainstream America. Stanley Wright of Fentress County, for example, following his discharge from the army in 1945, brought home under his arm the first radio ever owned by his family.

What about the soldiers who came back to the Upper Cumberland following World War I? They, too, had been touched by other peoples and other societies, but conditions along the Upper Cumberland at that time did not facilitate social change. Electricity, good roads, automobiles, radios, and telephones, along with better educational institutions and modern medicine—measures of a progressive, materialistic society and the tools by which change is accomplished—had not yet come to the Upper Cumberland in 1920. The region had all of them and more by 1950, however; at this time, the Upper Cumberland was ripe for change.

The oldest practicing physician in Kentucky in 1979, a ninety-nine-year-old lifelong resident of Burkesville, is critical of the new society of the Upper Cumberland. After some words of praise for electricity, indoor plumbing, and improved roads, Dr. W.F. Owsley pinpointed the problem: "People have changed. They've got no character. They've got no morals. They won't tell the truth. You can't put any dependence in them. They're not helping anybody; that helping business has done gone out."[18]

Brookie Owsley, R.N., disagrees with her husband's stand: "Well, I'll tell you, when you see how some of these parents and grandparents and great-grandparents act, I think young people today do mighty well."[19] Most people interviewed agreed with her assessment. At least 80 percent of them have no desire to go back to the days when life was simpler. They like to talk about those times and will bend your ear all day if you will listen. Yet, in the main, old-timers are present- and future-oriented. They like things as they are, and as they hope they will be.

191

Index of Migratory Legends, Folklore Motifs, and Traditional Beliefs

All of the legends, motifs, and beliefs listed here were told and apparently accepted as historical truth by narrators. The analytical distinctions made among the three are those of folklorists, not the narrators, who likely were unaware of the universality of these stories, story elements, and beliefs. The existence of these universal narrative patterns and elements in the oral historical traditions of the region does not invalidate the core of truth in accounts of hangings or encounters with wild animals. Instead, they provide the rich, descriptive, embellishmental detail that makes those accounts memorable and hence worth repeating.

Migratory Legends

Various narrative genres—anecdotes, folktales, and legends—are grouped here under the umbrella term *migratory legend* because they share in common the characteristics of being localized in the Upper Cumberland through association with local persons and places and being incorporated as factual history into the repertoires of the area's narrators.

Many of the events described in the legends could have occurred, but there is no way to prove or disprove their veracity. Thus, some of the legends summarized below may be fictional; others may be true. I have included both legends for which published parallels exist and those which present enough features of the migratory legend to warrant their inclusion, although they are not contained in the standard folklore indexes. (It should be pointed out that no complete index of American legendry exists.)

Summaries marked with a plus (+) symbol have recognizable analogues in the indexes. The indexes referred to are: Stith Thompson's *The Types of the Folktale* (Helsinki, 1961), Ernest Warren Baughman's *Type and Motif-Index of the Folktale of England and North America* (The Hague, 1966), and James T. Bratcher's *Analytical Index to Publications of the Texas Folklore Society* (Dallas, 1973), referred to herein as PTFS.

Motifs, keyed to Stith Thompson's *Motif-Index of Folk Literature* (Bloomington, Ind., 1955–58) and Baughman's index, are listed following each summary. Starred (*) items refer to Baughman entries. Page numbers refer to pages in the present volume.

1. *Hunter Steals Wife for Himself.* Hunting companion of Daniel Boone builds log cabin, sleeps on leaves. Returns East and steals a woman whose parents track her and start to return home with her. He overtakes the party, retrieves his wife. They raise a large family. Pp. 13–14.

2. (+) *Buried Gold Stolen by Thieves.* A frontiersman allegedly buries keg (or metal pot) containing gold. People spend years searching for the treasure. A freshly opened hole is found in the ground, and at the bottom of the hole is an impression left by the bottom of the container. P. 15. For sources containing possible parallels of this migratory legend, consult Richard M. Dorson, *Jonathan Draws the Long Bow* (Cambridge, Mass., 1946), p. 181; W. Prescott Webb, "Notes on the Folk Lore of Texas," *Journal of American Folklore* (1915), p. 291.

3. *Floating Twig Indicates Which Brave Will Marry Maiden.* Two braves in love with same maiden are told by their chief to toss a sprig of green into the stream to see which will travel the farthest. Nettle twig wins; stream, village, and brave are subsequently named Nettle Carrier. P. 17.

4. *Deaf and Dumb Lad Outwits Indians.* He is held captive by Indians for several years. During his captivity, the lad is taken blindfolded to treasure mine; compelled to carry loads of treasure. P. 18.

5. *Wolf Pack Attacks Two Hunters.* Two dogs are killed by the pack. Wolves turn on the hunters. Additional hunters arrive and drive away the animals. P. 20.

6. *Bear Attempts to Steal Pigs.* Pigs are heard squealing. Upon investigation, the owner finds a bear with pig held in its paws. Bear is shot and pigs are saved. P. 20.

7. (+) *The Panther on the Roof.* Panther on the roof of log cabin makes strenuous efforts to get at the occupants inside; straw burned in the fireplace prevents animal's entry into the cabin. P. 20. For additional references containing the panther on the roof, see William Lynwood Montell, *The Saga of Coe Ridge: A Study in Oral History* (Knoxville, 1970), p. 68; Robert R. Turner, "Ten-

nessee Legends: An Analysis in Terms of Motifs, Structure, and Style," (M.A. thesis, George Peabody College for Teachers, 1970), pp. 332-33, and PTFS, item 8.86.

8. (+) *The Panther in Pursuit.* Panther pursues woman who eludes the creature by ripping off pieces of her clothing and tossing them in the road to cause the animal to stop and smell. Pp. 20–21. This tale is related to Types 313–314, *The Magic Flight,* and is identified as Motifs D672, "Obstacle Flight," and R231, "Obstacle Flight—Atalanta Type." For a brief analysis of the Panther in Pursuit legend, consult Robert R. Turner, *Tennessee Legends* (Nashville, 1970), pp. 119–26.

9. (+) *Snake Charms Child.* Snake charms young girl and drinks milk from her cup. P. 22. This legend is Type 285, *The Child and The Snake,* widely known in Western tradition.

10. (+) *Snake Receives Sustenance from Weed.* Weed provides life-giving sustenance for snake locked in deadly struggle with another snake. Pp. 22–23. Motif D1338.2.1, "Rejuvenation by juice of plant."

11. *Military Commander Swaps Worn-out Steeds for Fresh Mounts.* Promises to return confiscated animals but never does. Pp. 61–62.

12. (+) *Forced Overeating.* Soldiers steal cakes (or pies) from kitchen (or kitchen window). (Thinking the theft too easy, the leader forces the man of the house to eat all of the cakes, poking the final bites down the man's throat with a pistol barrel.) See D.K. Wilgus and Lynwood Montell, "Beanie Short: A Civil War Chronicle in Legend and Song," *Journal of American Folklore* (1968), p. 142, for a note about the distribution of the forced overeating motif.

13. *Woman Keeps Sore Open on Horse's Back to Prevent Theft of Horse.* If it heals, soldiers would take the animal. Pp. 64–65.

14. *Guerrilla Vows to Kill One Hundred Federals in Retaliation for the Slaying of His Son.* P. 66.

15. *Guerrilla Vows to Kill All Twelve Men Who Molested His Wife and Daughter.* They were forced to undress, prepare a meal in the nude, and parade up and down the road in front of the men. P. 66.

16. *Hanged Guerrilla Does Not Die.* A convicted Confederate guerrilla is scheduled to die by hanging. Soldiers who are present allow him to drop from a loose knot through the scaffold into a casket below. He is whisked away from the scene by his wife and daughter. He is seen years later "out West," or near his old

home. Pp. 69–70. The account of the secret escape from the gallows is very similar to the manner in which Joe Coleman, a man hanged in 1845 in Cumberland County, Ky., reputedly escaped.

17. *Wife of Slain Soldier Dies of a Broken Heart.* Soldier is refused final request to see his young bride, who is only one-half mile away, before he is killed. Request denied. She dies soon thereafter. P. 77.

18. (+) *Excitable Pilot Jumps into Air; Log Raft Moves from Under Him.* Pp. 108–9. *Motif X1741.7, "Person jumps with disregard for gravity."

19. (+) *Theft of Turkeys with Owner's Assistance.* Raft pilot yells for owner to help him chase down an escaped turkey. Owner obliges, unaware that the bird belongs to him. Pp. 109–10. This legend incorporates Motif K345, "Sympathetic helper robbed."

20. (+) *Stolen Animal Is Disguised As Human So That Thief May Go Undetected.* Raft pilot steals beef, puts rubber boots on its back legs and rain slicker over the rest of it. Tells owner that his brother has just died of smallpox; owner runs away. P. 110. This legend contains Motifs K406, "Stolen animal disguised as person so that thief may go undetected," and K335.0.2.1, "Thieves steal pig and make it impersonate person with plague."

21. *Tired Raftsmen Stuff Wet Overalls into Stove Pipe.* Perplexed owner of hotel is unaware of the source of the smoke which fills the air. P. 115.

22. (+) *Man Refuses a Ride on Steamboat:* "No, thank you, I'm in a hurry." P. 144. Cf. Motif X1815.2(b), "Train goes no faster than man can walk."

23. *Wildcat Whistle on Steamboat Frightens All Within Earshot.* Farmer kills frightened mule thinking the animal made the noise. Pp. 145–46.

24. *Shy Man Finds Live Grasshopper (or Worm) in Food.* He cuts it in two pieces and eats it rather than push it aside on his plate. P. 172.

Folklore Motifs

Motifs are those elements of a story which move easily from one narrative to another, usually lending color and drama to stories into which they are incorporated. Again, the items listed below are keyed to the motif indexes prepared by Thompson and Baughman.

Motif C312.1, "Tabu: Man looking at nude woman." P. 66.

195

Motif D492.3, "Color of hair suddenly changed." Pp. 104–6.

Motif D672, "Obstacle flight." Pp. 20–21.

Motif D1338.2.1, "Rejuvenation by juice of plant." Pp. 22–23.

Motif *E422.1.11.5.1(e), "Ineradicable bloodstains as the result of blood shed during murder." P. 74.

Motif F1041.7, "Hair turns gray from terror." Pp. 104–6.

Motif K335.0.2.1, "Thieves steal pig and make it impersonate person with plague." P. 110.

Motif K345, "Sympathetic helper robbed." Pp. 109–10.

Motif K406, "Stolen animal disguised as person." P. 110.

Motif S100, "Revolting murders or mutilations." Pp. 63–79.

Motif X1741, "Lies about gravitation." Pp. 108–9.

Motif *X1741.7, "Person jumps with disregard for gravity." Pp. 108–9.

Traditional Beliefs

A number of the historical narratives which people in the Upper Cumberland recounted to me contained traditional beliefs. In many cases, the action or meaning of the story hinged on the belief itself. In the following list, traditional beliefs referred to in the book are keyed to items in three standard reference works: Wayland D. Hand, *Popular Beliefs and Superstitions from North Carolina*, Vols. VI and VII of the *Frank C. Brown Collection of North Carolina Folklore* (Durham, N.C., 1964), referred to here as *Brown*; Wayland D. Hand et al., *Popular Beliefs and Superstitions: A Compendium of American Folklore* (Boston, 1981), referred to as *Hand*; and Harry M. Hyatt, *Folklore from Adams County, Illinois* (Hannibal, Mo., 1965), referred to as *Hyatt*.

Viper will suck cattle. *Brown* 7528; *Hand* 31476-31481; *Hyatt* 1567. P. 21–22.

Chicken snakes and black snakes kept in a corncrib will rid barns and cribs of mice and rodents. Cf. *Hyatt* 1610. P. 22.

Whiskey, taken orally, will cure snake bite. *Brown* 2165; *Hand* 11267–11268, 11270. P. 22.

Flesh of newly killed chicken, applied to snake bite, will extract poison. *Brown* 2130; *Hand* 11239–11241. P. 22.

Smell of gunpowder rubbed on feet will keep away wolves. Cf. *Hand* 29883. P. 20.

Walking a figure eight on a log raft will prevent falling asleep and freezing to death. P. 106.

196

Glossary of Terms

A-harrow. A one-row, one-horse cultivator shaped like the letter A and containing numerous metal teeth which act as plows.

Band mill. Mill whose saws consist of a looping, toothed-steel belt mounted over pulleys.

Bed tick. Straw-filled mattress.

Bee gums. Hollow logs cut into lengths and used for housing honeybees for domestic use.

Block. Single-tier log raft, one log wide.

Bluffing. Rolling logs down a cleared path to the stream below.

Boom. Chain of floating logs enclosing an area of water to keep logs together and prevent them from floating downstream.

Bolt. Approximately one-sixth of a four-foot log from which staves are split.

Booster trip. Steamboat trip on which merchants rode free of charge.

Break-up. Rafting disaster caused by a collision.

Bucking mill. Mill that trimmed and shaped stave timber into staves.

Buhr. Millstone cut from buhrstone; used in grist mills.

Bull tongue plow. Named for its shape and large wooden beam; used for breaking virgin land.

Cant hook. Pole with an iron hook on one end used to move logs.

Capstan. Prong on the bow of a boat that channels the landing lines. Operated by a steam engine located in the hull of the boat.

Chaindog. Metal chains of eight or nine links containing a metal spike or wedge at each end.

Channeling logs. Rolling logs stranded in the stream banks and low, swampy

197

areas back into the stream channels so they may float downstream on the next tide.

Chopping-out hoe. Broad-bitted, hand-forged hoe used to groom crop rows when the plants are young and tender.

Chute. Inclined wooden flume through which water and logs are passed to a lower level of a stream; a cleared earthen path down which logs are permitted to roll into the water below.

Clevis. A U-shaped piece of iron with holes in the ends through which a pin is run to attach one thing to another.

Court day. Day when County Court was in session at the county seat.

Crab. Winch located on the bank of a stream, used for winding in the headworks of a boom float.

Cumberland River Rule. Measuring stick designed to measure logs in the water; used only along the Upper Cumberland and its tributaries.

Cutting coulter. Broad, sharpened metal blade inserted vertically through the tongue of a plow and extended downward to the ground; designed to cut roots.

Double float. Double block of logs, one behind the other.

Double shovel. A small, one-horse cultivating plow containing two legs with a small plow point on each.

Doubletree. Long wooden hitch to which two singletrees are attached when two horses are employed.

Doyle Rule. Measuring stick designed to measure logs on land.

Drift. A raft as large as three blocks of logs wide and three or more blocks deep.

Drifting. Catching loose logs floating down a river.

Drover. Person who drove livestock herds from farms to regional market centers.

Drummer. Salesperson who traveled in a horse-drawn vehicle filled with merchandise.

Eddy. Place in the stream channel where the water turns back against the current, often caused by rocks in the river.

Floater log. Buoyant log made from a softwood tree such as poplar.

Fodder. Coarse feed, especially dried corn leaves, for domestic livestock.

Freight run. Transporting freight in a mule-drawn wagon along established routes on a regular schedule.

Freight wagon. Horse- or mule-drawn wagon which regularly traveled established routes carrying farm and craft products to regional market centers.

198

Grist mill. Mill for grinding corn into meal.

Groundhog thresher. Machine used for separating grain or seeds from straw; powered by four teams pulling a sweep in a circle.

Heading. Oak timber used to form the ends of whiskey barrels.

Headwork. Floating platform attached on one side of the river and used to anchor the log float.

Hillside plow. Plow that enables hill country farmers to plow horizontally along the sides of hills. The hillside plow had a moldboard and landside that could be flipped onto the opposite side of the plow at the end of each row.

Hogshead. Large cask or barrel containing from 63 to 140 gallons, used for shipping farm products such as tobacco.

Hopper. Rectangular, funnel-shaped receptacle which can be emptied easily and evenly.

Huckster wagon. Peddler's merchandise wagon traveling along established routes on a regular schedule.

Jitney. Car that hauled passengers on a regular schedule over a fixed route.

Job-planter. Seed planter operated by hand.

Jumping coulter. Broad, dull metal blade inserted vertically through the tongue of a plow and extended toward the ground at an angle that causes the plow point to come out of the ground when large tree roots are encountered.

Log float. See Boom.

Moldboard plow. Plow designed to cut and turn the soil by means of a curved iron plate attached above a plowshare.

New ground. Land newly cleared of trees and ready for cropping.

Nigger whoop. A penetrating yell, often melodic, used in signaling someone at a distance.

North bank. Right side of a river, facing downstream.

Oar. Long pole, with a broad, flat blade at one end, used for propelling or steering a raft.

Oar stem. Pole part of the oar that one grips when rowing.

Overshot water wheel. Wheel that is powered counterclockwise by the weight of water passing across the top.

Packet. A licensed steamboat to carry passengers and cargo.

Padway. Thinly matted narrow path on the raft.

Peckerwood mill. Small, portable saw mill.

199

Pen-hooking. Practice of visiting local farms and communities seeking to buy livestock and, in turn, to sell the stock for a quick profit.

Pilot. Licensed operator of a boat.

Pilothouse. Small room, with windows, which houses the boat's steering equipment.

Pole road. See Tram road.

Raft pin. Wooden hickory pin, eight to eighteen inches long, used in raft construction to attach whaling to the logs.

River rat. Person who lives on or near the water and obtains food from the river by fishing and trapping.

Road crew. Community residents who constructed or improved roads for a specified number of days each year.

Roller mill. Mill designed to grind wheat into flour.

Rolling store. Merchandise and produce vehicle traveling along established routes on a regular schedule.

Runner. A raftsman.

Saw leg. A section of a tree trunk ready for sawing into lumber.

Scribner's Rule. Measuring stick designed to measure logs on land.

Shanty. Lean-to built on a raft where men sleep, eat, and store gear.

Shaving horse. Timber device used to hold raft pins and other wooden objects while they are shaved into shape.

Shin crack. Method of freeing grounded boats by using a rope, pole, or tree, e.g.

Shoals. Shallow places in a river.

Shroud. A cloth used for wrapping a corpse in preparation for burial.

Shucky beans. Beans hung on a string and dried.

Singletree. A one-animal hitch used on wagons, sleds, plows, etc.

Sinker log. Hardwood log that does not float.

Sixty-penny nail. Metal spike approximately ten inches long.

Slough. Inlet from the river; a marsh or swamp.

Snaking. Using beasts of burden in transporting individual logs from the woods to the river's edge.

South bank. Left side of a river, facing downstream.

Speedwagon. Wagon with high wheels, rubber tires, and a chain drive.

Spike pole (or pike pole). Pole with an iron hook on one end used to move logs.

Spring wagon. Light passenger wagon equipped with cushion springs.

Stateroom. Cabin and sleeping quarters for passengers.

Staves. Narrow, thin strips of wood set edge to edge to form the sides of a barrel.

Stave bolt. See Bolt.

Straw tick. Straw-filled mattress.

Stray log. Log that deviates from its proper course; stranded by low tides.

Surge pin. Pin used to position and secure the oar stanchions on the raft.

Swapping labor. Two or more neighbors teaming up to help each other.

Swing. A chain of floater logs with one end fixed securely to the opposite bank.

Tanner's beam. Split-log bench.

Tide. Condition of the river when swollen enough to permit driving or rafting logs.

Tier. Portion of the log raft that is one log wide.

Toll. Miller's payment for his services, usually one-eighth of the meal or flour ground.

Trace. Hand-blazed, rough trail, designed for horseback or ox-cart travel.

Trail. Catwalk part of the boom.

Tram road. Roadway for trams or pole cars composed of parallel, railroad-like tracks made with steel or wooden poles and metal pins.

Tuck. Ninety-degree turn in the river channel.

Turn. Sack of corn taken to the grist mill to be ground into meal.

Undershot water wheel. Wheel that is powered clockwise by the weight of water passing beneath the wheel.

Whaling. Long, thin strips of hickory used in raft construction.

Wheat fan. Machine used to separate the wheat kernel from the chaff.

Winding sheet. A cloth used for wrapping a corpse in preparation for burial.

Wood talk. Conversation about the timber trade.

Major Steamboat Landings, Downstream from Burnside to Carthage

Landing	Bank of River	Landing	Bank of River
Burnside	South	Bell's	North
Bronston	South	Plum Point	North
Waitsboro	North	Graham's	South
Mill Springs	South	Jones'	South
White Oak Creek	North	Daffron's	South
Robertsport	South	Leveradge's	South
Faubush	North	Wild Goose	South
Cub Creek	North	Rowena	North
Oats'	South	Indian Creek	South
Fall Creek	South	Rowe's	North
Morrow's	North	Kendall's	North
Norman's	South	Black Fish	North
Eads'	South	Helm's	North
Fox's	North	Blankenship	North
Bart Ramsey's	South	Olga	North
Lock 21	South	Creelsboro	North
Thomas Branch	North	opposite Creelsboro	South
Bart's	South	Winfrey's	South
Dockery's	North	Winfrey's Ferry	South
Harmon Creek	South	Winfrey's Ferry	North
Wolf Creek	North	Dove Branch	North
Gossage	North	Shoe String	North
Greasy Creek	North	Orchard's	South
Stokes'	South	Brownwood	[unknown]
Snow's	North	Lick Branch	[unknown]
Painted Creek	North	Albany (Whetstone)	South

Landing	Bank of River	Landing	Bank of River
Morgan's	North	opposite McMillan's	South
Phelps'	North	Chappell's	North
Morrison's	South	Martinsburg	North
Duff Allen Dick's	South	opposite Martinsburg	South
Bakerton	North	Poindexter's	North
Renox Creek	North	Eden's	North
Garmon's Ferry	North	Stephens'	North
Scott's Ferry	South	Overstreet's (Tenn.)	South
Burkesville	North	Celina	South
South Burkesville (Bow)	South	Knob Creek	North
Bear Creek	South	Bennett's Ferry	North
Neely's Ferry	South	Butler's Landing	North
Oliver's Ferry	South	Butler's Landing	South
Tobin (Champ) Shoals	South	Brimstone	North
Wright's Point	North	Gainesboro	South
Head Wilborn Bar	South	Lee's Landing	North
Will Cary's	North	Myers'	North
Galloway Creek	South	Montgomery's	South
Cary's Ferry	South	Cedar Hill	North
Arat	South	Bill Town	North
Cloyd's	South	Cub Creek	North
Bluff	North	Brook's Ferry	South
Mud Camp	North	Richmond	North
Stalcup Bar	South	Hackett's	North
Glasscock Branch	North	Highland	North
Judio Creek	South	Fort Blount	South
Dodson's	South	Wood Fork	North
Black's Ferry	South	Holleman's	South
opposite Black's Ferry	North	Granville	South
Richardson's	North	Church	North
Center Point	North	Craig's Point	North
Gerald's	North	West Point	North
McMillan's	North	Carthage	North

Biographies of the Narrators

Anderson, Landon B., born Dec. 28, 1901, in Gainesboro, Jackson County, Tenn., where he was a farmer and millwright in his younger days. He moved to Celina and married the daughter of a prominent riverman. Anderson was active in public life until 1980 and was Superintendent of the Celina Water Works for many years. Interviewed in Celina, Jan. 30, 1976, then jointly with Walter E. Webb at the Clay County Library, Feb. 7, 1976; again on March 12, 1976, with eight other persons during a videotaping session. He contributed much information on several occasions while riding with the author in an automobile across Clay and Jackson counties.

Anderson, Leon, born Aug. 9, 1909, at Gainesboro, Jackson County, Tenn., where he presently resides. His father and grandfather operated the warehouse at Gainesboro Landing. He was deputy county court clerk for seven years; deputy circuit court clerk for five to six years; and general sessions judge for sixteen years. Interviewed Sept. 10, 1975.

Baker, Lloyd "Dutch," born March 7, 1900, at Bronston, Pulaski County, Ky. He served as second mate and fireman on both the Upper and Lower Cumberland. He lives in retirement near Burnside, Ky.

Barnett, Arlo, born April 2, 1898, near Sawyer, Pulaski County, Ky. Barnett now resides at Honey Bee, McCreary County, Ky. Interviewed July 14, 1978, by Wilma J. Waters. Original tape and transcription on deposit in the Kentucky State Library, Frankfort.

Barton, Glenn, born 1921 in Forbus, Fentress County, Tenn. A former schoolteacher, he is now director of pupil personnel in the Fentress County schools. Interviewed in Jamestown, Tenn., June 18, 1979, by the author and Barbara Allen.

Barton, Ona, born 1901 in northern Fentress County, Tenn. A homemaker all her life, Mrs. Barton has been widowed since 1977. Her knowledge of

204

local history is seemingly endless. Interviews with her were always conducted in conjunction with other narrators on Aug. 7, 1978; Sept. 15, 1978; Nov. 10, 1978; June 18, 1979; and Aug. 3, 1979.

Baxter, Joshua K., born 1877 in Hestand, Monroe County, Ky., the son of a Union veteran. He was proprietor of a general store and postmaster at Hestand for many years. Interviewed by Patricia Walden, Dec. 19, 1975.

Beaty, Virgil, born April 6, 1895, on Harbin Creek near Bond Mountain, Pickett County, Tenn. Moved in 1905 to the Cedar Grove community, Pickett County, where he has always resided except for a brief stint in military service during World War I. Interviewed briefly Jan. 5, 1976; hesitant to be interviewed.

Bell, Judge Ira, born May 4, 1903, in Parmleysville, Wayne County, Ky. Presently resides in Monticello. Schoolteacher and principal for five years; Wayne County superintendent of schools for thirty-eight years; three additional years in Gallatin County, Ky. Presently an author and county judge in his fourth year. Interviewed Sept. 24, 1976.

Bilbrey, Albert, born April 2, 1900, at Pine Lick, Jackson County, Tenn. Resides as a farmer in his home area. Interviewed on videotape along with eight other authorities on local history at the Holland Memorial Library, Gainesboro, Tenn., March 12, 1976.

Bilbrey, Mrs. Albert, born July 8, 1908, at Pine Lick, Jackson County, Tenn. Interviewed March 12, 1976 (see interview comments regarding Albert Bilbrey).

Bilbrey, Reece, born Nov. 3, 1895, in Static, Pickett County, Tenn. Presently resides in Byrdstown, Tenn. Owned a small farm for fifty years but recently sold it. Worked in a machine shop during World War II. Taught school for twenty-three years. Interviewed by Linda White, July 4, 1972.

Birdwell, Dayton, born in Monroe County, Ky. Interviewed by Karen Walden, April 18, 1974.

Blair, Richard, born Sept. 18, 1907, at Gann's Bottom, Wayne County, Ky. Presently lives in retirement at Jamestown, Russell County, Ky. Farmed when young; taught school for ten years; worked in the insurance business for forty years. Interviewed by Robyn West, Jamestown, Sept. 23, 1976. Original tape and transcription are on deposit at the Kentucky State Library, Frankfort.

Brown, Earl, born ca. 1900 in southern Clinton County, Ky. Retired farmer and member of the courthouse whittling society in Albany, Ky. Interviewed Feb. 28, 1976.

Bryant, Ronnie, born Aug. 23, 1953, in Monroe County, Ky. Presently resides at Tompkinsville, Ky. Farmer and former assistant editor of the *Monroe County Messenger* newspaper. Interviewed by Mitzi Robertson, Dec. 15, 1973.

205

Burtram, Charlie, born 1901 in southern Wayne County, Ky. Although he carried the U.S. mail for a few years, he was a merchant most of his life in the Chestnut Grove community, Wayne County. Interviewed in his grocery store, Nov. 10, 1978.

Butler, Iva, born ca. 1908 at Whitleyville, Jackson County, Tenn. Taught public schools for several years; presently serving as librarian in the Holland Memorial Library, Gainesboro, Tenn. Interviewed Feb. 7, 1976 and Mar. 12, 1976.

Butler, James Franklin, born 1894, near Cloyd's Landing, Cumberland County, Ky., where he still resides as a farmer on his ancestral homeplace. Interviewed Feb. 27, 1976; Hiram Parrish was present during the interview. Interviewed again, by Frankie Hickey, June 21, 1978. Original tape and transcription are on deposit at the Kentucky State Library, Frankfort.

Byrd, Dovie, born 1913 at Chestnut Grove, Cumberland County, Ky. She presently lives at Speck, Clinton County, Ky., and is a homemaker. Interviewed Feb. 27, 1976.

Byrd, Elvin P., born Jan. 20, 1917, at Byrdstown, Pickett County, Tenn. Raised on Wolf River, he now lives at Speck, Clinton County, Ky., in semiretirement as a carpenter and farmer. Both of his parents were from Byrdstown, a community named for the informant's grandfather. His father was a blacksmith. Interviewed Feb. 27, 1976.

Byrd, Lucinda Zachary, born Sept. 8, 1892 at Byrdstown, Pickett County, Tenn. She presently resides in Albany, Ky. A homemaker; her late husband farmed and ran rafts on the Wolf River. Interviewed March 6, 1976 by Keith Byrd, a grandson.

Carter, Elsworth and Darlene, born ca. 1915 and 1920, near Rock Bridge, Monroe County, Ky. Elsworth was a farmer before and after serving in World War II. He died during the late 1960s. Darlene was a homemaker until his illness; she now works in a garment factory in Tompkinsville, Ky. Interviewed May 20, 1960.

Cassetty, Katherine, born ca. 1918 in Davidson County, Tenn. Her father was steamboat Captain Robert L. "Bob" Meadows. She was raised at Lee's Landing near Gainesboro, Tenn.; presently resides at Whitleyville, Tenn. She is a retired school teacher and school lunch supervisor. Interviewed March 12, 1976.

Chism, Trotwood K., born ca. 1868 in Tompkinsville, Ky., into one of the area's pioneer families. He was a jeweler most of his life. Interviewed with pencil and pad March 12, 1958.

Coe, Escar, born April 27, 1899 in Puncheon Camp Bottom, Russell County, Ky. He worked on steamboats from age eighteen in virtually every capacity— engineer, engineer's helper, clerk, mate, and pilot. Coe piloted the "Burnside," "Celina," and the "Rowena." He is one of the two surviving pilots on the Upper Cumberland. When steamboats ceased operation on the

Upper Cumberland, Coe went to work for Grissom-Rakestraw Lumber Co. in Burnside. He later worked for the WPA and other relief agencies and for the Ford Garage in Burkesville before being appointed postmaster at Burkesville in 1954, a position he retired from in 1969. Interviewed Oct. 30, 1975, and July 29, 1976. He was then interviewed by Frankie Hickey, June 27, 1979; this tape and its transcription are on deposit in the Kentucky State Library, Frankfort.

Coffey, Benjamin, born Jan. 8, 1917 in Monticello, Wayne County, Ky. He worked in small machine shops in Indianapolis and for General Motors from 1941 to 1975. He presently lives in Monticello and is chairman of a group that records cemeteries in Wayne County for the Kentucky Historical Society. Interviewed Sept. 10, 1976.

Crabtree, Emma, born May 29, 1886, near Gainesboro, Jackson County, Tenn. Her father, Booker Brooks, who drove drummer's wagons, was killed when she was twelve. She married Bill Crabtree when she was sixteen; they raised six children on the banks of the Roaring River, where Bill ran a ferryboat. Later, they moved to Bowling Green, Ky., so that their children could receive an adequate education. Interviewed May 19, 1976.

Crouch, Jason, born ca. 1905 at Moodyville, Pickett County, Tenn., where he presently resides in retirement after a lifetime devoted to farming. Interviewed Jan. 5, 1976, at the Upper Cumberland Regional Development District lunch for senior citizens in Moodyville.

Cummings, John I., born Aug. 8, 1901, near Lee's Chapel, Clinton County, Ky. A farmer-logger for many years, he is the last surviving raft pilot to run logs down the Wolf River to Celina. Interviewed Feb. 28, 1976.

Cummings, Mary, born Sept. 1894 at Cummings Mill, Jackson County, Tenn. She taught school for several years in Jackson and Putnam counties before becoming a hospital and x-ray technician in Chicago and Dallas. Interviewed with eight other persons on videotape at Gainesboro, Tenn., March 12, 1976.

Davidson, Quinn, born Jan. 17, 1905, in the house in which he presently resides on a ninety-acre farm near Chanute, Pickett County, Tenn. He and his sister, both unmarried, lived together until her death in 1962. Much of the poetry he writes commemorates her life; the rest of his poetry is based upon local persons and events. About fifteen of his compositions were set to music and recorded in Nashville at his own expense. Interviewed Jan. 6, 1976.

Dicken, Jean, born ca. 1938 in Clinton County, Ky. Interviewed May 11, 1981, by her son, Eric Dicken.

Dowell, Cicero "Bristow," born Nov. 12, 1905, in Smith Bottom, Russell County, Ky. Interviewed by Robyn West, Aug. 11, 1978 at Jamestown, Ky. Original tape and transcription are on deposit in the Kentucky State Library, Frankfort.

Edmunds, Benjamin Harrison, born Oct. 2, 1888, in the eastern part of Russell County, Ky. He resides in Russell Springs as a retired school teacher. Interviewed June 19, 1976.

Garrett, Robert "Bud," born Jan. 28, 1918, in Free Hills, overlooking Celina, Tenn. A self-employed businessman, he has engaged in restaurant, record shop, and garage businesses. He has recorded black blues vocal and guitar music and has played in the bands of numerous local musicians at various times. He has performed at home, in southern Kentucky, Nashville, Tenn., and Cordele, Georgia. He currently operates an automobile garage and drives a bus for the Head Start program in Celina. Interviewed Feb. 1, 1977.

Gaskin, E. Ray, born 1900 in Felix, Russell County, Ky., in a log cabin. He moved as a young man to Wartburg, Tenn., where he carved out an important niche in the logging business. A folk poet and writer, Gaskin likes to recall the days of his childhood in Russell County. Interviewed at home March 13, 1976; was present on June 19, 1976, at the Edmunds and Luttrell interviews and led the questioning and discussions from his own notes in those instances.

Goff, Lewis and Mae. He was born in White's Bottom, Cumberland County, Ky., Oct. 15, 1898; she was born on Clover Creek, same county, in 1906. They presently reside in White's Bottom and operate a productive farm. Interviewed July 29, 1976 with Becky Morse.

Gilreath, Eula, born ca. 1917 near Moodyville, Pickett County, Tenn. A resident of Jamestown, Tenn., she is the daughter of J.D. Lowrey, another narrator. She is a homemaker and garment factory worker. Interviewed Jan. 5, 1976 (see entry for Hiram Greene).

Greene, Hiram, born ca. 1900 in the Red Hill Community, Pickett County, Tenn. He is a retired farmer. Interviewed at Moodyville at a daily lunch program conducted in behalf of the senior citizens by the Upper Cumberland Region Development District, Jan. 5, 1976. Present at that interview also were Edd Moody, Eula Gilreath, and Jason Crouch.

Grissom, Mrs. T.B., Sr., born 1897 in Burnside, Ky. One of Burnside's community leaders, she is the widow of the co-owner of Grissom-Rakestraw Lumber Co. At one time Mr. Grissom was a clerk on one of the boats owned by the Cumberland Transportation Co. She has a valuable photograph collection of river life. Interviewed Oct. 12, 1976.

Hackett, Claude Cavett, born ca. 1900 in the Rough Point area of Jackson County, Tenn. He is a former steamboat clerk and state employee. Interviewed Feb. 7, and March 12, 1976 (see entry for Albert Bilbrey).

Hail, Jenny, born Sept. 18, 1888, in Pulaski County, Ky., in the same house in which she presently resides. Interviewed by a fieldworker for the Lake Cumberland Library District Oral History Project. Tape and

208

transcription are on deposit in the Kentucky State Library, Frankfort.

Hayes, Charles, Jr., born ca. 1920 in Monterey, Overton County, Tenn. He is currently employed by the Army Corps of Engineers, Nashville District, Nashville. Interviewed briefly in connection with other research business there on July 10, 1976.

Holloway, Bethel, born ca. 1900 in Putnam County, Tenn. He worked as a coal miner in the Monterey area during the 1920s and 1930s. Interviewed at his home in Calfkiller Valley, near Monterey, Nov. 9, 1979, by Brad Simpson, David Storie, and Ann Zachari.

Irvin, W. Kenneth, born Jan. 18, 1904, in Creelsboro, Russell County, Ky. Irvin is a merchant at Creelsboro. The family store there was the hub of economic activity for the entire area during river traffic days. Interviewed Feb. 4, 1976.

Jones, Will H., born on Bear Creek, Cumberland County, Ky., in 1888. He is a former deputy sheriff of Cumberland County. Interviewed by Jewell W. Thomas, Burkesville, Ky., April 20, 1977. Original tape and transcription are on deposit in the Kentucky State Library, Frankfort.

Kirkpatrick, Price, born ca. 1875 on Meshack Creek in Monroe County, Ky. His ancestors settled in the Cumberland River area just after the Revolutionary War. The president of People's Bank in Tompkinsville for many years, he died during the mid-1960s. Interviewed Aug. 21, 1961.

Koger, Sarah Jane, born Dec. 15, 1890, in rural Pickett County, Tenn. She is very familiar with the area's local history, as she and her husband ran a general store and operated sawmilling camps during the height of the sawmilling era of the 1920s and 1930s. Interviewed by the author and Barbara Allen, at her home in Jamestown, June 18, 1979, and Aug. 3, 1979. Ona Barton was present both times.

Kyle, Hugh, born Jan. 17, 1900, in Celina, Tenn. His grandfather helped to establish logging and rafting activities on the Upper Cumberland in the 1870s and 1880s. This narrator represents the third generation of Kyles who were prominent in the lumber business at Celina. Interviewed Feb. 12, 1976.

Langford, Rachel, born on Mitchell's Creek, Clay County, Tenn. Daughter of Bob Riley, of logging and rafting fame. She presently lives in Celina. Interviewed briefly Jan. 30, 1976.

Littrell, Mary, born ca. 1900 at Mt. Pisgah, Wayne County, Ky. She vividly recalled stavemilling activities and other facets of the timber industry. Interviewed in Albany, Ky., March 14, 1980, at a senior citizens function.

Lowrey, J.D., born March 28, 1889, near Moodyville, Pickett County, Tenn. He resides in retirement near Moodyville, after many years spent in

209

various facets of logging and sawmilling activities. Interviewed March 27, 1976.

Luttrell, A.V., born Apr. 26, 1896, on Goose Creek, Russell County, Ky. He taught school, worked in banks and operated a motion picture theater. His father ran one of the first bucking mills in Russell County and was a leader in the area's early stave industry. Interviewed June 19, 1976.

Martin, Lena Howell, born Feb. 29, 1892, in Highland, Jackson County, Tenn. Her people were river merchants and her own memory is sharp along these lines. Interviewed March 12, 1976, during a group interview at the Holland Memorial Library, Gainesboro (see entry for Albert Bilbrey).

Massey, Kenneth, born 1890 in Burnside, Ky. He was a steamboat pilot and later general manager of Burkesville and Burnside Transportation Co. He presently resides in Pittsburgh and was connected with the steel industry until his retirement. Interviewed Oct. 4, 1976, May 10, 1977, by Colleen Garland; and Oct. 12, 1976, by Mrs. T.B. Grissom, Sr.; all in Burnside.

Maxey, Walter, born June 17, 1895, in the black section of Burkesville, Ky. He worked at various positions on the steamboats from about 1915 to 1930, especially as steward and cook. Interviewed Dec. 29, 1975; died two days later. His philosophy of life was one of almost total subservience to whites. He was very pleased to be the subject of an interview.

Meadows, Ernest, born July 8, 1900, in Jackson County, Tenn. Retired steamboat pilot, he was one of the two living former pilots on the Upper Cumberland; lived in Free State, Jackson County. Interviewed in Gainesboro, Tenn., Feb. 7, 1976, March 12, 1976 (see entry for Albert Bilbrey) and at his home on Aug. 12, 1976. He died in 1979.

Miller, Nora, born at Creelsboro, Russell County, Ky. A widely traveled, retired schoolteacher, she once clerked in the W.K. Irvin general store at Creelsboro. Interviewed Sept. 23, 1976, by Mrs. Ethel Gaskin.

Mitchell, Adele, born ca. 1910 in Metcalfe County, Ky. She presently lives in retirement near Edmonton, Ky., following a lifelong teaching career. Interviewed by Carolyn Best, Jan. 28, 1976.

Mitchell, Bernice, born ca. 1900 near Campbellsville, Ky. She moved with her parents to Burnside, Ky., just prior to her teenage years. She has collected photographs and other historical data across the years. She and her brother in North Carolina still exchange newsy letters with much historical information in them. She was employed as secretary most of her life by Grissom-Rakestraw Lumber Co. and its successor, Hamer Lumber Co. Contacted for bits of information on several occasions; major interviews Oct. 2, Oct. 12, Nov. 8, and Dec. 8, 1976.

Montell, Hazel, born March 2, 1909, in Rock Bridge, Monroe County, Ky. She is a former homemaker and store clerk. Informal interview Feb. 3, 1981, Bowling Green, Ky.

Montell, Willie, born Aug. 16, 1908, at Mt. Gilead, Monroe County, Ky. He was a farmer, road-grader operator, store proprietor, school bus driver, and director of local Neighborhood Youth Corps program until his death in June 1979. He provided information at various times during the period of research, especially Dec. 25, 1976, and Jan. 16, 1977.

Moody, Edd, born Nov. 1, 1897, at Moodyville, Pickett County, Tenn. He was a lifelong farmer. Interviewed Jan. 5, 1976 (see entry for Hiram Greene).

Owsley, Brookie, born ca. 1908. She is a registered nurse and anesthetist. Interviewed Dec. 29, 1975.

Owsley, Dr. William F., born July 1879 in Burkesville, Ky. He was the oldest practicing physician in Kentucky at the time of his death in 1979. His grandfather, Dr. Joel Owsley, came to Burkesville in 1810. He began practicing medicine when the horse and buggy were the only means of reaching patients' homes. He recalls compounding medicines from his own bulk pharmaceuticals; resented modern medicine. Interviewed Dec. 29, 1975.

Page, O.B., born April 7, 1905, in Monroe County, Ky. A retired farmer-carpenter, he has been minister and song leader in the Church of Christ since the 1920s. Interviewed by Karen Walden, Nov. 28, 1973.

Page, Vada Tooley, born ca. 1900 in Monroe County, Ky., near Tompkinsville. She is the daughter of Coyle Tooley, a merchant and driver of a huckster wagon. She is a retired school teacher. Interviewed Nov. 28, 1973.

Parrish, William Hiram, born Sept. 5, 1897, in Swan Pond Bottom (now Scott's Bottom) near Burkesville, Ky. He moved to Burkesville with his parents in 1913. A farmer all of his life, he served ten years in the local Agricultural Stabilization Office. In 1967 he served as county judge for eight months. Parrish went with the author on numerous visits to contact and interview other narrators. He was first interviewed at home on Dec. 23, 1975.

Patton, George, born ca. 1900 at Jamestown, Tenn.; died at Jamestown in 1975. Interviewed by Linda White, July 1972.

Peavyhouse, Will, born April 4, 1901, in Buffalo Cove, Fentress County, Tenn. A farmer, logger, public servant, he lives in semiretirement near the place of his birth. Interviewed Jan. 31, 1976, during the time

211

when he was helping to build a new sanctuary for the West Fentress Baptist Church.

Perdew, Quentin, born ca. 1920 in Clinton County, Ky. Interviewed by Timothy Perdew, Albany, Ky., May 10, 1980.

Phillips, Ray B., born 1907 in Byrdstown, Tenn., where he presently resides in retirement. A schoolteacher for forty years, he has since worked for the Human Resources Agency, Byrdstown. Interviewed by Linda White, July 13, 1972.

Pitman, Bea, born Feb. 14, 1914, in Byrdstown, Tenn. She is a farm homemaker. Interviewed by Keith Byrd, March 6, 1976.

Powell, Henry, born ca. 1900 in Wayne County, Ky. Interviewed by Bennie Coffey, Feb. 12, 1979. Original tape and transcription are on deposit in the Kentucky State Library, Frankfort.

Prenn, Guillelmine Cummins, born 1901 at Cummings Mill, Jackson County, Tenn. She is a professional artist, and retired supervisor of instruction for the Jackson County schools. Interviewed March 12, 1976 (see entry for Albert Bilbrey).

Pyle, Willie, born Dec. 23, 1909, in Byrdstown, Tenn. A farmer, he worked at saw mills and rock quarries as a seasonal employee and for seventeen years for a public power company. He died in 1974. Interviewed by Linda White, July 3, 1972.

Ray, Wade, born Jan. 26, 1892, near Mitchell's Creek, Overton County, Tenn. He resides in retirement near Allons, Tenn., following a career of farming and logging. He worked on log rafts with Bob Riley. Interviewed briefly March 13, 1976.

Reid, Effie, born in Smith County, Tenn. Her father was Benton Lowe, Sr., clerk on the steamboat "W.T. Hardison." Mrs. Reid and her husband published a newspaper in Carthage for many years. Interviewed April 2, 1976.

Rich, Willie M., born Feb. 2, 1894, in Pickett County, Tenn. He is presently a resident of the Faix community. Many of his people, including himself, were farmer-loggers on the Obey River. Later he worked at stave and heading mills. His father was among the first persons to raft logs to Celina; the narrator was one of the last. Still active despite his years, Rich was called from the woods and woodcutting activities in order for the author to interview him, Jan. 6, 1976.

Rogers, Henry H., born 1894 in Fentress County, Tenn. He is a retired livestock dealer. Interviewed in Jamestown, Tenn., June 18, 1979.

Rush, Clarence, born Oct. 1, 1906, at Bear Creek, Cumberland County, Ky., where he presently resides. He is a Civil War buff and authority on local history. Interviewed Jan. 9, 1976.

Scott, William Hamilton, born March 27, 1874, in the Hickory Ridge section of Monroe County, Ky. He spent his lifetime as a farmer in Monroe County except for a few months in Texas as a young man. At the time of his death May 11, 1976, at a nursing home in Tompkinsville, Ky, he had 113 great-grandchildren and 22 great-great-grandchildren. Interviewed by Patricia Waldon, Dec. 20, 1975.

Shearer, Mrs. Matt, born 1893 in Wayne County, Ky. Her ancestral home was flooded by the waters of Lake Cumberland. Interviewed by Elizabeth Simpson, Monticello, Ky., May 13, 1977. Original tape and transcription are on deposit in the Kentucky State Library, Frankfort.

Simpson, Elizabeth, born Wayne County, Ky. Presently resides in Monticello. Interviewed Sept. 24, 1976.

Smith, Randolph, born Burkesville, Ky. He is descended from early families of the county (Cumberland), is a pharmacist and recognized authority on local history and genealogy, and has published books in the field of genealogical research. He was not formally interviewed but was telephoned on numerous occasions.

Stone, Gladys, born Sept. 16, 1914, as Martha Gladys Smith on Neely's Creek, Clay County, Tenn. She married Amos Stone and spent the rest of her life as a farm homemaker on his ancestral place at Stone's Landing, on the Cumberland about two miles above Celina. Presently a widow, she manages the family farm which is tilled by her son and grandsons. Interviewed April 16, 1976, by Becky Morse.

Stone, John, born Aug. 28, 1900, in Irish Bottom, Cumberland County, Ky. He worked on riverboats from 1916 to 1926, mainly as watchman and mate. He lives in retirement near Irish Bottom. Interviewed Dec. 26, 1975.

Storie, Carlos, born April 2, 1897, the third generation of his line to be born in what is now Pickett County, Tenn. A retired farmer-logger, he resides near the Forbus community. Interviewed Jan. 5, 1976.

Upton, Butler and Edwina, born Clay County, Tenn. Husband-wife mortuary team who operate the Upton Funeral Home in Celina. She was born at Willow Grove; he in the Mitchell's Creek area. Both of their ancestral homeplaces are inundated by Dale Hollow Reservoir. The Uptons are local history buffs and were extremely willing to cooperate and to lend important documents from their private collection. Interviewed Jan. 30, 1976; numerous other short visits.

Van Norman, Emma, born southern Metcalfe County, Ky. She is a homemaker. Interviewed by Kay Harbison in 1972.

Van Zant, Ruth, born ca. 1900 in Metcalfe County, Ky., where she has lived all her life. She taught in a one-room school for several years, then worked as a reporter for an Edmonton newspaper. She presently writes the weekly column "Happenings" for the *Edmonton Herald*. Interviewed by Carolyn Best, Feb. 8, 1976.

Walden, Judge Cass, born 1903 in Monroe County, Ky., where he knew the river and river people for several years. He moved to Edmonton, Ky., where he was a lawyer for many years prior to becoming circuit

213

judge, a position that he held for a long time. He also served as state senator. Interviewed by Carolyn Best, Jan. 31, 1976.

Walker, Garnet, born June 17, 1919, three miles from Mill Springs, Wayne County, Ky. Lived in rural Wayne County until 1973 at which time he retired from educational administration and moved to Monticello, Ky. He taught five years in a one-room school, served three years as school attendance officer, six years as supervisor of instruction, one year as high school English teacher, and seventeen years as an elementary school principal. He is a local historian. Interviewed Sept. 10 and Sept. 24, 1976.

Wallace, Gilbert, born 1905 in Metcalfe County, Ky. He was elected on various occasions to county offices such as sheriff and county judge. He also served as deputy warden at LaGrange Penitentiary and was a state employee immediately prior to retirement. Interviewed by Carolyn Best, Feb. 16, 1976.

Walters, Rev. Gifford, born 1908. A retired Baptist minister and associational missionary, he presently resides in Monticello, Ky. Interviewed Sept. 24, 1976.

Watson, Arnold, born Nov. 29, 1894, in Peytonsburg, Cumberland County, Ky. A former schoolteacher, factory worker, and rural mail carrier at Peytonsburg (1926–46), he lived in retirement in the community of his birth. After our first interview on Dec. 26, 1975, he urged, "Hurry back; I'm an old man and won't live forever." I went back for the second interview on Jan. 9, 1976. He died a few months later.

Watson, Sam, born Metcalfe County, Ky., ca. 1890. He spent much of his life in Washington, D.C. Interviewed by Kay Harbison in 1972.

Webb, Walter E., born March 5, 1915, on the Obey River, Celina, Tenn. A former schoolteacher, principal, ballistician, and supervisory physicist of naval ordnance materials for twenty years, he presently lives in retirement at Dale Hollow Lake. Interviewed Feb. 7, 1976.

White, Clyde "Bully," born Monroe County, Ky., where he has lived all of his life. Interviewed by Steve Hurt, Karen Walden, and Sharon Walden, Dec. 19, 1973.

Williams, Edith, born ca. 1891 near Hestand, Monroe County, Ky. She married Cloyd Williams, who operated the warehouse at McMillan's Landing for eight years, then ran the general store there until the 1950s. Their home was the same house in which Benton McMillan, governor of Tennessee, was born. She never worked in the family store, but she cooked on numerous occasions for log raftsmen and steamboat rousters. Interviewed May 14, 1976.

Williams, Luida, born Luida Ellington in Salt Lick Bend, Cumberland County, Ky., in 1876. Her parents were slaves. She married Nathan Williams. A widow, Mrs. Williams now resides in a nursing home in Greensburg, Ky., where she was interviewed by Frankie Hickey,

214

Aug. 22, 1979. Original tape and transcription are on deposit in the Kentucky State Library, Frankfort.

Williamson, Cecil, born Jan. 30, 1893, at Granville, Jackson County, Tenn., on the banks of the Cumberland River. He was a veteran of World War I, a Jackson County schoolteacher, and an employee of Firestone Tire and Rubber Co., Akron, Ohio, for several years (see Albert Bilbrey).

Winningham, Anne Harrison, born July 13, 1895, in Pickett County, Tenn., near Wolf River. She was married to William Winningham in 1913 at age 18. They moved to Albany, Ky., at the end of World War I. She was appointed sheriff of Clinton County to fill the unexpired term of office of her slain husband. Interviewed by Timothy Perdew, May 10, 1980.

York, Luther M., born in Three Forks of the Wolf River, Fentress County, Tenn. He was a retired farmer at the time he was interviewed by Linda White, July 1, 1972.

Bibliography of Written Sources

Anderson, Landon Butler. "Brief History of Clay County [Tennessee]." Unpubl. manuscript, n.d. Manuscript in possession of Landon Anderson, Celina, Tenn.

Army Corps of Engineers. "Flood in Celina, Tennessee—How to Avoid Damage." [Nashville, 1968].

Austin, J.P. *The Blue and The Gray: Sketches of the Unwritten History of the Great American Civil War.* Atlanta: Franklin Printing and Publishing Co., 1899.

Bandy, Lewis David. "Folklore of Macon County, Tennessee." M.A. thesis, George Peabody College for Teachers, 1940.

"B.B. Sherrill, Clay Resident, Celebrates 100th Birthday." *The Celina Globe,* 5 Jan. 1961, p. 1.

Bratcher, James T. *Analytical Index to Publications of the Texas Folklore Society, Volumes 1–36.* Dallas: Southern Methodist Univ. Press, 1973.

Cherry, Kyle J. "Raft Tide." Unpubl. manuscript, n.d. Manuscript in possession of Mary Elizabeth Cherry, Celina, Tenn.

Collins, Richard H. *History of Kentucky.* 2 vols. Covington, Ky.: Collins and Co., 1882.

Connelly, Thomas Lawrence. *Army of the Heartland; the Army of Tennessee, 1861–1862.* Baton Rouge: Louisiana State Univ. Press, 1967.

Dale, A.L. "History of My Life." Unpubl. manuscript, n.d. Manuscripts of A.L. Dale in possession of Grandstaff Dale, Nashville.

———. "Memoirs of A.L. 'High' Dale." Unpubl. manuscript, n.d.

———. "Old Time Steamboating on the Cumberland River." Unpubl. manuscript, n.d.

———. "Record of A.L. Dale's People." Unpubl. manuscript, n.d.

Davenport, Lawrence C. *Local Historical Research by a Class in Local Historical Research.* Somerset, Ky.: Somerset Community College, 1966.

"Diary of a Tie Lady." *Koppers News,* 19 (Dec. 1947–Jan. 1948), 22–23.

Dorson, Richard M. *Jonathan Draws the Long Row: New England and Popular Tales and Legends.* Cambridge: Harvard Univ. Press, 1946.

Douglas, Byrd. *Steamboatin' On the Cumberland.* Nashville: Tennessee Book Co., 1961.

Duke, Basil W. *A History of Morgan's Cavalry.* Cincinnati: Miami Printing and Publishing Co., 1867.

Evans, George E. *The Days That We Have Seen.* London: Faber and Faber, 1975.

Fitzgerald, Isaiah. "Points of Historic Interest in Clay County." Unpubl. manuscript, n.d. Copy of manuscript in possession of Landon Anderson, Celina, Tenn.

Fry, Gladys-Marie. *Night Riders in Black Folk History.* Knoxville: Univ. of Tennessee Press, 1975.

Gardenhire, Kibbie Tinsley Williams. "Memoirs of Kibbie Tinsley Williams Gardenhire." Unpubl. manuscript, 1939. Copy of manuscript in possession of Margaret Tinsley Elliott and Landon Anderson, Celina, Tenn.

Gaskin, E. Ray. "Folktales of the Kentucky Hills." Unpubl. manuscript, 1968.

"Glasgow to Burkesville Stage Carried Mail." *Glasgow Daily Times,* 14 Nov. 1965, Sect. II, 6–7.

Goodpasture, Albert V. "Overton County, Address of Albert V. Goodpasture, delivered at Livingston, Tennessee, July 4, 1876." Published 1877. Rpt. Nashville: B.C. Goodpasture, 1954.

Goodpasture, Albert V., and W.H. Goodpasture. *Life of Jefferson Dillard Goodpasture; to Which is Appended a Genealogy of the Family of James Goodpasture.* Nashville: Cumberland Presbyterian Publishing House, 1897.

Gray, Charles P. "The Saga of Uncle Bob Riley." Unpubl. manuscript, n.d. Manuscript in possession of Rachel Langford, Celina, Tenn.

"Grissom-Rakestraw Story," *National Hardwood Magazine* (March 1962), n.p.

Guthrie, Charles S. "Corn: The Mainstay of the Cumberland Valley." *Kentucky Folklore Record,* 12 (Oct.–Dec. 1966), 136–42.

———. "Tobacco: Cash Crop of the Cumberland Valley." *Kentucky Folklore Record,* 14 (April–June 1968), 38–43.

217

Hale, Will T., and Dixon L. Merritt. *A History of Tennessee and Tennesseans.* 3 vols. Chicago: Lewis Publishing Co., 1913.

Harrison, Lowell H. *The Civil War in Kentucky.* Lexington: Univ. Press of Kentucky, 1976.

Hogue, Albert R. *History of Fentress County, Tennessee.* Baltimore: Regional Publishing Co., 1975.

———. *Mark Twain's Obedstown and Knobs of Tennessee: A History of Jamestown and Fentress County, Tennessee.* Jamestown, Tenn.: Cumberland Printing Co., 1950.

———. *One Hundred Years in the Cumberland Mountains Along the Continental Divide.* McMinnville, Tenn.: Standard Printing Co., 1933.

Huddleston, Tim. *History of Pickett County, Tennessee.* Collegedale, Tenn.: College Press, 1973.

Hull, Cordell. *The Memoirs of Cordell Hull.* 2 vols. New York: Macmillan, 1948.

Hyatt, Harry M. *Folklore from Adams County, Illinois.* Hannibal, Mo.: Alma Egan Hyatt Foundation, 1965.

Ives, Edward D. *Joe Scott: The Woodsman-Songmaker.* Urbana: Univ. of Illinois Press, 1978.

"J.K. Baxter, 96, Still Going Strong." *Tompkinsville News,* 18 Sept. 1975, p. 2.

Johnson, Augusta P. *A Century of Wayne County, Kentucky, 1800–1900.* Louisville: Standard Printing Co., 1939.

[Johnson, Leland]. "Engineers on the Twin Rivers: 1769–1975." Nashville: Unpubl. document, Nashville District Corps of Engineers, United States Army, 1975.

Joyner, Charles W. *Slave Folklife: Antebellum Black Culture in the South Carolina Low Country.* Urbana: Univ. of Illinois Press, 1981.

Kentucky Writer's Project. *Fairs and Fairmakers of Kentucky.* Frankfort: Kentucky Dept. of Agriculture, 1942.

Killibrew, J.B. *Iron and Coal of Tennessee.* Nashville: Tavel and Howell, 1881.

Knight, George A. *My Album of Memories.* Knoxville: Southeastern Composition Services, 1971.

———. *Our Wonderful Overton County Heritage.* Knoxville: Southeastern Composition Services, 1972.

Knox, Jack. *The Riverman.* Nashville: Abingdon Press, 1971.

Langford, Rachel R. "Rafts and Rafting." Unpubl. manuscript, n.d. Manuscript in possession of Rachel Langford, Celina, Tenn.

Laws, Malcolm P. *Native American Ballads.* Philadelphia: American Folklore Society, 1964.

Lawson, Ernest M. *Awakening of Cumberland County, or The Last Fifty Years.* Burkesville, Ky.: Cumberland County Printing Co., 1973.

Leslie, John E. "Early Days in Monroe County." Unpubl. manuscript, n.d. (ca. 1930). Manuscript in possession of Kentucky Library, Western Kentucky Univ., Bowling Green.

Maxey, Hampton. "History of Clay County [Tennessee]." Unpubl. manuscript, n.d. Manuscript in possession of Curtis and Edwina Upton, Celina, Tenn.

McClain, G. Lee. *Military History of Kentucky.* Frankfort: Military Dept. of Kentucky, 1939.

Miller, Wayne. "Gibson's Recipe for Success . . . Good Men, Good Timber, Good Equipment." *National Hardwood Magazine,* 47 (Aug. 1973), 52–58.

Montell, William Lynwood. *Monroe County History, 1820–1970.* Tompkinsville, Ky.: Tompkinsville Lions Club, 1970.

———. *The Saga of Coe Ridge: A Study in Oral History.* Knoxville: Univ. of Tennessee Press, 1970.

Nashville District Corps of Engineers. *Flood Plain Information: Cumberland River, Obey River, Celina, Tennessee.* Nashville: United States Army Corps of Engineers, 1968.

Peavyhouse, Will C., and Merle Peavyhouse. *A History of Buffalo Cove, Fentress County, Tennessee.* Privately published, n.d.

Pyles, Aaron E. *Genealogy of the Coonrod Pyle Family.* Campbellsville, Ky.: Privately published by the author, 1978.

Rich, Jesse W. *Cutting, Rafting and Running Logs Down the Obey River: 1880–1920.* Privately published, 1972.

Ridley, Bromfield L. *Battles and Sketches of the Army of Tennessee.* Mexico, Mo.: Missouri Printing and Publishing Co., 1906.

———. "Champ Ferguson." *Confederate Veteran,* 7 (Oct. 1899), 442–43.

Schulman, Steven A. "Logging in the Upper Cumberland Valley: A Folk Industry." M.A. thesis, Western Kentucky Univ., 1973.

———. "Reminiscences of Logging along the Cumberland." *Kentucky Folklore Record,* 18 (Oct.–Dec., 1972), 96–98.

Seals, Monroe. *History of White County.* Sparta, Tenn.: Privately published by Mrs. Monroe Seals, 1935.

Sensing, Thurman. *Champ Ferguson: Confederate Guerrilla.* Nashville: Vanderbilt Univ. Press, 1942.

Smith, Lewis K. "Jackson County, History of Gainesboro." Unpubl. manuscript, n.d. Copy of manuscript in possession of Landon Anderson, Celina, Tenn.

219

Smith, Winston S. "Escar Olin Coe on the Upper Cumberland: Reminiscences of a River Pilot." *Kentucky Folklore Record,* 20 (July–Sept. 1974), 59–83.

Stone, William C., Sr. "Historical Sketches of Clay County, Tennessee." Unpubl. manuscript, 1962. Manuscript in possession of William C. Stone, Sr., Nashville.

———. "History of Clay County, Tennessee." *Clay County Centennial 1870–1970 Commemorative Brochure.* Celina, n.p., 1970.

Swiggett, Howard. *The Rebel Raider: Life of John Hunt Morgan.* Indianapolis: Bobbs–Merrill, 1934.

Tarrant, E. Sergeant. *The Wild Raiders of the First Kentucky Cavalry.* Lexington: Henry Clay Press, 1969.

"The Tourist's Pocket Map of the State of Tennessee, Exhibiting Its Internal Improvements." Philadelphia: n.p., 1938.

Tibbals, Alma O. *A History of Pulaski County, Kentucky.* Bagdad, Ky.: Grace Owens Moore, 1952.

Turner, Robert R. "Tennessee Legends: An Analysis in Terms of Motifs, Structure, and Style." M.A. thesis, George Peabody College for Teachers, 1970.

"Uncle Fate Biography is Pickett History." *Pickett County Press,* 15 Jun. 1972, p. 4.

Walker, Garnet. *Exploring Wayne County.* Privately published. Rpt. and rev., 1966.

Watson, Eddie H. "There and Now." Willow Grove Homecoming Edition, *Livingston Enterprise,* 31 Aug. 1969.

Waugh, Butler H. "The Child and the Snake in North America." *Norveg,* 7 (1960), 153–82.

Webb, W. Prescott. "Notes on the Folklore of Texas." *Journal of American Folklore,* 28 (1915), 290–99.

Wells, Joseph W. *History of Cumberland County.* Louisville: Standard Printing Co., 1947. Rpt. Burkesville, Ky.: David Wells, 1971.

———. *This or That.* Louisville: Standard Printing Co., 1966.

Wilgus, D.K., and Lynwood Montell. "Beanie Short: A Civil War Chronicle in Legend and Song." In *American Folk Legend: A Symposium,* ed. Wayland D. Hand. Berkeley: Univ. of California Press, 1971, pp. 133–56.

———. "Clure and Joe Williams: Legend and Blues Song." *Journal of American Folklore,* 81 (Oct.–Dec. 1968) 295–315.

Wilhelm, Eugene. "Animal Drives in the Southern Highlands." *Mountain Life and Work*, 42 (Summer 1966), 6–11.

Wirt, Alvin B. *The Upper Cumberland of Pioneer Times.* Washington, D.C.: Alvin B. Wirt, 1954.

Wright, J.C. *Autobiography of Reverend Absalom B. Wright of the Holston Conference, M.E. Church.* Cincinnati: Cranston and Curts, 1896.

Notes

Notes to the Introduction

1. Books which successfully combine the methodologies of folklore and oral history include William Lynwood Montell, *The Saga of Coe Ridge: A Study in Oral History* (Knoxville: Univ. of Tennessee Press, 1970); Gladys-Marie Fry, *Night Riders in Black Folk History* (Knoxville: Univ. of Tennessee Press, 1975); George E. Evans, *The Days That We Have Seen* (London: Faber and Faber, 1975); Edward D. Ives, *Joe Scott: The Woodsman-Songmaker* (Urbana: Univ. of Illinois Press, 1978); and Charles W. Joyner, *Slave Folklife: Antebellum Black Culture in the South Carolina Low Country* (Urbana: Univ. of Illinois Press, 1981).

2. In *The Saga of Coe Ridge*, my pioneering work demonstrating that oral sources can successfully be employed to reconstruct history in the absence of formal records, I outlined five cardinal tenets regarding such uses of the spoken word, four of which bear repeating here: (1) narrators do not consciously falsify information; (2) they often improvise details to preserve the core of historical truth; (3) several oral accounts of an event should be searched and compared for points of agreement and disagreement to arrive at a composite account; and (4) narrators and other community residents date events by association with other events that occur at about the same time (pp. 192–97).

With Barbara Allen, I recently considered these points at greater length, devoting an entire chapter in the book *From Memory to History: Using Oral Sources in Local Historical Research* (Nashville: American Association for State and Local History, 1981) to the internal and external tests which may be applied to oral narratives in attempting to assess their historical validity (pp. 67–87). We devoted an additional chapter in that work to the question of interpreting narrator values, attitudes, beliefs, and feelings reflected in such stories (pp. 89–100).

3. Escar Coe, tape-recorded interview, Burkesville, Ky., Oct. 30, 1975; Leon Anderson, tape-recorded interview, Gainesboro, Tenn., Sept. 19, 1975. Unless otherwise noted, all of the interviews were conducted by the author; unless otherwise stated in the notes, all of the original tapes are housed in the Archive of

Folklore, Folklife, and Oral History, Western Kentucky University, Bowling Green.

4. *Clay County Tribune,* Dec. 30, 1899, p. 2.

5. *Celina Herald,* Sept. 13, 1906.

6. *Ibid.*

7. The insider–outsider points of view in historical reconstruction are discussed at length in *From Memory to History,* pp. 8–14.

Notes to Chapter 1

1. Landon Anderson, "Brief History of Clay County [Tennessee]," *Celina Globe,* ca. 1969, p. 1; also, Landon Anderson, tape-recorded interview, Celina, Tenn., Jan. 31, 1976.

2. Willie Pyle, tape-recorded interview by Linda White, Jamestown, Tenn., July 3, 1972.

3. Gladys Williams, Pall Mall, Tenn., Aug. 7, 1978. Coonrod Pyle may not have been a Long Hunter but simply the earliest person to discover the Wolf River Valley. Aaron E. Pyles, in *Genealogy of the Coonrod Pyle Family* (Campbellsville, Ky., Privately published by the author, 1978), pp. 8, 11, records that Coonrod was born in 1766. Such being the case, he could not have been one of the original Long Hunters. The story of the stolen bride may be a migratory legend; the account of the gold buried in a keg and then stolen most assuredly is. Both legends are indexed in Appendix A.

4. William Curtis Stone, Sr., "Historical Sketches of Clay County, Tennessee" (unpubl. manuscript), p. 1. Manuscript provided by Landon Anderson.

5. A.L. Dale, "Memoirs of A.L. 'High' Dale" (unpubl. manuscript), p. 1.

6. Tim Huddleston, *History of Pickett County, Tennessee* (Collegedale, Tenn.: College Press, 1973), p. 1.

7. George Allen Knight, *My Album of Memories* (Knoxville: Southeastern Composition Services, 1971), p. 4.

8. The Big South Fork settlement was centered on a stockade that was built at Parmleysville to protect white settlers. Another stockade for defense in the Kentucky region was built in 1790 three miles south of present-day Columbia. For more information about these stockades, consult Garnet Walker, *Exploring Wayne County* (Monticello, Ky.: Privately published, 1960), p. 3; also see Judge Joseph W. Wells, *History of Cumberland County* (Louisville: Standard Printing Co.; 1947), p. 10.

9. Walker, *Exploring Wayne County,* p. 3.

10. Albert V. Goodpasture, "Overton County" (address delivered at Livingston, Tenn., July 4, 1876); rpt. Nashville, 1954, pp. 5–6.

11. Albert R. Hogue, *One Hundred Years in the Cumberland Mountains along the Continental Divide* (McMinnville, Tenn.: Standard Printing Co., 1933), p. 7.

12. Albert V. and W.H. Goodpasture, *The Life of Jefferson Dillard Goodpasture* (Nashville: Cumberland Presbyterian Publishing House, 1897), p. 7. Prophetically enough, the present town of Sparta in White County, Tenn., was laid out in city lots in 1802, while the area was still an Indian reservation. See Monroe Seals, *History of White County* (Sparta, Tenn.: Privately published by Mrs. Monroe Seals, 1935), p. 6.

13. A fuller account of their civilization is given in George Allen Knight, *Our Wonderful Overton County Heritage* (Knoxville: Southeastern Composition Services, 1972), pp. 5–10.

14. Hogue, *One Hundred Years*, pp. 9–10. Hogue, born in the early 1870s, talked with Samuel Walker of Scott County, one of the soldiers who assisted in the removal of the Indians to the west of the Mississippi. Hogue recounts some stories obtained during that visit in *History of Fentress County, Tennessee* (Nashville, 1916; rpt. Baltimore: Regional Publishing Co., 1975), pp. 61–62. The contest for the maiden is likely a migratory legend and is included in Appendix A.

15. Sarah Jane Koger, tape-recorded interview, Jamestown, Tenn., Aug. 3, 1979.

16. Price Kirkpatrick, tape-recorded interview, Tompkinsville, Ky., Aug. 21, 1961.

17. Hogue, *History of Fentress County*, p. 63. Davy Crockett's personal history recounts the same story but locates it in Hawkins County, Tenn. This is a mistake on Crockett's part, according to Hogue. The account is included in Appendix A as a possible migratory legend.

18. Tape-recorded interview, Jamestown, Tenn., Aug. 3, 1979.

19. Verda Cook Wright, Letter to the Editor, *Pickett County Press*, Aug. 4, 1966; rpt. in Huddleston, *History of Pickett County*, p. 144. For a note regarding the use of gunpowder to keep away wolves, see Appendix A. The story of the panther in the tree is strikingly similar to a migratory legend identified in note 20 and listed in Appendix A.

20. Ona Barton, tape-recorded interview, Jamestown, Tenn., Aug. 3, 1979. For texts, more detailed comments, and a bibliographic note on panther legends, consult Montell, *Saga of Coe Ridge*, pp. 87, 104–105. See also Appendix A.

21. Sarah Jane Koger, Aug. 3, 1979.

22. Lena Howell Martin, tape-recorded interview, Gainesboro, Tenn., March 12, 1976. For a note regarding the belief that snakes will suck cattle, see Appendix A.

23. Tape-recorded interview, Gainesboro, Tenn., March 12, 1976; also Mrs. Albert Bilbrey, Gainesboro, March 12, 1976. For a note regarding the belief that snakes kept in corn cribs will kill rodents, see Appendix A.

24. March 12, 1976.

25. March 12, 1976. For notes regarding the beliefs that whiskey and chicken flesh are effective against snake bite, see Appendix A.

26. This legend complex as known in North America was studied by Butler Waugh, "The Child and the Snake in North America," *Norveg*, 7 (1960), 153–82. A migratory legend note is included in Appendix A.

27. Elsworth Carter, tape-recorded interview, Rock Bridge, Monroe County, Ky., June 10, 1960. This story contains Motif D1338.2.1, "Rejuvenation by Juice of Plant," and has been included as a migratory legend in Appendix A.

28. Published sources based on oral tradition include Knight, *Overton County Heritage*, p. 56; Seals, *White County*, p. 15; E.R. Gaskin, "Folktales of the Kentucky Hills" (unpub. manuscript, 1968), p. 4. A lengthy oral account of clearing and preparing a new ground was provided by Richard Blair, tape-recorded interview by Robyn West, Jamestown, Ky., Sept. 23, 1976. Original tape and transcription on deposit in the Kentucky State Library, Frankfort.

29. Virgil Beaty, tape-recorded interview, Byrdstown, Tenn., Jan. 5, 1976.

30. Albert Bilbrey, tape-recorded interview, Gainesboro, Tenn., March 12, 1976.

31. All of these names are from the author's own family oral traditions.

32. Bilbrey, March 12, 1976.

33. Landon Anderson, Lena Martin, Mr. and Mrs. Albert Bilbrey, March 12, 1976.

34. Clyde "Bully" White, tape-recorded interview by Karen and Sharon Walden, Center Point, Monroe County, Ky., Dec. 19, 1973.

35. Richard Blair, Sept. 23, 1976.

36. Lewis David Bandy, "Folklore of Macon County, Tennessee," M.A. thesis, George Peabody College for Teachers, 1940, pp. 48–49.

37. Prospective proprietors had to first appear in court and petition the local authorities for the right to construct a mill. An investigation team was delegated to examine the site and report that no damage would be done to the property of others, and that the passage of fish and navigation vehicles would not be obstructed. See Lawrence R. Davenport, *Local Historical Research by a Class in Local Historical Research* (Somerset, Ky: Somerset Community college, 1966).

38. Gaskin, "Folktales," p. 2.

39. Will H. Jones, tape-recorded interview by Jewell Thomas, Burkesville, Ky., April 20, 1977. Original tape and transcription on deposit in the Kentucky State Library, Frankfort.

40. Charlie Burtram, tape-recorded interview, Sunnybrook, Ky., Nov. 10, 1978.

41. Alvin B. Wirt, *The Upper Cumberland of Pioneer Times* (Washington, D.C.: Privately published, 1954), p. 41.

42. Gladys Stone, tape-recorded interview, Celina, Tenn., April 16, 1976.

43. Landon Anderson, March 12, 1976.

44. Lena Martin and Landon Anderson, March 12, 1976.

45. A.V. Luttrell and E.R. Gaskin, tape-recorded interview, Russell Springs, Ky., June 19, 1976.

46. Landon Anderson, March 12, 1976; see also Knight, *Overton County Heritage*, p. 151.

47. Mrs. Matt Shearer, tape-recorded interview by Elizabeth Simpson, Monticello, Ky., May 13, 1977. Original tape and transcription on deposit in the Kentucky State Library, Frankfort.

48. Arnold Watson, tape-recorded interview, Kettle, Ky., Dec. 26, 1975; Gilbert Wallace, tape-recorded interview by Carolyn Best, Edmonton, Ky., Feb. 16, 1976; Ruth Van Zant, tape-recorded interview by Carolyn Best, Edmonton, Ky., Feb. 8, 1976.

49. Clyde White, Dec. 19, 1973.

50. W. Kenneth Irvin, tape-recorded interview, Creelsboro, Ky., Feb. 4, 1976.

51. James F. Butler, tape-recorded interview, Cloyd's Landing, Ky., Feb. 27, 1976.

52. Vada Tooley Page, tape-recorded interview by Patricia Walden, Tompkinsville, Ky., Nov. 28, 1973. Her father, Coyle Tooley, ran a store and a huckster wagon before and after 1900.

53. James F. Butler, June 21, 1978.

54. Richard Blair, Sept. 23, 1976.

55. Ruth Van Zant, Feb. 8, 1976.

56. Arlo Barnett, tape-recorded interview by Wilma Waters, Honey Bee, McCreary County, Ky., July 14, 1978. Original tape and transcription on deposit in the Kentucky State Library, Frankfort.

57. Henry Powell, tape-recorded interview by Bennie Coffey, Wayne County, Ky., Feb. 12, 1979. Original tape and transcription on deposit in the Kentucky State Library, Frankfort.

58. Daily Crouch, tape-recorded interview, Forbus, Tenn., Jan. 5, 1976.

59. Ira Bell, tape-recorded interview, Monticello, Ky., Sept. 24, 1976.

60. Ira Bell, Sept. 24, 1976.

61. Kentucky Writer's Project, *Fairs and Fairmakers of Kentucky* (Frankfort: Kentucky, 1942), Dept. of Agriculture, p. 68.

62. Glenn Barton, tape-recorded interview, Jamestown, Tenn., June 18, 1979.

63. Hiram Parrish, tape-recorded interview, Burkesville, Ky., Dec. 23, 1975.

64. Quoted by Hiram Parrish, Dec. 23, 1975.

65. Eugene Wilhelm, "Animal Drives in the Southern Highlands," *Mountain Life and Work*, 42 (Summer 1966), 12.

66. Elvin P. Byrd, tape-recorded interview, Lee's Chapel, Clinton County, Ky., Feb. 27, 1976.

67. Henry H. Rogers, tape-recorded interview, Jamestown, Tenn., June 18, 1979.

68. Carlos Storie, tape-recorded interview, Forbus, Tenn., Jan. 5, 1976.

69. Mary Littrell, tape-recorded interview, Monticello, Ky., March 14, 1980.

70. Perry M. Cross, tape-recorded interview by David Cross, Albany, Ky., May 10, 1980.

71. Mary Littrell, March 14, 1980.

72. Henry H. Rogers, June 18, 1979.

73. Sarah Jane Koger, June 18, 1979.

74. Sam Watson, tape-recorded interview by Kay Harbison, Summer Shade, Ky., July 1, 1971.

75. Judge Cass Walden, tape-recorded interview by Carolyn Best, Edmonton, Ky., Jan. 31, 1976; Clyde White, Dec. 19 1973.

76. Sam Watson, July 1, 1971.

77. Will Peavyhouse, tape-recorded interview, Buffalo Cove, Fentress County, Tenn., Jan. 31, 1976.

78. Willie Montell, tape-recorded interview, Tompkinsville, Ky., Jan. 15, 1977.

79. Carlos Storie, Jan. 5, 1976.

80. James F. Butler and Hiram Parrish, tape-recorded interview, Cloyd's Landing, Ky., Feb. 27, 1976.

81. Lena Martin, March 12, 1976.

82. Virgil Beaty, Jason Crouch, and Edd Moody, tape-recorded interview, Moodyville, Tenn., Jan. 5, 1976.

83. Edd Moody, Jan. 5, 1976.

84. Jason Crouch, Jan. 5, 1976.

85. Quoted in Ernest M. Lawson, *Awakening of Cumberland County, or The Last Fifty Years* (Burkesville, Ky.: Cumberland County Printing Co., 1973), p. 161.

86. Joshua Baxter, tape-recorded interview by Patricia Walden, Hestand, Ky., Dec. 19, 1975.

87. Arnold Watson, Jan. 9, 1976.

88. Arnold Watson, Jan. 9, 1976; Gladys Stone, April 16, 1976.

89. Hiram Parrish, Feb. 27, 1976.

90. Gladys Stone, April 16, 1976.

91. James F. Butler, Feb. 27, 1976; Gladys Stone, April 16, 1976; Virgil Beaty, Jan. 5, 1976.

92. *Kentucky Folklore Record*, 12 (1966), 87–93.

93. James F. Butler, Feb. 27, 1976.

94. John I. Cummings, tape-recorded interview, Lee's Chapel, Clinton County, Ky., Feb. 28, 1976.

95. Several published sources describe the harvesting and threshing processes. See, e.g., Joseph W. Wells, *This or That* (Louisville: Standard Printing Co., 1966), p. 10; Seals, *White County*, pp. 14–15; Huddleston, *History of Pickett County*, p. 41; John E. Leslie, "Early Days in Monroe County" (unpubl. manuscript, ca. 1930), n.p.

96. Willie Montell, Jan. 15, 1977.

97. Huddleston, *History of Pickett County*, p. 41.

98. Virgil Beaty, Jan. 5, 1976.

99. A.L. Dale, "Old Time Steamboating on the Cumberland River" (article from the files of Mr. and Mrs. Butler Upton), p. 4.

100. Carlos Storie, Jan. 5, 1976; Virgil Beaty, Jan. 5, 1976.

101. Charles S. Guthrie presents the vocabulary of tobacco growing in "Tobacco: Cash Crop of the Cumberland Valley," *Kentucky Folklore Record*, 14 (1968), 38–43.

102. Willie Rich, tape-recorded interview, Faix, Tenn., Jan. 6, 1976.

Notes to Chapter 2

1. J.C. Wright, *Autobiography of Rev. Absalom B. Wright of the Holston Conference, M.E. Church* (Cincinnati: Cranston and Curts, 1896), p. 41. The population of what is now Pickett County, Tenn., was virtually depleted in this manner; see Huddleston, *History of Pickett County*, p. 36.

2. Cordell Hull, *The Memoirs of Cordell Hull* (New York, Macmillan, 1948), I, p. 7; Hogue, *History of Fentress County*, p. 48, observes, "There is scarcely a public road in this section that has not been marked by the blood of a soldier."

3. Published sources of information regarding the battle at Mill Springs are many, including Thomas L. Connelly, *Army of the Heartland; the Army of Tennessee, 1861–1862* (Baton Rouge: Louisiana State Univ. Press, 1967), pp. 97–99; Lowell H. Harrison, *The Civil War in Kentucky* (Lexington: Univ. of Kentucky Press, 1976), pp. 23–28; G. Lee McClain, *Military History of Kentucky* (Frankfort: Military Dept. of Kentucky, 1939), pp. 174–75.

4. Jean Dicken, tape-recorded interview by Eric Dicken, Albany, Ky., May 11, 1980.

5. Jenny Hail, tape-recorded interview, n.d., Pulaski County, Ky. The original tape and transcription are on deposit in the Kentucky State Library, Frankfort.

227

6. Quinn Davidson, tape-recorded interview, Chanute, Pickett County, Tenn., Jan. 6, 1976.

7. Cordell Dishman, tape-recorded interview, Sunnybrook, Ky., Nov. 10, 1978.

8. "Away up on Fishing Creek" was sung by Mrs. S. Hagan, Wayne County, Ky., in 1938 and recorded by Gertrude Vogler for the Federal Writers Project.

9. "The Ballad of Mill Springs" is identified as item A 13 in Malcolm Laws' index of *Native American Ballads* (Philadelphia: American Folklore Society, 1964), p. 125. "The Battle of Mill Springs" was recorded somewhere in Tennessee by Howard W. Odum from the singing of J.D. Arthur. Another wartime song, actually only a flute tune to which words were locally applied, was called "Little Jimmy Walden." According to T.K. Chism, approximately 90 years old, pencil and pad interview, Tompkinsville, Ky., Mar. 12, 1958, Jimmy Walden was flutist for Kentucky's 37th Infantry Battalion, which mustered at Tompkinsville. The words are:

> Little Jimmy Walden,
>   Toodle lollie day;
> Old Billy Patterson,
>   Toodle lollie day;
> fulton, Fulton,
>   Toodle lollie day.

10. Lynwood Montell, *Monroe County History, 1820–1970* (Tompkinsville, Ky.: Tompkinsville Lions Club, 1970), pp. 23–28.

11. Arnold Watson and Hiram Parrish, tape-recorded interview, Kettle, Cumberland County, Ky., Jan. 9, 1976. This legend is listed in Appendix A as a possible migratory legend.

12. Clarence Rush, tape-recorded interview, Bear Creek, Cumberland County, Ky., Jan. 9, 1976.

13. Bethel Holloway, tape-recorded interview by Brad Simpson, David Storie and Ann Zachari, Calfkiller Valley, Putnam County, Tenn., Nov. 9, 1979.

14. Jenny Hail. Both of these stories have certain earmarks of migratory legends and are so identified in Appendix A.

15. Published sources utilized in this sketch of Champ Ferguson's life include J.P. Austin, *The Blue and the Gray: Sketches of the Unwritten History of the Great American Civil War* (Atlanta: Franklin Printing and Publishing Co., 1899), pp. 89–91; Bromfield L. Ridley, "Champ Ferguson," *Confederate Veteran*, 7 (Oct. 1899), 442–43; Basil Duke, *A History of Morgan's Cavalry* (Cincinnati: Miami Printing and Publishing Co., 1867), pp. 182–83, 416–18; Will T. Hale and Dixon L. Merritt, *A History of Tennessee and Tennesseans* (Chicago: Lewis Publishing Co., 1913), III, pp. 644, 650–57; Augusta P. Johnson, *A Century of Wayne County, Kentucky, 1800–1900* (Louisville: Standard Printing Co., 1939), pp. 131, 136; Thurman Sensing, *Champ Ferguson, Confederate Guerrilla* (Nashville: Vanderbilt Univ. Press, 1942); Howard Swiggett, *The Rebel Raider: Life of John Hunt Morgan* (Indianapolis: Bobbs-Merrill, 1934), p. 60; E. Sergeant Tarrant, *The Wild Raiders of the First Kentucky Cavalry* (Lexington: Henry Clay Press, 1969), pp. 39, 68, 76, 132, 158, 203.

Tape-recorded oral traditions came from the following persons whose names will not be used in connection with specific information because of persisting personal and family tensions over Champ Ferguson: Landon Anderson, Celina, Tenn., Feb. 7, 1976; Reece Bilbrey, interviewed by Linda White, Static, Pickett County, Tenn., July 4, 1972; Quinn Davidson, Jan. 6, 1976; Jean Dicken, May 11, 1980; Bethel Holloway, Nov. 9, 1979; Edd Moody, Moodyville, Pickett County, Tenn., Jan 5, 1976; Will Peavyhouse, Buffalo Cove, Fentress County, Tenn., Jan. 31, 1976; Ray B. Phillips, interviewed by Linda White, Byrdstown, Tenn., July 13, 1972; Willie Pyle, interviewed by Linda White, Jamestown, Tenn., July 3, 1972; Clarence Rush, Jan. 9, 1976; Arnold Watson, Dec. 26, 1975; Walter E. Webb, Celina, Tenn., Feb. 7, 1976; Anne H. Winningham, interviewed by Timothy Perdew, Albany, Ky., May 10, 1980; Luther M. York, interviewed by Linda White, Three Forks of the Wolf, Fentress County, Tenn., July 1, 1972.

16. One biased published source claims that the daughter was murdered while the mother pleaded for the child's life. Two other published sources claim that the 12 men (one states 16) killed them both, then burned their bodies in the house.

17. Jean Dicken, May 11, 1980.

18. There is speculation that Smith may have been Champ's brother, James. George William Patterson, a great-grandson of James Ferguson, wrote, however, in a letter to the author on Feb. 1, 1981, that Lt. Smith was a brother-in-law of Champ's first wife. Patterson also believes that it was Smith who was in charge of the 12 men who insulted Champ's wife and daughter.

19. Seals, *White County*, p. 102, claims that Ann later married George Metcalf.

20. The survival portion of the Ferguson legend is not unlike the recent rumors that, instead of being burned to death, Hitler sought refuge in South America and that President Kennedy still lives on although in an unnatural state. While no parallels to Ferguson's escape from the gallows have been uncovered, this sounds strangely like a migratory legend and is so identified in Appendix A.

21. A study of his life and activities during the Civil War was made by D.K. Wilgus and Lynwood Montell, "Beanie Short: A Civil War Chronicle in Legend and Song," in *American Folk Legend: A Symposium*, ed. Wayland D. Hand (Berkeley: Univ. of California Press, 1971), pp. 133–56. Recent information about Short's activities and death was tape recorded from Clarence Rush, Jan. 9, 1976; Arnold Watson, Jan. 9, 1976; Joshua K. Baxter, interviewed by Patricia Walden, Hestand, Ky., Dec. 19, 1975; Landon Anderson and Walter E. Webb, Celina, Tenn., Feb. 7, 1976; Edith Williams, Tompkinsville, Ky., May 14, 1976; James F. Butler, Cloyd's Landing, Cumberland County, Ky., Feb. 27, 1976; and Ronnie Bryant, interviewed by Mitzi Robertson, Tompkinsville, Ky., Dec. 15, 1973.

22. Clarence Rush, Jan. 9, 1976.

23. Arnold Watson, Dec. 26, 1975.

24. Arnold Watson, Jan. 9, 1976. The ineradicable bloodstain which resulted as a result of the killing of Short and Ashlock is Motif E422.1.11.5.1(e).

25. Sung by Mrs. Louise Sartin, Willow Shade, Metcalfe County, Ky., July 6, 1956, for D.K. Wilgus, then of Western Kentucky University. Tape courtesy of Dr. Wilgus.

26. Goodpasture and Goodpasture, *Life of Jefferson Dillard Goodpasture*, p. 75.

229

27. Albert R. Hogue, *Mark Twain's Obedstown and Knobs of Tennessee: A History of Jamestown and Fentress County, Tennessee* (Jamestown, Tenn: Cumberland Printing Co., 1950), p. 60; Huddleston, *Pickett County*, p. 27.

28. Hogue, *History of Jamestown and Fentress County*, pp. 46–47; Amp Poore described these events to Hogue personally in 1929.

29. Will Peavyhouse, Jan. 31, 1976.

30. Tape-recorded interviews, Jan. 5, Jan. 6, March 27, 1976.

31. Hogue, *History of Jamestown and Fentress County*, p. 48, mentions these episodes attributed to the Wolf Gang.

32. Sarah Jane Koger, tape-recorded interview, Jamestown, Tenn., Aug. 3, 1979.

33. Reece Bilbrey, July 4, 1972.

34. Quinn Davidson, Jan. 6, 1976.

35. Tape-recorded interview, Jan. 6, 1976.

36. Hogue, *History of Jamestown and Fentress County*, p. 48. Hogue's authority was Amp Poore, a contemporary who personally recounted the Wolf Gang's story for Hogue.

37. Edd Moody, Jason Crouch, Hiram Greene, tape-recorded interview, Moodyville, Tenn., Jan. 5, 1976.

38. Emma Crabtree, tape-recorded interview, Bowling Green, Ky., May 19, 1976.

39. Judge Ira Bell, tape-recorded interview, Monticello, Ky., Sept. 24, 1976.

40. Judge Cass Walden, tape-recorded interview by Carolyn Best, Edmonton, Ky., Jan. 31, 1976.

Notes to Chapter 3

1. Knight, *Album of Memories*, p. 115.

2. Between 1885 and 1895 White County, Tenn., alone exported more than $1 million worth of walnut timber, aside from great quantities of other timber. See Seals, *History of White County*, p. 60. During the period 1890 to 1910, Clay County's actual property value exceeded $11 million. After the timber was cut over and erosion claimed much of the topsoil, the property value fell below $2 million. See Hampton Maxey, "History of Clay County [Tennessee]" (unpubl. manuscript), p. 4.

3. Willie Rich, tape-recorded interview, Faix, Pickett County, Tenn., Jan. 6, 1976. Also, tape-recorded interviews with Hugh Kyle, Celina, Tenn., Feb. 12, 1976; Elvin Byrd, Lee's Chapel, Clinton County, Ky., Feb. 27, 1976; and James F. Butler, Cloyd's Landing, Cumberland County, Ky., Feb. 27, 1976, all attest to the importance of logging to the area's economy.

4. Knight, *Album of Memories*, p. 100.

5. Virgil Beaty, tape-recorded interview, Forbus, Tenn., Jan. 5, 1976.

6. Hiram Parrish, tape-recorded interview, Cloyd's Landing, Cumberland County, Ky., Feb. 27, 1976. Similar testimonies were stated in tape-recorded interviews with John I. Cummings, Lee's Chapel, Clinton County, Ky., Feb. 28, 1976; and Edd Moody, Moodyville, Tenn., Jan. 5, 1976.

7. [Leland Johnson], "Engineers on the Twin Rivers: 1769–1975" (unpubl. manuscript, United States Army Corps of Engineers, Nashville, 1975), p. 304.

8. Jesse Rich identified some of these men in his booklet, *Cutting Rafting, and Running Logs Down the Obey River, 1880–1920* (n.p.: Privately published, 1972), p. 4. Those identified from the Celina, Tenn., area were Captain A.C. Dale, William Hull, Hugh H. Kyle, J.D.H. Hatcher, Captain Jim Davis, Pleas and Hobart Harrison; from Gainesboro, Tenn., were Colonel M.L. Gore and George Birdwell; from Kentucky were J.M. Stephenson and J.A. Vaughn from Rowena; and Will Henry and L.C. Ross, location unknown. Others from Celina, identified by William Curtis Stone, Sr., "History of Clay County, Tennessee" (unpubl. manuscript, 1962), p. 9, include W.C. Keen, Jim Gamble, Buck Baker, Clabe Beaty, and M.M. Smith.

9. See, e.g., the oral testimony of Virgil Beaty, Jan. 5, 1976. Saw mills were in the Upper Cumberland region as early as the 1820s. Steam-driven mills were there by the 1850s. Varney Andrews of Celina, Tenn., chartered a steamboat and moved his family and steam-powered mill to Texas in 1858, according to Butler Upton, tape-recorded interview, Celina, Jan. 30, 1976. Upton was quoting from a local manuscript written by Will L. Brown.

10. Rich, *Cutting, Rafting and Running Logs*, p. 11.

11. Willie Rich, Jan. 6, 1976, dated the birth of Obey River rafting about 1885, since his father, who was born in 1870, helped as a very young man to open the Obey to rafting activities. Hogue, *History of Jamestown and Fentress County*, p. 17, claims that Obey River rafting activities date from 1870.

12. Statistics extracted from J.B. Killibrew, *Introduction to the Resources of Tennessee* (Nashville: Tavel and Howell, 1874) are cited in Rich, *Cutting, Rafting and Running Logs*, p. 4. Rich notes that in 1884 Nashville received 1,400 rafts from the Upper Cumberland. That year Nashville mills sawed a total of 86,165,000 board feet of lumber.

13. Jack Knox, *The Riverman* (Nashville: Abingdon Press, 1971), p. 14.

14. Rich, *Cutting, Rafting and Running Logs*, pp. 9–10; Carlos Storie, tape-recorded interview, Forbus, Tenn., Jan. 5, 1976; Virgil Beaty, Jan. 5, 1976; John I. Cummings, Feb. 28, 1976; Willie Rich, Jan. 6, 1976.

15. Edd Moody, Jan. 5, 1976.

16. Rich, *Cutting, Rafting and Running Logs*, p. 10.

17. Virgil Beaty, Jan. 5, 1976.

18. Steven A. Schulman, "Logging the Upper Cumberland River Valley: A Folk Industry," M.A. thesis (Western Kentucky Univ., 1973), p. 39.

19. Will Peavyhouse, tape-recorded interview, Fentress County, Tenn., Jan. 31, 1976. Joseph W. Wells, *This or That* (Louisville: Standard Printing Co., 1966), p. 18, states the rule: "Get diameter at small end in inches, subtract four; multiply this by half of the last diameter; multiply this by length in feet and divide by eight."

20. E.R. Gaskin, tape-recorded interview, Russell Springs, Ky., June 19, 1976. Hiram Parrish and J.F. Butler agreed that this was a buyer's rule, not a seller's rule.

21. Virgil Beaty, Jan. 5, 1976; also Jason Crouch, tape-recorded interview, Moodyville, Ky. Jan. 5, 1976.

22. Rich, *Cutting, Rafting and Running Logs*, p. 10. Lieberman, Loveman, and O'Brien was the company to make the deepest impact on regional historical legendry, but numerous other companies, mainly Nashville-based, either bought logs onsite or purchased rafts from the Upper Cumberland in Nashville, including Indiana Lumber, John B. Ransom, Norwell and Wallace, Farris, Goldhurner-

Leauman, Hicks and Green, Kirkpatrick, Farris Hardwood, Prewitt-Spurr, Goldberg and Rich, Streight and Sutherland, and Nashville Hardwood. B and B Lumber Co. was located in Jamestown, Tenn.; its chief buyer was Will Peavyhouse. Stave and tie companies are dealt with elsewhere in this chapter.

23. Rich, *Cutting, Rafting and Running Logs*, p. 9.

24. Hugh Kyle, Feb. 12, 1976.

25. Bernice Mitchell, letter to Lynwood Montell, Mar. 21, 1976.

26. Hugh Kyle, Feb. 12, 1976.

27. Willie Rich, Jan. 6, 1976; Will Peavyhouse, Jan. 31, 1976. Prices per 1,000 board feet paid to the farmers varied according to the year and the species of logs. Generally the prices ranged from $1.00 to $20, according to various sources.

A.L. Dale, "Old-Time Steamboating" (unpubl. manuscript), p. 6, writes that log buyers made a lot of money while farmers made very little. Log buyers received around $60 per 1,000 at Nashville during zenith years of the timber industry.

28. Will Peavyhouse, Jan. 31, 1976.

29. This manner of deceit was also attested to by James F. Butler, Feb. 27, 1976.

30. James F. Butler, Feb. 27, 1976.

31. Judge Cass Walden, tape-recorded interview by Carolyn Best, Edmonton, Ky., Jan. 31, 1976. Pirates were seldom caught and jailed, according to Elvin Byrd, Feb. 27, 1976.

32. Virgil Beaty, Jan. 5, 1976; Garnet Walker, tape-recorded interview, Monticello, Ky., Sept. 10, 1976.

33. The *Southern Lumberman*, March 1, 1882, p. 2, contains an account of log piracy following a flood on the Cumberland. An agent of Arch Mancourt and Company, Burnside, reported finding many of his company's logs with the brand still on them made into rafts by parties having no right to them.

34. Elvin Byrd, Feb. 27, 1976.

35. Gladys Stone, tape-recorded interview, Celina, Tenn., April 16, 1976.

36. Kyle J. Cherry, "Raft Tide" (unpubl. manuscript), pp. 3–5; Arnold Watson, tape-recorded interview, Kettle, Ky., Dec. 26, 1975, described how his father shod oxen by using a winch and cables to hoist their hindquarters into the air.

37. Edd Moody, Jan. 5, 1976; Hiram Green, tape-recorded interview, Moodyville, Tenn., Jan. 5, 1976; J.D. Lowrey, Moodyville, Mar. 27, 1976; Eula Gilreath, tape-recorded interview, Moodyville, Jan. 5, 1976; Coyle Copeland and Jonathan Allred, tape-recorded interviews, Crawford, Ky., June 18, 1976; Arnold Watson, Dec. 26, 1975.

38. Rich, *Cutting, Rafting and Running Logs*, p. 7; corroborated orally by A.V. Luttrell, tape-recorded interview, Russell Springs, Ky., June 19, 1976.

39. Elvin Byrd, Feb. 27, 1976.

40. Willie Rich, Jan. 6, 1976.

41. Lloyd "Dutch" Baker, tape-recorded interview, Burnside, Ky., Oct. 12, 1976. Willie Rich, Jan. 6, 1976, described a boom in essentially the same terms.

42. Bernice Mitchell, tape-recorded interview, Burnside, Ky., Oct. 12, 1976.

43. Willie Rich, Jan. 6, 1976.

44. *Cumberland Commercial*, Nov. 26, 1904. According to Bernice Mitchell, Oct. 12, 1976, the Chicago Veneer Co. was sold to Hoffman Veneer Co., which in turn passed ownership to the Burnside Veneer Co. The latter closed as a result of the construction of the Wolf Creek Dam.

45. Hugh Kyle, Feb. 12, 1976; Landon Anderson, tape-recorded interview, Celina, Tenn., Feb. 1, 1977.

46. Will Peavyhouse, Jan. 31, 1976; James F. Butler, Feb. 27, 1976; and Arnold Watson, Jan. 9, 1976.

47. Cherry, "Raft Tide," p. 9.

48. Rafts were constructed with the logs lined up perpendicular with the river and put under small oak or hickory saplings, 4 to 6 inches in diameter, called *whaling* or *stringers*. One length of whaling, overlapping at the ends, was placed across the top of the logs on both sides of the raft 12 to 18 inches from the end of the logs. A five-quarter hole was drilled through the whaling and into each log by means of an auger (or gimlet). A raft pin (a seasoned white hickory pin, 8 to 18 inches long, trimmed to a sharp point on one end and to a head on the other) was driven through the hole in the whaling and into the log, much as a railroad spike is driven into a crosstie. The men who owned the logs furnished the raft pins. A number of people, generally old men, whittled raft pins with Bowie knives, drawknives, or jackhorses and sold them at 20 to 25 cents per 100 count. When seasoned, the pins were hard enough to drive into any log and, after swelling, were virtually impossible to pull out.

As a precaution against loss, sinker logs were rafted with *chaindogs*, metal chains of 8 or 9 links containing a metal spike on each end. The chaindog was placed over the whaling and the spikes were driven into the log on each side until the chain was tight over the whaling.

Oars were used to guide the rafts down the river. On a small, single-tier raft there were 2 oars, one on the bow and one on the stern. Rafts measuring 3 to 5 tiers in width often had 3 oars on the bow and 2 on the stern. Oar stems, 8 to 9 inches in diameter, were made from white poplar saplings 16 to 18 feet in length. The butt end of the oar was trimmed and tapered to a thickness of about 3 inches and was inserted into the mortise in the oar stem and secured with wooden pins. The end that went into the water to serve as the oar blade was tapered to about 1 inch in thickness.

Holes were bored in the middle of the bow and stern logs, and the oar stanchions were positioned into the holes and secured to the raft by means of a board called a *surge pin*. Another piece, called a *bridle*, was used to brace the oar stem. The entire steering apparatus was called a *sweep*; it required at least 2 men to handle it during periods of stress. Information provided from tape-recorded interviews with Virgil Beaty, Jan. 5, 1976; James F. Butler, Feb. 27, 1976; Elvin Byrd, Feb. 27, 1976; John I. Cummings, Feb. 28, 1976; Hiram Parrish, Feb. 27, 1976; Will Peavyhouse, Jan. 31, 1976. Beaty provided considerable detail about the making of raft pins: "They had a shaving horse they called it, a piece of timber eight or ten feet long and two holes bored into one end of it and a log put in so it'd set up there. And then they had a hole mortised in that; they called it a nigger's head. . . . That would hold the raft pins so they could shave it with a drawknife. And there's old men that followed making raft pins." Cummings addressed the point of caring for the chaindogs in a letter to the author dated March 29, 1976: "Lumber company representatives at the destination removed the chaindogs and kept them for the pilot until his next trip. They were carried home in grass-sacks."

Written descriptions of raft construction include Charles P. Gray, "The Saga of Uncle Bob Riley" (unpubl. manuscript), p. 11; Knight, *Album of Memories*, p. 100; and Rich, *Cutting, Rafting and Running Logs*, p. 8.

49. Hugh Kyle, Feb. 12, 1976.

50. Edd Moody, Jan. 5, 1976; also Elvin Byrd, Feb. 27, 1976.

51. John I. Cummings, Feb. 28, 1976.

52. Elvin Byrd, Feb. 27, 1976.

53. Earl Brown, informal interview, Albany, Ky., Feb. 28, 1976.

54. John I. Cummings, Feb. 28, 1976.

55. Elvin Byrd, Feb. 27, 1976.

56. Eddie Hayes Watson, "There and Now," *Willow Grove Homecoming Edition*, Celina *Statesman*, Aug. 31, 1969, p. 1.

57. Rich, *Cutting, Rafting and Running Logs*, p. 13; Will Peavyhouse, Jan. 31, 1976.

58. Rich, *Cutting, Rafting and Running Logs*, p. 13.

59. Letter from Jerry Mitchell to Bernice Mitchell, Oct. 22, 1976.

60. Lloyd "Dutch" Baker described the process of multiplying by 4, Oct. 12, 1976.

61. Letter from Jerry Mitchell to Bernice Mitchell, Sept. 1, 1976.

62. W.K. Irvin, tape-recorded interview, Creelsboro, Ky., Feb. 4, 1976.

63. Hugh Kyle, Feb. 12, 1976.

64. John I. Cummings, Feb. 28, 1976.

65. J.D. Lowrey, March 27, 1976.

66. Elvin Byrd, Feb. 27, 1976.

67. Will Peavyhouse, Jan. 31, 1976.

68. John I. Cummings, Feb. 28, 1976.

69. Lloyd "Dutch" Baker, Oct. 12, 1976.

70. Edd Moody, Jan. 5, 1976; also Jason Crouch, Jan. 5, 1976. Whitley Rock was located in the main channel of the Cumberland below Gainesboro. Legend attributes the naming of this rock to an 1840 break-up on the rock of a flatboat loaded with horses which belonged to a man named Whitley and his partner. See A.L. Dale, "Old Time Steamboating on the Cumberland River" (unpublished manuscript), pp. 5–6.

71. Will Peavyhouse, Jan. 31, 1976.

72. Will Peavyhouse, Jan. 31, 1976. The belief that hair turns gray suddenly is Motif D492.3; see Appendix A.

73. John I. Cummings, Feb. 28, 1976. Heretofore unrecognized as a traditional motif, I have listed in Appendix A the belief that one should walk in a figure eight to prevent freezing to death.

74. Wells, *This or That*, p. 18.

75. Figures vary considerably here, running the gamut from 40,000 to 50,000 board feet per raft. Logically, the size of the raft was dictated by the size of the order from Celina or Nashville. W.K. Irvin specified 1,600 logs in a drift; Hugh Kyle said that the Kyles rafted between 2,000 and 3,000 logs in a drift.

76. Hugh Kyle, Feb. 12, 1976, specified that the locks were 300 feet long and that the rafts were 280 feet in length. Corroborated by Cherry, "Raft Tide," pp. 6–7.

77. W.K. Irvin, Feb. 4, 1976.

78. Hugh Kyle, Feb. 12, 1976; also Carlos Storie, Jan. 5, 1976.

79. Willie Rich, Jan. 6, 1976.

80. Will Peavyhouse, Jan. 31, 1976.

81. John I. Cummings, Feb. 28, 1976.

82. James F. Butler, Feb. 27, 1976. This account has been indexed in Appendix A to indicate its likely traditional existence as a migratory legend.

83. Judge Cass Walden, Jan. 31, 1976.

84. Landon Anderson, Feb. 1, 1977.

85. Hiram Parrish, Feb. 27, 1976; Knox, *The Riverman*, p. 17.

86. Hiram Parrish, Feb. 27, 1976.

87. The turkey story is retold by Riley's daughter, Rachel Langford in "Rafts and Rafting" (unpubl. manuscript), pp. 2–3; also by Gray, "Bob Riley," p. 34, who relates two other stories about Riley's exploits, pp. 35–36. The turkey story is included in Appendix A as a migratory legend and contains Motif K345, "Sympathetic helper robbed."

88. Cherry, "Raft Tide," p. 10. The same story, a migratory legend, is told about Jim Guthrie, a Clinton Countian who rafted on the Cumberland just after the Civil War. See Charles Guthrie, "Folktales and Legends of the Cumberland Valley," *Kentucky Folklore Record*, 15 (1969), pp. 61–62. See also Appendix A, which identifies Motif K335.0.2.1, "Thieves steal pig and make it impersonate person with plague."

89. Hiram Parrish, Dec. 23, 1975.

90. John Stone, tape-recorded interview, Irish Bottom, Cumberland County, Ky., Dec. 26, 1975.

91. Hugh Kyle, Feb. 12, 1976.

92. Edith Williams, tape-recorded interview, Monroe County, Ky., May 14, 1976.

93. Knight, *Album of Memories*, p. 101; John I. Cummings, Feb. 28, 1976, described the shanty in similar terms, noting also that a layer of boards was nailed beneath the straw. James F. Butler, Feb. 27, 1976, and Cherry, "Raft Tide," p. 8, noted that quilts were taken along for sleeping needs.

94. Elvin Byrd, Feb. 28, 1976.

95. Will Peavyhouse, Jan. 31, 1976; see Rich, *Cutting, Rafting and Running Logs*, p. 21, for very similar comments.

96. "Diary of a Tie Lady," *Koppers News*, 19 (Dec. 1947–Jan. 1948), p. 23.

97. Will Peavyhouse, Jan. 31, 1976.

98. Elvin Byrd, Feb. 27, 1976. Edith Williams, formerly of McMillan's Landing, Monroe County, Ky., stated on May 14, 1976, that she often cooked for raft crews, even in the middle of the night. She recalled that they were always well-mannered.

99. Hugh Kyle, Feb. 12, 1976. Judge Cass Walden, Jan. 31, 1976, had heard that young boys would hide atop the bluffs overlooking the Cumberland near Gerald's Landing in Cumberland County, Ky., and throw rocks at the raftsmen. The raftsmen would shoot over the heads of these pranksters, but no personal animosities on either side were involved.

100. John I. Cummings, Feb. 28, 1976.

101. John I. Cummings, Feb. 28, 1976.

102. Elvin Byrd, Feb. 27, 1976. Other narrators could not recall a log house in Lillydale which served as a hotel.

103. John I. Cummings, Feb. 28, 1976.

104. Rich, *Cutting, Rafting and Running Logs*, p. 23.

105. James F. Butler, Feb. 27, 1976.

106. Rich, *Cutting, Rafting and Running Logs*, pp. 23–24. I have indexed the episode of the rain-soaked overalls being stuffed in the chimney in Appendix A as a possible migratory legend.

107. Knox, *The Riverman*, p. 17; Cherry, "Raft Tide," p. 11. Hiram Parrish claimed on Dec. 23, 1975, that nobody between Glasgow and Burkesville, Ky., would keep raft hands overnight since they were wet and dirty and perhaps had been drinking.

108. Cherry, "Raft Tide," p. 11. Earlier the deck passage fare was about $1.50 for the trip to Celina, according to Gray, "Bob Riley," p. 34.

109. Willie Rich, Jan. 6, 1976. Later, they rode the train to Livingston and walked from there home, according to Rich.

110. According to a feature story entitled, "B.B. Sherrill, Clay Resident, Celebrates 100th Birthday," *Celina Globe*, Jan. 5, 1961, p. 1, the raftsmen would trot about 30 minutes, then slow their pace to a walk for a mile, stopping long enough at a crossroads store to get food and water.

111. Garnet Walker, Sept. 10, 1976.

112. John I. Cummings, Feb. 28, 1976.

113. Carlos Storie, Jan. 5, 1976.

114. John I. Cummings, Feb. 28, 1976.

115. [Johnson], "Engineers on the Twin Rivers", p. 305; Knight, *Album of Memories*, p. 102.

116. Hugh Kyle, Feb. 12, 1976; John I. Cummings, Feb. 28, 1976. Kyle noted that the last logs purchased by the Kyles came out of the East Fork of the Obey in the late 1930s. John I. Cummings, Feb. 28, 1976, stated, "We rafted a lot of logs in the Depression. That's the only way we had of making any money."

117. John I. Cummings, Feb. 28, 1976; Wade Ray, tape-recorded interview, Allons, Tenn., March 13, 1976.

118. Ayer and Lord was a Chicago-based outfit. Ayer and Lord bought out the Boland Tie Company, Burnside, Ky., then eventually transfered ownership to the Wood Preserving Corporation, which also bought out the Grissom-Rakestraw Lumber Company of Burnside. WPC now operates in Burnside as a subsidiary of the Koppers Corporation and produces laminated flooring.

119. J.D. Lowrey, March 27, 1976. Lowrey worked as a buyer for Ches-Wyman for 11 years.

120. Jason Crouch, Jan. 5, 1976.

121. Mrs. T.B. Grissom, Sr., and Bernice Mitchell, tape-recorded interview, Burnside, Ky., Oct. 12, 1976. The Kentucky Lumber Co., headquartered at Williamsburg, Ky., was destroyed in 1917 when a flood broke the booms at Burnside and caused the loss of several thousand logs, according to Bernice Mitchell.

122. *Pickett Countian*, Nov. 3, 1926, p. 1; *Bill Fiske's Bugle*, Jan. 25, 1912, p. 1.

123. Will Peavyhouse, Jan. 31, 1976.

124. Arnold Watson, Jan. 9, 1976. Farm wages during that period were 50 cents daily at best. E.R. Gaskin, June 19, 1976, observed that saw mill pay in Russell County, Ky., was between 60 and 75 cents daily.

125. E.R. Gaskin, June 19, 1976.

126. A.V. Luttrell and E.R. Gaskin, June 19, 1976. Neither made mention of money earned.

127. [Johnson], "Engineers on the Twin Rivers", p. 305.

128. The first saws in water-powered mills were called *whip saws,* and they operated like the present-day crosscut saw. The water-powered sash saw was an improvement over the whip saw as it was locked in a wooden frame which operated in an up-and-down fashion. The log was fed into the saw by means of a carriage. The sash saw was popular in Monroe County, Ky., until 1857, when the first steam-powered mill began operation, according to John E. Leslie, "Early Days in Monroe County" (unpubl. manuscript, ca. 1930), pp. 4–5.

129. Benjamin Edmunds, tape-recorded interview, Russell Springs, Ky., June 19, 1976.

130. Charlie Burtram, tape-recorded interview, Chestnut Grove, Wayne County, Ky., Nov. 10, 1978.

131. E.R. Gaskin, June 19, 1976.

132. Sarah Jane Koger, tape-recorded interview, Jamestown, Tenn., Aug. 3, 1979.

133. "The Grissom-Rakestraw Story," *National Hardwood Magazine* (article reprint, March 1962), n.p.

134. Wayne Miller, "Gibson's Recipe for Success . . . Good Men, Good Timber, Good Equipment," *National Hardwood Magazine,* 47 (Aug. 1973), pp. 52–58 *passim.* I visited the premises on Dec. 23, 1975 and talked with Walter Gibson and Mrs. Charles Gibson.

135. Willie Rich, Jan. 6, 1976; Hugh Kyle, Feb. 12, 1976.

136. Some timber boundaries have been reduced to scrub timber within recent years. It became necessary for most hill country residents to go back to farming on a heavier scale than ever before, according to Virgil Beaty, Jan. 5, 1976; Knight, *Album of Memories,* p. 103, notes that the Depression, coupled with the decline of timber, caused him to revert to farming, which "was not my first love."

137. "Logging in the Upper Cumberland," p. 3.

Notes to Chapter 4

1. Leslie, "Monroe County."

2. Oral sources are unclear in dating precisely the emergence of flatboats on the river. Leslie, in "Monroe County," bases his opinion on oral tradition passed on to him in the 1880s, and he gives 1790 as the year flatboat operations began. Flatboating could not logically have commenced in Kentucky until 1797, however—the year that the disputed military land grants were populated—according to Randolph Smith of Burkesville, Ky., in a telephone conversation, Oct. 18, 1976. [Johnson], "Engineers on the Twin Rivers," p. 19, gives an 1802 diary citation to demonstrate that flatboats were already in existence that year. William Stone, Sr., "History of Clay County, Tennessee," *Clay County Centennial 1870–1970 Commemorative Brochure* (Celina, Tenn.: n.p., 1970), p. 8, dates the first construction of flatboats around Celina as 1804.

3. Landon Anderson, tape-recorded interview, Celina, Tenn., Jan. 31, 1976; Judge Cass Walden corroborated the statement that shipments were made to New Orleans in the early days in a tape-recorded interview on Jan. 31, 1976, in Edmonton, Ky., conducted by Carolyn Best.

4. Knight, *Overton County Heritage*, 69. See also Knight, *My Album of Memories*, p. 99.

5. Arnold Watson, tape-recorded interview, Kettle, Ky., Jan. 9, 1976; Quinn Davidson, tape-recorded interview, Chanute, Tenn., Jan. 6, 1976; Landon Anderson, Jan. 31, 1976; Gladys Stone, tape-recorded interview, Celina, Tenn., April 16, 1976; Stone, "Clay County," p. 8, and [Johnson], "Engineers on the Twin Rivers," p. 23.

6. James F. Butler, tape-recorded interview, Cloyd's Landing, Ky., Feb. 27, 1976; [Johnson], "Engineers on the Twin Rivers," p. 19; Gray, "Bob Riley," p. 2.

7. Oral descriptions were also provided by Clarence Rush, tape-recorded interview, Bear Creek, Cumberland County, Ky., Jan. 9, 1976; Gladys Stone, April 16, 1976; Arnold Watson, Dec. 26, 1975. Printed sources drawn from oral tradition include Leslie, "Monroe County" and Gray, "Bob Riley," p. 2.

8. Arnold Watson, Dec. 26, 1975.

9. Stone, "Clay County," p. 9.

10. Escar Coe, tape-recorded interview, Burkesville, Ky., Oct. 30, 1975; Davenport, *Local Historical Research*, gives 1832 as the date the "Jefferson" reached Burnside, Ky.

11. Escar Coe, July 29, 1976.

12. Knight, *Overton County Heritage*, p. 70.

13. *Nashville Republican Banner*, March 13, 1872.

14. Byrd Douglas, *Steamboatin' on the Cumberland* (Nashville: Tennessee Book Company, 1961), p. 148.

15. Landon Anderson, Aug. 8, 1976. Anderson placed the blame for the fire on Confederate troops who were located on the Celina side of the river at that time.

16. Kibbie Gardenhire, "Memoirs of Kibbie Tinsley Williams Gardenhire" (n.p.: Unpubl. Manuscript, 1939), p. 14.

17. Landon Anderson, Aug. 11, 1976.

18. Joshua K. Baxter, tape-recorded interview by Patricia Walden, Hestand, Ky., Dec. 19, 1975; Landon Anderson, Feb. 7, 1976.

19. Gladys Stone, April 16, 1976.

20. In Kentucky, Glasgow and Somerset were rail centers as early as the 1880s. In Tennessee, Cookeville, Carthage, and Sparta had railroads by the late 1880s, and Monterey and Crossville were included about 1900.

21. Goodpasture and Goodpasture, *Life of Jefferson Dillard Goodpasture*, p. 5.

22. The story, long told on the Tompkinsville team, was repeated Oct. 25, 1980, by Kenneth Sidwell, coach of that first team, at a dinner honoring Monroe County School Superintendent Darrell Carter, who had been the captain of the team.

23. Hiram Parrish, tape-recorded interview, Burkesville, Ky., Dec. 26, 1975.

24. "Uncle Fate Biography Is Pickett History," *Pickett County Press*, June 15, 1972, p. 4.

25. Judge Cass Walden, Jan. 31, 1976. Ruth Van Zant attested in a tape-recorded interview by Carolyn Best, Edmonton, Ky., Feb. 8, 1976, that her father often traveled to Louisville by wagon to purchase goods for his store.

26. "J.K. Baxter, 96, Still Going Strong," *Tompkinsville News*, Sept. 18, 1975, p. 2.

27. "The Tourist's Pocket Map of the State of Tennessee, Exhibiting Its Internal Improvements" (Philadelphia: n.p., 1838).

28. Alma Owens Tibbals, *A History of Pulaski County, Kentucky* (Bagdad, Ky.: Grace Owens Moore), p. 71.

29. Hiram Parrish, Dec. 26, 1976.

30. "Glasgow to Burkesville Stage Carried Mail," *Glasgow Daily Times,* Nov. 14, 1965, Sect. 6–7. The information pertaining to Beaumont was also attested to orally by Judge Cass Walden, Jan. 31, 1976.

31. Judge Cass Walden, Jan. 31, 1976.

32. Alta Barber Garnett, tape-recorded interview, Columbia, Ky., undated (ca. 1977).

33. Mrs. T.B. Grissom, Sr., tape-recorded interview, Burnside, Ky., Oct. 12, 1976. Original tape and transcription on deposit in the Kentucky State Library, Frankfort.

34. Hiram Parrish, Dec. 26, 1975.

35. Corroborated by Rachel Langford, tape-recorded interview, Celina, Tenn., Jan. 30, 1976.

36. John Stone, tape-recorded interview, Cumberland County, Ky., Dec. 26, 1975.

37. The United States Army Chief of Engineers *Report for 1935,* pp. 349, 352, indicates 326 miles. Richard H. Collins, *History of Kentucky* (Covington, Ky.: Collins and Co., 1882), II, pp. 630–31, cites an earlier U.S. government survey which indicates that the round trip mileage from Lee's Landing to Burnside was 362.

38. Escar Coe, July 29, 1976.

39. The CNO & TP was eventually purchased by the Southern Railroad.

40. Escar Coe, July 29, 1976; restated in a tape-recorded interview with Frankie Hickey, June 27, 1979. That tape and transcription are on deposit in the Kentucky State Library, Frankfort.

41. Noted in Lawson, *Awakening of Cumberland County,* p. 23.

42. Hugh Kyle, tape-recorded interview, Celina, Tenn., Feb. 12, 1976. R.M. Langford, who lived to be almost 100 years old, operated the Kyle warehouse for a number of years.

43. Kenneth Massey, tape-recorded interview by Colleen Garland, Burnside, Ky., May 10, 1977.

44. Escar Coe, Oct. 30, 1975.

45. Escar Coe, Oct. 30, 1975.

46. Escar Coe, Oct. 30, 1975.

47. W.K. Irvin, tape-recorded interview, Creelsboro, Ky., Feb. 4, 1976.

48. Escar Coe, Oct. 30, 1975 and July 29, 1976.

49. Landon Anderson, Jan. 31, 1976.

50. Hugh Kyle, Feb. 12, 1976.

51. Edith Williams, tape-recorded interview, Tompkinsville, Ky., May 14, 1976; Judge Cass Walden, Jan. 31, 1976, also attested to the importance of McMillan's Landing.

52. Tape-recorded interview, Gainesboro, Tenn., Mar. 12, 1976.

53. Mrs. Matt Shearer, tape-recorded interview by Elizabeth Simpson, Mon-

ticello, Ky., May 13, 1977. Original tape and transcription are on deposit in the Kentucky State Library, Frankfort.

54. Lewis Goff, Cumberland County, Ky., July 29, 1976.

55. Gladys Stone, Apr. 16, 1976. This narrative, likely migratory, has been indexed in Appendix A and contains Motif X1815.2(b), "Train goes no faster than man can walk."

56. Escar Coe, July 29, 1976. See also Winston S. Smith, "Escar Olin Coe on the Upper Cumberland: Reminiscences of a River Pilot," *Kentucky Folklore Record*, 20 (1974), 59–83.

57. John Stone, Dec. 26, 1975; Albert Bilbrey, tape-recorded interview, Gainesboro, Tenn., Mar. 12, 1976; Hiram Parrish, Feb. 27, 1976.

58. Arnold Watson, Jan. 9, 1976.

59. Tape-recorded interview by Frankie Hickey, Greensburg, Ky., Aug. 22, 1979. Original tape and transcription on deposit in the Kentucky State Library, Frankfort. The account of the wildcat whistle and the mule has been indexed in Appendix A as a possible migratory legend.

60. Escar Coe, Oct. 30, 1975; also tape-recorded interview by Frankie Hickey, Burkesville, Ky., June 27, 1979.

61. Kenneth Massey, tape-recorded interview by Colleen Garland, Burnside, Ky., Oct. 4, 1976. Lloyd "Dutch" Baker, tape-recorded interview, Burnside, Oct. 12, 1976; also *Cumberland Commercial*, Apr. 26, 1904; and *Somerset Journal*, May 10, 1904. The CNO & TP is now the Southern Railroad.

62. Kenneth Massey, Oct. 4, 1976.

63. Escar Coe, July 29, 1976.

64. Hiram Parrish, Feb. 27, 1976.

65. Lewis Goff, July 29, 1976.

66. Escar Coe, July 29, 1976.

67. Hiram Parrish, Feb. 27, 1976.

68. Landon Anderson and Claude Hackett, March 12, 1976; John Stone, Dec. 26, 1975.

69. Kenneth Massey, tape-recorded interview by Colleen Garland, Burnside, Ky., Aug. 11, 1976.

70. Garnet Walker, tape-recorded interview, Monticello, Ky., Sept. 10, 1976.

71. Kenneth Massey, Aug. 11, 1976.

72. John Stone, Dec. 26, 1975.

73. Claude Hackett, tape-recorded interview, Gainesboro, Tenn., March 12, 1976.

74. John Stone, Dec. 26, 1975.

75. John Stone, Dec. 26, 1975; Claude Hackett, March 12, 1976. The quote is Hackett's.

76. Landon Anderson, March 12, 1976.

77. Escar Coe, Oct. 30, 1975.

78. Willie Rich, tape-recorded interview, Faix, Pickett County, Tenn., Jan. 6, 1976.

79. Details provided by Landon Anderson, Jan. 31, 1976; John Stone and Hiram Parrish, Dec. 26, 1975; and Escar Coe, Oct. 30, 1975. Douglas, *Steamboatin' on the Cumberland*, p. 250, corroborates these oral testimonies.

80. For a full consideration of the legends and songs surrounding the Williams boys, see D.K. Wilgus and Lynwood Montell, "Joe and Clure Williams: Legend and Blues Song," *Journal of American Folklore*, 81 (1968), 295–315.

81. Recorded by the author and Dr. D.K. Wilgus, then of Western Kentucky Univ.

82. Leslie, "Monroe County," n.p.

83. Claude Hackett, Landon Anderson, March 12, 1976; Cecil Williamson, tape-recorded interview, Gainesboro, Tenn., March 12, 1976; William Scott, tape-recorded interview, Tompkinsville, Ky., Dec. 20, 1975; Escar Coe, July 29, 1975; Garnet Walker, Sept. 10, 1976; Joshua K. Baxter, tape-recorded interview, Hestand, Ky., Dec. 19, 1975.

84. Garnet Walker, Sept. 10, 1976.

85. Benjamin Edmunds, tape-recorded interview, Russell Springs, Ky., June 19, 1976, spoke of the Greasy Creek Pike, one of the many toll roads in the area. Individuals were required to have permits for the construction of toll roads and the subsequent collection of toll, according to E.R. Gaskin, tape-recorded interview, Russell Springs, July 19, 1976; and Arnold Watson, Jan. 9, 1976.

86. E.R. Gaskin, tape-recorded interview, Wartburg, Tenn., March 13, 1976.

87. Edd Moody and Jason Crouch, tape-recorded interview, Moodyville, Tenn., Jan. 5, 1976; Hiram Parrish, Dec. 26, 1975.

88. William Scott tape-recorded interview by Patricia Walden, Monroe County, Ky., Dec. 20, 1975.

89. John Stone, Dec. 26, 1975.

90. Escar Coe, July 29, 1976.

91. Escar Coe, July 29, 1976.

92. Tape-recorded interview by Frankie Hickey, Cumberland County, Ky., June 21, 1978. Original tape and transcription on deposit in the Kentucky State Library, Frankfort.

93. Oral tradition identified the 12 named in the text. Douglas, *Steamboatin' on the Cumberland*, pp. 327–51, identified 3 other boats that went down, but he does not list all those talked about in oral tradition.

94. Landon Anderson, Jan. 30, 1976.

95. Smith, "Escar Olin Coe," p. 73; Hiram Parrish, Dec. 26, 1975; Edith Williams, May 14, 1976; Walter Maxey, tape-recorded interview, Burkesville, Ky., Dec. 29, 1975; information about the disaster was also included in the papers of Bernice Mitchell, Burnside, Ky.

96. Douglas, *Steamboatin' on the Cumberland*, pp. 348–49, claims that the "Fountain City" went down at Bart Landing at an unknown date.

97. Information furnished by Ernest Meadows, tape-recorded interview, Free State, Jackson County, Tenn., Aug. 12, 1976; Lena Martin, tape-recorded interview, Gainesboro, Tenn., March 12, 1976; Landon Anderson and Claude Hackett, March 12, 1976; Hiram Parrish, Dec. 26, 1975; and Escar Coe, July 29, 1976.

98. Cicero "Bristow" Dowell, tape-recorded interview by Robyn West, Jamestown, Ky., Aug. 11, 1978. Original tape and transcription on deposit in the Kentucky State Library, Frankfort.

Notes to Chapter 5

1. Sarah Jane Koger, tape-recorded interview, Jamestown, Tenn., Aug. 3, 1979.

2. Willie Montell, noted with pencil and pad, Rock Bridge, Monroe County, Ky., Dec. 25, 1976.

3. Willie Montell, Dec. 25, 1976.

4. Quentin Perdew, tape-recorded interview by Timothy Perdew, Albany, Ky., May 10, 1980.

5. Temporary migration from the Upper Cumberland was common between 1890 and 1920 when young men, most often single, went each wheat harvest season to follow the big grain binders northward from Oklahoma to the Dakotas. My grandfather and my former father-in-law did this several times.

6. Hazel Montell, noted with pencil and pad, Bowling Green, Ky., Feb. 3, 1981. This realistic narrative is likely a migratory legend; I have recorded two other versions of someone's eating a worm or a grasshopper under almost identical circumstances. Because it could be a migratory legend, it has been indexed in Appendix A.

7. Tape-recorded interview, Russell Springs, Ky., June 19, 1976.

8. E.R. Gaskin, tape-recorded interview, Russell Springs, Ky., June 19, 1976.

9. Quentin Perdew, tape-recorded interview by Timothy Perdew, Albany, Ky., May 10, 1980.

10. Information on floods and flooding may be gleaned from Lawson, *Awakening of Cumberland County*, pp. 301–307; Nashville District Corps of Engineers, *Flood Plain Information [,] Cumberland River [,] Obey River [,] Celina [,] Tennessee* (Nashville: United States Army Corps of Engineers, 1968), pp. 2–34; Army Corps of Engineers, "Flood in Celina, Tennessee—How to Avoid Damage," ([Nashville], 1968). Oral accounts are abundant. Floods were discussed by Judge Cass Walden, tape-recorded interview by Carolyn Best, Edmonton, Ky., Jan. 31, 1976; Gladys Stone, tape-recorded interview, Celina, Tenn., April 16, 1976; Edith Williams, tape-recorded interview, Tompkinsville, Ky., May 14, 1976; Hiram Parrish, tape-recorded interview, Burkesville, Ky., Dec. 23, 1975.

11. There is no apparent rationale to support the construction of yet another dam on the Upper Cumberland; still, the Corps of Engineers has been contending for years for the construction of the Celina Dam to be located on the state line near the mouth of Kettle Creek. Wells, *This or That*, p. 135, states that such a move would "preach the dedicatory funeral of life-giving valleys that met an untimely death in watery graves."

12. Huddleston, *History of Pickett County*, p. 79.

13. Published with permission of the composer, Mrs. W.T. Cherry, Madison, Tenn., Feb. 24, 1981.

14. [Johnson], "Engineers on the Twin Rivers, p. 420. Numerous residents of Burnside shared their stories of relocation with me.

15. See statistics and comments in Montell, *Monroe County History*, pp. 78–79.

16. The unemployment figures for each relevant county were as follows: Macon, 5.1; Clay, 6.2; Pickett, 9.2; Fentress, 10.9; Overton, 9.1; Jackson, 12.0; Smith, 6.9; Dekalb, 7.8; Putnam, 11.0; White, 12.0; Cumberland, 12.7. These figures were issued by the State of Tennessee, Department of Economic Security,

Research and Statistics Section, and were provided through the courtesy of the Byrdstown office.

17. *Clay County Statesman*, July 2, 1970, Sect. 5, p. 1.
18. Tape-recorded interview, Burkesville, Ky., Dec. 29, 1975.
19. Tape-recorded interview, Burkesville, Ky., Dec. 29, 1975.

Index

Don't Go Up Kettle Creek was composed on the Mergenthaler Linotron 202N in ten point Trump Medieval type with three points of spacing between the lines. Canterbury initials are used in display. The book was designed by Dwight Agner, composed by Williams of Chattanooga, printed offset by Thomson-Shore, Inc., and bound by John H. Dekker & Sons. The paper on which the book is printed bears the watermark of S.D. Warren and is designed for an effective life of at least three hundred years.

THE UNIVERSITY OF TENNESSEE PRESS : KNOXVILLE